IMAGES THAT INJURE

DECEMBER, 1996
"The Poynter"

For Joann —

"... and may
great kindness
come of it
in the end."

All the best,

JCS

IMAGES THAT INJURE

Pictorial Stereotypes in the Media

Edited by
PAUL MARTIN LESTER

Westport, Connecticut
London

Library of Congress Cataloging-in-Publication Data

Images that injure : pictorial stereotypes in the media / edited by
   Paul Martin Lester.
        p.   cm.
     Includes bibliographical references and index.
     Partial Contents: General overview—Ethnic stereotypes—Gender
   stereotypes—Age stereotypes—Physical stereotypes : disabled,
   blind, large women—Sexual preference stereotypes—Miscellaneous
   stereotypes : teachers, police officials, politicians, lawyers,
   religious followers, media personnel, media victims—A
   photographic display : images that heal—Concluding remarks.
     ISBN 0–275–94928–1.—ISBN 0–275–95357–2 (pbk. : alk. paper)
     1. Stereotype (Psychology) in mass media.   I. Lester, Paul
   Martin.
   P96.S74I45   1996
   303.3'85—dc20   95–34418

British Library Cataloguing in Publication Data is available.

Library of Congress Catalog Card Number: 95–34418
ISBN: 0–275–94928–1
         0–275–95357–2 (pbk.)

First published in 1996

Praeger Publishers, 88 Post Road West, Westport, CT 06881
An imprint of Greenwood Publishing Group, Inc.

Printed in the United States of America

The paper used in this book complies with the
Permanent Paper Standard issued by the National
Information Standards Organization (Z39.48–1984).

10 9 8 7 6 5 4 3 2 1

Contents

Preface

Everette E. Dennis

Stereotypes have come a long way since Walter Lippmann first proffered his formulation of "pictures in our heads." On the one hand, stereotypes are rather negatively defined as "a conventional, formulaic and oversimplified conception, opinion or image," while on the other they communicate dramatically and well.

For visual communicators, whether photographers, videographers, filmmakers, cartoonists, or graphic artists, stereotypes are useful devices because they are easily understood and make a clear, if unfair and at times hurtful, point. For cartoonists, such depiction is part of their job description, but for communicators charged with an accurate representation of news and information, even entertainment fare, they can be damaging and dangerous.

Visual messages play a profound role in social memory, as photographs of the flag raising on Iwo Jima or the anguished student at Kent State clearly indicate. Some dramatic portrayals that were once fresh and imaginative can become, when overused, hackneyed material that is eventually parodied because it is so predictable. Of far greater social consequence, however, are what Paul Lester and his contributors to this volume call "images that injure," that is, "pictorial stereotypes in the media." In the essays and pictures that follow, a distinguished gathering of communication, visual communication and graphics experts take up hurtful images—mostly along demographic lines, treating ethnic and racial stereotypes but also those involving gender, age, physical disabilities, sexual preference and other characteristics. Overt and subtle characterizations are considered here, as are representations that are deliberate and accidental. Always, there is a concern with the impact of the image on the audience generally and on individual audience segments and people, as well. Here this book cuts new ground by addressing impact and consequences of visual messages, as well as the motivations—innocent and malicious—of those who crafted and communicated them.

The result here is a thoughtful and provocative volume, one that assuredly contains its share of serious, critical (some would say, politically correct) comment, as well as important questions about the origins of the visual material, the intent of its producers and the resulting impact on consumers of information, entertainment, opinion fare and advertising.

This useful volume, edited by a gifted and creative scholar (stereotypical terms, no doubt) will stimulate useful discussion and debate among media studies and communication students, as well as professionals in the field and the general public.

Introduction

Paul Martin Lester

When a friend of mine read the list of topics for this book, he immediately E-mailed a message to me in mock consternation to the effect that this work had no value for him because it did not include a discussion of Italian Americans (his ethnic heritage). When I offered to include a chapter if he would write it, he respectfully declined. I soothed his ethnic pride with the hope that perhaps in the next edition there would be such a discussion.

What other stereotypes could be in a future edition or volume? The list is as varied and complex as the number of people who have ever lived, are living, and have yet been born. For example, stereotypes that might be included in a future book could concern each country you or your family comes from, whether your political views are conservative or liberal, whether you come from a small or large family, your economic situation, what kind of job you have, whether you live in an apartment or in a house, the color of your hair, whether you have a New York or Texas accent, whether you are short or tall, what kind of music you prefer, whether you wear glasses, your unhealthy habits, the number of children you have, whether you exercise regularly, your primary leisure activity, whether you prefer baseball or football, whether you like to drive a Ford or Chevy automobile, whether you have had a major illness or life trauma, and so on.

Assigning classifications is a necessary function of the brain. It is a way for the organ to sort and remember a symbolic representation of the input from the senses in order to immediately determine whether something is helpful or harmful. This higher brain function is both natural and necessary. We all notice a person's skin color, sex, age, clothing, accent, and other characteristics. But stereotyping is a mental activity that is neither natural or necessary. Because of laziness, upbringing, or coincidental experiences, the stereotyping of individuals results in harmful generalizations that deny an individual's unique contribution to humanity. When the media engage in stereotyping, misleading representations about members from diverse cultural groups are confirmed. Without adequate experiences and educational references, stereotypes lead to prejudice and discrimination. As Walter Lippmann wrote, "Whether right or wrong, . . . imagination is shaped by the pictures seen . . . . Consequently, they lead to stereotypes that are hard to shake."[1] In this visually stimulated, alarmingly cautious world, imagination is more often than not shaped by mediated, rather than direct images.

There were two reasons that I put together this collection of essays, one obvious and one a bit devious. The obvious reason is to demonstrate how prevalent media stereotyping is in all manner of media and for all cultural groups, with the aim of urging present and future media personnel to do better. A clue to the other, hidden agenda of this work can be found by knowing a bit about each contributor's résumé: Almost all of them have word, rather than image backgrounds. Having an assignment to write about the impact of visual messages is an excellent way to further the cause of visual literacy, which I firmly believe is needed at all levels of education.

Early on in the process of this book, Bill Enteman sent me this message:

The best editors climb inside the author's head and then help us communicate with the rest of the world of what I call normal people—of which we are distinctly—and proudly—not a part.

I am humbled and honored to be a part of such a thoughtful and sensitive group of communicators who have graciously let me inside their heads.

Anthropologist Mary Catherine Bateson, in her excellent book, *Peripheral Visions*, writes a great deal about stereotypes. As a resident of several countries while living with her parents or conducting research as an adult, Bateson is well qualified to comment on the causes and effects of cultural stereotyping. In a chapter titled "Learning from Strangers," she writes:

For a member of a dominant group, the sense of self is enhanced by a conviction of the inferiority of the other. Colonists may become more British or more French than they would have been at home. Any nation that has suffered or benefited from foreign occupation rapidly develops stereotypes and theories to explain behavior that seems bizarre. Such situations of sustained contact and contrast often find their own equilibrium, and, in doing so, cease to be contexts for learning. Instead they become layered with rage and frustration.[2]

This book is a testament for all those media professionals, academics, students, and viewers struggling to end the rage and frustration caused by media stereotypes that injure.

PART I

GENERAL OVERVIEW

1

Ethical and Moral Responsibilities of the Media

Deni Elliott

Pictures sell. From the crass person-on-the-street observation that an offensive news photo was published because "they only want to sell newspapers" to the complicated alchemy of turning psychology and design into successful product sales, it is clear: Visual messages work. Publishing images that injure or are aesthetically pleasing makes economic sense. But that's not ethics.

Pictorial stereotypes are legal. And they are often compelling. But neither legal nor aesthetic arguments suffice in justifying when it's morally permitted to publish images that injure.

This chapter is about ethics. Specifically, it is about the moral[1] responsibilities of mass media concerning the presentation of images that injure. I argue that mass media engage in morally questionable behavior when they publish images that injure. Publishing such images requires good moral (not economic, legal, or aesthetic) reasons to justify the harms caused.

The bulk of this chapter is definitional and conceptual. An understanding of what media should do in regard to pictorial stereotypes depends on getting clear on such terms as "injury" and "moral causality" and on the relationship between power and moral responsibility. A summary of what moral responsibilities for media follow from this conceptual work and criteria for justifying the use of injurious images complete the chapter.

THE MORAL SCOPE

Economics, aesthetics, and First Amendment aside, it is wrong in a prima facie sense to do things that cause harm to other human beings. This tenet fits with 2,000 years of moral philosophy. Whether one studies the history of utilitarianism, duty-based ethics, or virtue theory, an operative principle is how one justifies causing another to suffer harms. Different theoretical bases provide different answers to that question, but all theories of justification address the problems of the causing of human suffering. More important, the notion of this prima facie wrong fits our own moral intuitions. If people are going to cause us to suffer harms, we want to know why. The morality of their action depends on how good a reason they can provide. For example, I cause some students emotional pain and deprive many more of pleasure when I schedule an exam. My reason—testing their understanding of course material—provides justification for the harm that I cause.

Any situation, including the publication of visual messages, becomes morally questionable (that is, worthy of concern and analysis) when an individual perceives himself or herself as suffering a harm or as being likely to suffer a harm. When people say that they have been offended, when they claim to have suffered emotional or physical pain, or when they feel that they have been deprived of pleasure, they perceive themselves as having been harmed.[2]

Now, the fact that people perceive themselves as having been harmed[3] doesn't imply that someone else is necessarily at fault. The perception of harm is nothing more (and nothing less) than the opportunity for a conversation in the moral realm. Perception of harm is the usual indicator that further analysis is needed to determine if there is a problem of moral concern.

We can see how this scope of moral concern is different from economic, legal, or aesthetic concerns. Economics is important in the running of a media business, whether the primary purpose is to inform, persuade, or to entertain. The mass communication industries are not the only industries that rely on an economically stable base from which to operate. Physicians in private practice, for example, are financially dependent on their patients for income, but we would not excuse unethical activity by pointing to the doctor's need to make money. Doctors who receive kickbacks from labs and specialists in exchange for patient referrals are quite rightly accused of having a conflict of interests. Doctors are expected to place their patients' needs ahead of their own fiscal desires. In an analogous way, it is illegitimate to justify the use of images that injure by appeal to economics. Whether a picture "works" in a marketing sense is morally insignificant.

Neither is a harmful image justified when reducible to law. The law provides a set of minimum standards. Practitioners may be held accountable for violating these standards. It is legally permissible to publish any non-libelous, non-obscene image. However, the fact that almost any image *can* be published doesn't imply that all such images *should* be published. The answer to the question of which images should be published is found through moral rather than legal analysis.

Aesthetics is often at the core of an argument to publish a picture that may be morally troublesome. If the photo lacks aesthetic appeal, no one will argue for its publication. However, the fact that it's a "damn good picture" doesn't provide justification for publishing a picture that will cause someone to suffer harm.

SUFFERING IS IN THE PAIN OF THE BEHOLDER (SORT OF)

The moral scope delineates the activity for which we are accountable to other people. People vary in their sensitivities, and what is one person's injury may easily be another's joke. But the starting place for the moral discussion must be the harm suffered by an individual or the harm that could reasonably be foreseen to be suffered by an individual.[4]

Sometimes no one is to blame, morally speaking, or the harm caused may be strongly justified. But the person harmed serves as the obvious starting place for the conversation. If no one claims harm, if no one claims that another more vulnerable individual has been or is likely to be harmed, then there is no moral problem. A discussion in the moral realm is still possible, but it starts at a far different level, the level of ideal behavior. For example, it may be morally ideal for media managers to strive to provide images that heal vulnerable individuals or groups. However, it is morally required that they refrain from publishing photos that unjustifiably cause injury.

Injury, for purposes of this book, then can be defined simply as perceived harm. The injury may be great or slight, depending upon the perception of the injured person. Certainly the claim of injury gains credence through the number of voices claiming injury, but even the voice of one cannot be ignored, morally speaking.

MORAL CAUSALITY

Sometimes people suffer harm, and it's no one's fault. If I go to my favorite restaurant, which does not take reservations, and find that all of the tables are filled and that other prospective diners are lined up in front of me, no one there is to blame for my continuing hunger and my disappointment at an hour's wait outside the restaurant's door. If, while I wait, I fall victim to an unusual western Montana drive-by shooting, the diners in front of me are not to blame for my untimely demise, even though it is because of them that I am standing outside. That someone is what Aristotle would call the proximate cause of my harm does not imply that that person is morally blameworthy for what I suffer.

Moral blameworthiness requires either an intention to cause harm or a relationship through which one incurs special responsibilities. Intention is rarely a factor when images that injure are published. Pictorial stereotypes are rarely produced with malice or with the plan to cause harm to individuals or to the community. But the power and influence of mass market media create special responsibilities for image providers to be aware of the harm that they do or could cause.

Power creates special moral obligations. Any time that there is an inequality in power in a relationship, the more powerful party incurs special responsibilities in regard to the more vulnerable party. The clearest example of a power relationship is the parent-child relationship. I have particular responsibilities toward my son that I don't have toward those who aren't vulnerable to my power.

For example, if I wear my Gay Rights button as I walk through the local city streets, there is likely to be some individual who is offended by the pink triangle and its symbolic reference. I am not responsible for the harm that person suffers. I don't have a special relationship in regard to that homophobic individual. Convention and the primacy of the American value of free expression allow individuals to hold and express beliefs that may offend others. Unless I am intentionally seeking to cause suffering in that person on the street by wearing my Gay Rights button, I am no more morally blameworthy for his suffering than I would be if he suffered by my buying the last ticket to a football game.

However, if I wear the same button to my son's Little League baseball game, I have become morally accountable because of my relationship to my son. My relationship gives me power over him, including the responsibility for harm that I cause him to suffer. It is reasonable for me to predict that some of the more conservative parents and my son's teammates will react to that button in a way that has negative consequences for him.

Unlike the situation in which I offended the man on the street, I need to justify causing my son to suffer harm. I may justify my act by deciding that asserting my beliefs will increase the level of tolerance that gay and lesbian people have in the community and that it will teach my son how to take responsibility for his family's beliefs even if they are unpopular. My justification for causing my son to suffer pain may be weak or strong, but justification of some sort is necessary because, unlike the person on the street, my son is vulnerable to my power.

Individuals who hold power over another, whether it is within the classic parent-child relationship or within the professional-client or professional-community relationship, have special responsibilities in regard to those who are vulnerable to them.

MEDIA AND POWER

Media institutions are powerful. The connection between the expressive media and receptive audience creates an amazing description of a mediated public:

- Children between the ages of two and seventeen watch an average of twenty-five hours of television each week; adults are estimated to spend half of their leisure time watching television or consuming other media,
- Sixty million copies of the 1,500 daily newspapers and the 7,600 weekly or semi-weekly papers are sold each day,
- The number of different periodicals totals 60,000, with 40,000 new books each year.[5]

How "evil" an influence this creates is a point of contention among scholars.[6] But it's a given that media of all types sell more than information, products, or pleasure. Through choosing who's news, in deciding which physical images promote sales, and in building contexts for situation comedies, television executives promote some lifestyles and dissuade the audience from valuing others.

Media are also powerful in that they are unavoidable. Either from direct viewing or reading, or from secondhand reports, media provide the lion's share of our knowledge and beliefs concerning life outside of our direct experience.

This influence carries moral responsibilities associated with power for media practitioners. These practitioners are responsible for the impact of their work on individuals in the audience even if there is no intention on the part of the practitioner or the industry to cause harm. Individuals in the audience are necessarily vulnerable to the impact of the media in all of its social functions.

Media institutions fulfill social functions. News media tell citizens what they need to know for effective self-governance; persuasive media sell their clients' messages to an audience; and entertainment media sell their clients' brand of pleasure. All media institutions, of course, have the economic function "to attract and hold a large audience for advertisers,"[7] but that is irrelevant to a discussion in the moral realm. That is, economic realities don't provide justification for causing people to suffer harms. Neither does doing one's job necessarily provide justification for causing harms.

People are morally required to meet their role-related responsibilities, but they ought not do so at any cost. My parenting duties, for example, require me to provide for my child as best I am able, but it's not okay for me to steal from another child to provide for my own. Transplant surgeons cannot take organs without permission, even if they have the best intention of saving their patient's life. The executive branch of government should protect the country but ought not subvert the democratic process in a zealous attempt to do what's best for the country. Media should fulfill their social functions as well, but like the others, media practitioners cannot do their job at any cost.

The cost of pictorial stereotypes is the harm suffered by individuals of pictured groups and by individuals outside of the group who are affected by the negative depictions. Because of the inequality of power between the media presenter and the audience recipient, media have a responsibility to justify causing individuals to suffer harms.

JUSTIFICATION FOR PUBLISHING IMAGES THAT INJURE

Justification is the process by which a morally questionable act becomes a more or less morally permissible act. It becomes more or less morally permissible based on whether the questionable act is strongly or weakly justified. Although there are moral limits on how one does one's job, role-related responsibilities, fulfilling one's social function, can sometimes themselves justify morally questionable acts. Professors giving exams provide a handy example of a time that it is strongly justified for an individual to cause others to suffer harms.

Under what conditions is it morally permissible to portray an individual in a way that injures that individual or other members of his or her group? When doing so is the only way that the media in question can fulfill its social function. If police are searching for a suspect who happens to be an African American man, the need for news media to fulfill its social function of alerting the community to this explains why it is justified for the presentation of the image. If advertisers are promoting a product to meet the needs created by a disability, such as a hearing loss, it is justified to present a person as limited without the product. Even the societal need for entertainment can provide justification. Presenting a young Anglo attractive woman as vulnerable or a swarthy male detective as fearless is not necessarily a moral position. The problem arises when the norm of presentation is the African American criminal, the limited disabled person, the vulnerable Anglo woman and the fearless man.

Unjustified uses are difficult to pick out except in their most extreme cases: feature stories that celebrate the ordinary when performed by people with disabilities, news stories that needlessly identify criminals as African American and assume that no color identification implies Anglo, and public service announcements that offer disability as the fate worse than death that results from drinking alcohol or using drugs. These portrayals assume and reinforce negative stereotypes. Deciding whether a specific instance of pictorial stereotype is justified requires analysis by analogy: Is the case in question more like those justified by social function or is it more like those that needlessly reinforce negative stereotypes?

2

Stereotyping, Prejudice, and Discrimination

Willard F. Enteman

It seems both ironic and appropriate that we should turn our attention to stereotyping in the field of journalism. While the origin of the word "stereotype" has been almost entirely lost in the dim recesses of linguistic history, it is most closely associated with journalism as a trade. The older print people among us will remember that the original stereotype was called a *flong*, which was a printing plate that facilitated reproduction of the same material. The typesetter could avoid recasting type by using the stereotype. Thus, a stereotype imposes a rigid mold on the subject and encourages repeated mechanical usage.

The term "prejudice" has a more direct history. It was meant to convey what it does: prejudgment. It is ironic, however, that as journalists we should be concerned about our own prejudgments. The craft of journalism is dedicated to helping people make judgments based on facts and evidence in order to liberate them from prejudice. Nevertheless, we dare not evade the truth here. There is stereotyping and prejudice in journalism in general and, sadly, in pictorial journalism in particular. People may, of course, be unaware of their prejudices. Discrimination, as we shall use it here, moves beyond prejudice. It is not an unintentional prejudgment; it is intentional. Even thoughtless discrimination arises out of a studied desire to evade conflicting evidence.

We have taken the term "stereotype" beyond its original intent to a metaphorical one that retains overtones of the original. Those who promulgate a metaphorical stereotype do not want to respond to actual nuances of actual situations. They use a metaphorical stereotype as a substitute for careful analysis. However, the purposes of the stereotype are the same as in the print history: They are grounded in laziness. In standard economics, efficiency is another term for laziness. The person who substitutes a stereotype for careful analysis simply does not want to work harder than necessary to achieve a superficially acceptable result. Professors do the same when they treat each class as if it were just like the last one and each student as if she or he were no different from any other. When we are tempted with the use of stereotypes, we are attempting to evade the need to think anew about situations and people.

The combination of stereotypes with prejudice and discrimination is lethal. A productive manner in which to understand what has happened is to borrow a term from the legal community, that of artificial person. In law, an artificial person is an unreal and constructed person. Stereotyping converts real persons into artificial persons. In our stereotypical acts, we ignore the individuality of people and treat them as proxies for some group we have decided they should represent. We stop treating them as real persons in their own right and treat them instead as artificial persons, which means as extensions of a category we have constructed. In short, we deny them their humanity. Prejudice and discrimination magnify the dangers of stereotyping because the natural laziness that is a historical part of stereotyping is extended by another natural laziness: tenuous generalization.

The combination of stereotyping and prejudice becomes even more virulent in the context of pictorial imagery. The hackneyed phrase has it that a picture is worth a thousand words. We might suggest a new one to the effect that even a million words may not be able to undo the negative impact of a bad picture.

If we are to challenge pictorial stereotyping ethically, we should pay attention to some prerequisites for the consideration of ethical issues. There are two such conditions that I think are particularly appropriate for our topic: choice and commitment.

In regard to choice, fortunately, we do not have to enter into or resolve the messy, complex, and confusing debate among philosophers in regard to free will versus determinism. What we can say, I think, is that ethics demands choice. Where there is no choice, there is no room for sensible ethical judgments. If eventually scientists conclude that free will is a superstition, we shall be forced to revise radically our thinking about ethics. In the meantime, we should note that the scientific stand in favor of determinism is at most a presumption of science; its evidence is not entirely compelling.

The second precondition of ethics is one of a commitment to do what is right. As a philosopher, I have no special insight that enables me to persuade immoral people to abandon their way of life. I may, however, be able to help the committed person determine what is right in a particular situation. Throughout this chapter, I shall assume that we are dealing with people who have choices and who are committed to doing what is right.

We are led, then, to ask why it is wrong to engage in stereotyping, prejudice, and discrimination. Some readers may be impatient with the notion that such a question needs to be asked. However, as I tell my students, conclusions are only part of an argument and usually not the most important part. What is important is the reasoning that leads to the conclusion. If the reasoning is adequate, we can use it elsewhere. Thus, I hope to identify good reasons for believing that stereotyping, prejudice, and discrimination are wrong. Once that is established, I would hope to extend the reasoning to the subject at hand and that process will lead us to a more complete understanding of the ethics of journalism in general and pictorial imagery in particular.

PERSONALISM

The subject of prejudice brings to mind the ethical philosopher Immanuel Kant. He argued for making a distinction between persons and things. In elucidating his view, he said that we may divide the existing universe between that which has a price and that which has dignity. Things that have a price can be exchanged, one for the other, as the price changes. In the marketplace, this is accomplished most efficiently with money. Here we have the origin of the expressions, "Every*thing* has its price" and "Image is every*thing*."

Kant contrasts that which has a price with that which he says is beyond all price. The latter refers to people. Karl Marx would pick this point up later in his complaint that capitalism turns everything, including people, into a commodity. People have what Kant called a dignity, and the invasion of that dignity cannot be justified, no matter what price someone is willing to pay. The expression, "Every*body* has his or her price," is cynical and should be rejected morally for just the reasons Kant suggests: People are not things. Since we all view ourselves as persons, not things, the only consistent view to take is that everyone should be treated as a person and not as an object to be manipulated. Thus, Kant argues that the consistent rule, or in his term, categorical imperative, is that we should treat each person with dignity.

The very nature of such stereotyping, prejudice, and discrimination is that they make real persons artificial and treat human beings as objects. Since few would complain about manipulating objects, through logical distortion, they legitimize the manipulation of humans. Thus, a common tactic of those who would strip others of their dignity is to deny that they are humans.

By way of contrast, utilitarianism is the ethical perspective that suggests that we should make our ethical decisions by selecting the course of action that is most likely to lead to the greatest happiness for the greatest number of people. For example, editors may justify the printing of gruesome automobile accident pictures in an effort to get readers to drive more carefully. Beyond such concerns with reforming people's behavior, I have even heard journalists offer utilitarian justifications for occasions on which, in the name of the story or the picture, they accept stereotyping that ends up taking advantage of or manipulating other persons. Listed below are some examples:

Harmlessness

There are those who argue that some cases of exploitation are harmless or nearly so. For example, some think it is acceptable to stereotype white Anglo males. They sometimes suggest first that such stereotyping is an appropriate corrective for prejudices of the past and, second, that such people retain so many levers of power that such stereotyping is harmless. But if the underlying principle is that treating people as objects is wrong, there is no justification for compensatory prejudice. Stereotyping those with power may be less morally obnoxious than stereotyping those without power, but it remains morally obnoxious in any event. The cure for decades, indeed millennia, of stereotyping and prejudice is not more refined and sophisticated stereotyping and prejudice; it is cessation.

Communication

I have heard some journalists argue that stereotyping, prejudice, and discrimination can be justified in the interest of communicating to the broader audience. Since the basic job of journalism is to communicate, they say that whatever aids in the process of communication is justified. In short, as the utilitarian would have it, undermining the rights of a few may be defended if it is to the advantage of many. However, as our advertising colleagues could tell us, usually it is more than the surface message that is communicated to an audience. The use of stereotypes, especially in pictorial form, ends up communicating much more than may have been intended; it communicates a history of ignorance and exploitation.

Professional Obligations to Readers, Listeners, or Viewers

This is, perhaps, the most frequent justification I have heard from journalists for stereotyping activities. In the context of this rationalization, we can find all sorts of pictorial actions as when we show pictures of grieving parents or severely injured persons or picture after picture of arrests that consistently show people from diverse cultures being arrested when, as a matter of fact, Anglos are arrested in greater numbers than any other ethnic group. Journalists do have obligations to readers, viewers, and listeners, but they have obligations to others, also. Journalists do not withdraw from the human race when they pick up their note pad or their camera. The issue should always be whether there are other ways of getting the story told without stereotyping someone else and reinforcing prejudice. A journalist should always have choices for reporting a story.

History

Utilitarian journalists sometimes justify their stereotyping activities by suggesting that they are contemporaneous historians leaving a record of events as they have happened. Thus, even though living people may be exploited, they think that is justified if future generations can learn valuable lessons. The historical argument is strengthened from a utilitarian perspective, because by referring to future generations, it increases the number of people affected and thus extends the greatest number to find the greatest good. Such justifications may be challenged on a number of grounds. First, if the purpose is to leave a record of stereotyping and prejudice, it is enough to do that without engaging in it to prove the point. Suppose, for example, I wanted to be sure that future historians would be aware of the fact that there is in the United States at the end of the twentieth century a substantial industry in child pornography. It seems preposterous to suggest that the best way for me to leave that record would be to reproduce numerous examples of child pornography. I always have the option of describing what exists without continuing the exploitation of the children. Second, there is plenty of independent corroborating evidence without adding to or duplicating the exploitation.

Entertainment

Another justification I hear regularly for stereotyping and prejudice is that it is entertaining. As often as not, the entertainment sought is a humorous one, so it is even more difficult to object. I believe the news media has set itself on a dangerous course in accepting the role of entertainer as part of its central responsibilities. Certainly, we want readers, viewers, and listeners to pay attention to what we do, and my call is not to turn papers or magazines into academic journals. Nevertheless, too much questionable activity is admissible under the guise of entertainment for us to be entirely comfortable with that role. In the pictorial area, the temptation is even greater because of the potential impact of pictures. There is no doubt that people make fools of themselves visually, but we need to be careful that in our effort to entertain we do not perpetuate stereotypes, prejudice, and discrimination.

ROLES NOT RULES

As increasing numbers of occupations have clamored for recognition as professions, their spokespeople have developed and promulgated codes of ethics for the newly minted profession. With one eye on prospective lawsuits and the other on a skeptical public, they have developed codes in increasing detail. Rules and regulations are usually designed to be negative they tell us what not to do. However, the fundamental task of journalism is to accomplish something, not to avoid doing something wrong. To put the matter too simply, what is needed is roles, not rules. I am not denying the positive potential that well-drawn codes might have. I am, however, suggesting that the ethical problems in journalism spring more often from people who are avoiding their professional responsibilities than from people who are pursuing them too aggressively. What we need are examples of journalists who have solved the problems that have been articulated even within this area of journalistic ethics. We need to hear from or about journalists who have faced some of the issues identified above and overcome them successfully. Committed journalists want to communicate. They want to get the real story across; they want to have pictures and videotapes that tell the real story. They do not want to deal in stereotypes, prejudice, discrimination, and the substitution of artificial persons for real ones. Committed journalists want to aid readers, listeners, and viewers as persons just as committed teachers want to help students as persons, committed physicians want to help patients as persons, and committed clergy want to help parishioners as persons.

A newsroom with narrowly selected reporters and editors does not recognize it has choices because there is no palpable articulation of them. From the perspective of the accurate presentation of the news, it is critically important that newsrooms be diversified. Talk of a pluralistic society is often little more than political cant, but it is also revelatory of an observable fact of our society. As much as some might like to deny it, the fact is that we have a remarkably diverse and diversified society. It is not enough to imagine how others with different experiences, different backgrounds, and different aspirations might react. It is important for people with that diversity to be living witnesses in order to expand choices.

My argument here is not for preferential hiring. It is not the condescending view that some groups of people need a hand up rather than a hand-out. Both sides of that equation reinforce stereotypes and prejudice. The argument here is directly related to improving the quality of the news and serving the readers, viewers, and listeners.

The pictorial media should be at the forefront on this issue. Visual messages are necessarily a product of one's perspective. The people in the pictorial media know better than anyone else that different pasts yield different perspectives. They also know the richness that comes from diversity. Communication is improved when real contact can be made with the audience. Real contact only arises when the audience understands. Diversity of background in the newsroom is essential to gain the news.

Failures among those who are committed along these lines come from what I identified earlier as laziness. Of course, it is difficult to diversify a newsroom, but it is neither impossible nor as difficult as many would like to persuade us. And notice, please, that I am not speaking of laziness as a character flaw; I am speaking of professional laziness, which leads to a failure to present the news. It is as inexcusable as the professional laziness of a professor who fails to keep up with the field or a student who fails to show up for a class.

At the same time, imagery is perhaps more susceptible to the use of stereotypes and the reinforcement of prejudice. When it comes time to prepare verbal communication, reporters and editors still have at their command the whole range of choices given by the language in terms of vocabulary and syntax. When it comes time to prepare pictures or videotape back in the newsroom, they are constrained to choose from among the alternatives that appear before them. Thus, it is important that their choice be as wide and as competent as possible. The bedeviling problems that occur when editors and others are presented with choosing the lesser of evils will not all be solved by the development of choice, but they may be moderated. The task of the pictorial person is to present a wide choice of alternatives developed from a multitude of perspectives and to enter into the discussion of them as the final news product is being prepared.

It is not easy for journalists or anyone else to maintain the same enthusiasm for the profession that enlivened them at the start. In addition, as John Dewey recognized, habit is like the flywheel of the human mind. We fall into habitual patterns because if we did not, if everything was always up for grabs at all times, soon enough we would find that we could not do anything well. Thus, there should be processes in which journalists are continually informed about new developments. In some professions, this is called continuing education. Instead of stereotyping people, we should be celebrating them in all their individuality and diversity. The pictorial message should be looking for what is remarkable, what is noteworthy, what is singular about the subjects, not what makes them representative of some preconceived image. The pictorial message should extend the vision of the viewer; it should not confine or constrain that vision. News is not the repetition of the old and hackneyed; it is the presentation of what is news. People already have prejudices and stereotypes. Reinforcing them is not part of the news beat; extending the perspective of the viewer is. The issues we face in our society are too complex and too important to be reduced to thinking by stereotypes. That does not contribute to the national dialogue; it distracts from it.

If we ensure that we have a diversified newsroom of committed journalists who have been continually educated and who are presented with a wide array of genuine choices, we can have some faith that the conclusions of that newsroom will ensure that we do not stretch the bounds thoughtlessly. Obviously, even the most diversified, conscientious, and well-educated newsroom can make mistakes. The notion that we might reach perfection comes from an unjustified human arrogance. However, we can do better. We can create the conditions under which prejudicial, discriminatory, and stereotyping behavior is minimized. The choice is ours to determine whether we are committed.

3

Media Methods that Lead to Stereotypes

Travis Linn

"Hi, honey, I'm home!"

For most situation comedy (sitcom) programs on television, a man's role begins and ends with that exclamation (it also identifies the role of the woman as the patient homemaker). The image of a man is shallow, usually depicting him as a bumbling idiot, having to rely on his wife for almost everything around the house, and inept at raising the children.[1]

Such a stereotype arouses the righteous anger of many men and women. Stereotypes used in humor are particularly harmful when they are based on race, gender, and other characteristics that are both inevitable and irrelevant to personal worth.

And yet, stereotypical views of others are part of our shared culture. We participate in them even when we consciously reject them. It is this reality upon which the writers of sitcoms rely.

The job of a sitcom is to make people laugh, and that is done by prejudices and stereotypes that are common to the culture. The Polish joke, the Jewish joke, the Catholic joke, the New Englander joke—all these play upon images that may or may not have any basis in fact. Certainly they're prejudicial in that they characterize classes of people. Yet they're considered funny because either we share those prejudices or we're aware of them and sufficiently accepting of them that we can laugh while telling ourselves that we don't believe. In fact, the humor depends partly on the recognition that the stereotypes are stereotypes, that they are not universal truths. The jokes about Jews' obsession with wealth wouldn't be jokes if we believed that all Jews were so obsessed. Instead of laughing, we would nod knowingly. At the same time, they wouldn't be understandable if we didn't share at least the knowledge of the stereotype. Our reaction would be, "What's that about?"

The use of stereotypes is equally common, however, in dramatic programs that purport to represent life as it really is (at least to the point of credibility). Gang members on television are almost always Latino or African American. Southern women are blonde, tough, and wise underneath a layer of practiced charm, and so on. Stereotypes are used as a way of gaining credibility. A stereotype is, after all, an artifact of common belief. Most people believe that most gang members are Latino or African American because law enforcement officers tell us that's the case, and the evening news confirms it. The truth is that there are many Anglo gangs. Thus, the use of this stereotype in a dramatic program is one that appears to fit reality, and because it appears to fit reality, the program gains the confidence of the viewer in that regard.

The use of an ethnic stereotype tends to reinforce the common belief that it relies upon, thus hardening attitudes about multicultural groups. Stereotypes lead viewers to believe that only Latino and African Americans are gang members. The writer of the dramatic program is thus faced with a paradox: Casting Latinos as gang members reinforces an ethnic stereotype and is injurious and prejudicial, but taking another course—perhaps having an interracial gang—is at odds with common belief to the extent that the dramatic presentation is robbed of some of its credibility, and thus its power.

THE JOURNALIST FACES A SIMILAR DILEMMA

In news, one could argue, stereotypes have no legitimate role. Humor is not the objective of the newscast (at least one would not think so!). It would seem an appropriate goal of the journalist to portray people as they are, not as we think them to be. Indeed, journalism is most compelling when it shows us that reality is different from what we have assumed it to be. Yet the journalist inevitably leans on the same stereotypes as the writer of comedy or drama, but for somewhat different reasons. The journalist also faces a different dilemma, but one no less central to the craft.

WHY JOURNALISM STEREOTYPES

One of the most obvious ways that journalists preserve stereotypes is in the selection of examples, or cases, to illustrate stories. A sales tax increase is proposed. The assignments editor calls for a story that shows how the increase might affect "a typical family." What is a "typical" family in our society? The answer used to be that it is an Anglo family with a working male, a stay-at-home wife, and two children, aged about three and about six. Now, chances are the wife will have a job, but the rest will be the same. On the other hand, the reporter may be keenly aware of societal changes that are going on, and so she may seek out an unmarried Latina mother of three children. This family may actually be less "typical" than the traditional one.

The problem in this scenario, as far as a discussion of stereotyping goes, is not the selection of one family or another. It is the concept of picking a "typical" family. In American society, diversity is so widespread and variety so pronounced that it is too much of a stretch to designate any family as being "typical." Focusing on one kind of family—any family—as being illustrative is a practice that ignores the majority of society.

When, then, is the solution? Should the journalist use three, five, ten different examples? This technique would provide some context and perspective, but it would take up a prohibitive amount of time or space. Should the journalist avoid examples altogether, presenting only statistics that can describe the whole population? This procedure would avoid stereotyping, but it would make the story dull and, to many, incomprehensible. Certainly it would take the humanity out of the story, leaving it cold and bloodless.

Thus, the journalist's dilemma comes from the role as a storyteller. If a story is to be meaningful and interesting, it has to be about people, specific people. But when that is done, imbalance is introduced. It is similar to the dilemma of a researcher. When the researcher uses anecdotal evidence, the research has life and meaning, but it loses "significance" because anecdotes can and do distort; they leap out from their contexts and assume unwarranted importance. Statistics, fairly presented, maintain the balance and are "significant" (or at least they can be), but they are also dull and possibly incomprehensible. The compromise that is often adopted is to present the statistical tables accompanied by anecdotes or quotations that illustrate the major findings. This improves the report and makes it more understandable, but it is a compromise. The anecdotes and quotations that are used tend to be remembered more vividly than the dry statistics that provide the context.

For the journalist, it is the same. Most of us who were conscious at the time have vivid memories of the 1968 Democratic Convention in Chicago. We remember the riots, the pictures we saw on television of protesters throwing rocks, bottles, and excrement at the police; the pictures we saw on television of the police tear-gassing and clubbing the protesters. Most people would say that the television coverage focused on the rioting, diverting attention from the convention itself. Yet only a small fraction of the television coverage was of the rioting. The vast majority of television time was taken up by the activities in the convention hall and the related meetings. The coverage was not balanced in favor of the rioting, but our attention was and our memory is. Furthermore, if the journalists at the time had told the television audience, "They're rioting outside, and police are hauling away hundreds of people, but we're not going to show you that activity because it's minor compared to the selection of a presidential candidate," the home viewer might have rioted.

This "selective perception" is a phenomenon so familiar that it is standard to textbooks on communications. It affects those who send messages as well as those who receive them, and it is based upon and reinforces stereotypical thinking. All of us evaluate new information by comparing it with the perceptions that we already have—perceptions that we accept as true, as having stood the tests of previous comparisons. Occasionally, we allow the new information to change our perceptions, but more frequently we accept, reject, or reshape the new information in such a way as to preserve our existing perceptions, perceptions that could be called "world view" or "prejudice."

Here is another paradox. If we see all new information in the light of beliefs already held, we are bound to preserve prejudices and to ignore new insights. If, on the other hand, we set aside previously held beliefs—as if that were possible—we would have no basis on which to judge new information, and for us every day would be our first day in the world.

How, then, are we—how is the journalist—to resolve these paradoxes? There can be no true resolution, of course. Otherwise these examples would not be paradoxes. But there can be honest grappling with the issues. What follows are a few suggestions or thoughts on ways that journalists can avoid the unconscious use of stereotypes.

ENERGETIC, THOROUGH REPORTING

In journalism, laziness and stereotypical thinking go together. The reporter asks two or three questions, gets a good quote or sound bite, and moves on. The first line of defense against prejudice in journalism is thorough reporting. The more questions asked, the more observations made, the more concrete and particular the reporter's notes, then the more the journalist is focusing on a person, a family, or an incident, rather than taking a face and a name and plugging those into a set of assumptions.

SUSPENSION OF BELIEF

Writers of fiction hope for "suspension of disbelief." They want their readers to set aside rationality for the moment and accept the sometimes unlikely premises of their creations. In journalism, we should seek suspension of belief. We should consciously recognize the assumptions that lace "common knowledge" and suspend our belief in those assumptions as we consider the facts of a given situation. We cannot erase long-held perceptions from our minds, but we can suspend their application until we get the facts of the situation at hand. Too often, as reporters, we (literally or in principle) write the first draft of the story in the car, en route to the scene, subject only to minor adjustments to accommodate obvious contradictions.

AVOIDANCE OF GENERALITIES AND QUALITATIVE ADJECTIVES

Journalists unconsciously add opinion and prejudice to stories through the use of generalities and qualitative adjectives.

Generalities such as "when it gets hot, we get lazy" or "kids need action; just listening to someone talk isn't fun" assign behaviors to groups or classes. They are per se stereotypical. Such generalities are often used as "soft leads" to stories, so that we can contrast an individual case. The rest of the sentence is "but John Smith gets busier as the temperature goes up" or "but these kids turn off their video games to hear their teacher explain something."

Qualitative adjectives are those that apply judgment to the subject rather than describing something that can be observed. "Angry" is a qualitative adjective in that it is the application of the writer's judgment rather than the observation of behavior. "Slamming the telephone down" is a modifying phrase that describes behavior. It is also a more powerful image than "angry." Description of attributes and action is simultaneously less judgmental and more powerful than the attribution of qualities. Words like "normal," "ordinary," "unusual," and "rare" apply the journalist's (often unfounded) opinion to people and events.

The inevitable conclusion is that stereotypical thinking and writing are linked with lazy journalism. A reporter who fails to do enough background research and fails to ask all the questions falls into the trap of using generalities to fill the gaps. The writer who fails to find the precise words allows stereotypical phrases to creep into the copy. The photographer who relies on visual clichés perpetuates harmful stereotyping. Simply put, an energetic, thorough journalist has no room in a story or photograph for vague generalities and convenient stereotypes.

PART II

ETHNIC STEREOTYPES

4

Newspaper Stereotypes of African Americans

Carolyn Martindale

Negative stereotypes of African Americans have been deeply ingrained in Anglo American culture ever since Africans were first brought to this country in chains. The stereotypes served an essential purpose; they justified Anglo enslavement of Africans. The captured Africans were presented as dangerous and violent pagans who would benefit from the civilizing influence of Christian slave holders. They also were presented as feckless, ignorant, child-like beings who needed the fatherly care of the slave owner.

These stereotypes of Africans, defined by Joseph Boskin as the savage and the Sambo images, have been reinforced in millions of ways by Anglo American culture for nearly 400 years.[1] And 130 years after the end of slavery, they are still alive today because they serve the same purpose. These harmful stereotypes reinforce the Anglo American's belief in Anglo superiority over the African American.

In a largely segregated society such as America's, few Anglos grow up in integrated neighborhoods, go to schools with a truly racially mixed student body, or attend churches or participate in social groups that are integrated. Few have much close contact with or knowledge of people of another race. Thus, Anglos can be influenced by media images: a shot of an African American youth wrestled to the ground by an Anglo police officer, a photo of African American babies in incubators used to illustrate a story on crack-addicted babies, an illustration of an African American woman's hand holding a pencil that a local TV station projects in the background as a commentator discusses welfare fraud.

These images send a powerful subliminal message to Anglos that the majority of African Americans are violent, criminal, drug-addicted, and on welfare. And because these images come from the news media, which claim to represent reality and to provide unbiased information about society, Anglos tend to believe the images are true. News media visual messages have a credibility that the portrayal of a violent African American man in a movie or an ignorant African American teenager on a TV show does not.

When Anglos see negative media photos and stories about their own culture, they sense that those portrayed are the exception, the aberration, not the people they know from daily experiences to make up the bulk of the Anglo population. But lacking any real knowledge or experience of the world of African Americans, it is easy for Anglos to assume, without consciously realizing what they are thinking, that these media images represent the reality about African Americans.

News media images reinforce a set of stereotypes about African Americans that Anglos absorbed from their culture as they were growing up. These images were conveyed in movies, books, radio, TV programs, in cartoons and advertisements, in comments and jokes overheard, in insults that friends used, in pejorative terms and in assumptions about African Americans that underlay Anglo culture and were rarely questioned. And these stereotypes are reinforced by the news media Anglos turn to for accurate information about the world in which they live.

CHANGING IMAGES OF AFRICAN AMERICANS

Today's more enlightened and realistic news media coverage of African Americans has occurred slowly, but it has been clouded by a dark counterpoint of new negative images of African Americans. These images have continued to shore up Anglo Americans' convictions of their superiority over African Americans and to justify their distrust of and hostility toward them.

One longitudinal study showed that throughout the late 1950s and the 1960s, when Civil Rights was one of the hottest running stories of the period, leading newspapers did not follow their usual practice of providing sidebar stories and background pieces exploring the history of the current situation. Thus readers were denied information that would have explained the blatant oppression and injustices against which African Americans were rebelling. At the same time, readers were bombarded with portrayals of African American leaders conducting protest marches, African American citizens agitating for change, urban dwellers looting stores as cities burned, and militants with clenched fists upraised, threatening another "long, hot summer."[2]

Perhaps it is not surprising that in 1967, after the Civil Rights movement had been underway for a decade, a Gallup poll of Anglo Americans revealed that 75 percent of those interviewed believed that African Americans were treated the same as Anglos. The poll also found that the Anglo public blamed the current racial unrest on "outside agitators" and "Negroes demanding too much."[3] The fact that Anglos were still abysmally ignorant of the real conditions of African American life and thought they were demanding too much, after ten years of media coverage of the Civil Rights movement, is a powerful testimony to the media's failure to explain the causes of the movement—the problems African Americans were trying to solve.

During the 1970s, some newspapers began, however belatedly, to provide coverage of the problems facing African Americans. Stories explored inequities and oppressive situations on both the national and the local level. Perhaps the coverage occurred because the confrontational events and the urban riots of the 1960s had largely ceased and African Americans were seen by media executives as less of a threat. It is possible that executives thus were willing to devote some space and reporting resources to examining the complaints and charges African Americans had been voicing since the 1950s.[4]

In the 1970s and throughout the 1980s, as African Americans took advantage of their right to vote in the Deep South states and leaders began organizing political movements, more and more African Americans were elected to office, first on the local level, then as mayors of major cities and as state legislators, and finally as members of Congress. The news media reflected this change in the reality of American political and cultural life, and coverage of African American elected officials going about the business of running a city or state became increasingly common.[5] This kind of coverage helped to counteract the belief of many other Americans that African Americans were somehow different from them.

At the same time, however, it became common to find stories about charges of legal or ethical wrongdoing on the part of African American elected officials. Several research studies have shown that a number of federal law enforcement agencies have attempted to discredit some African American political officials by setting out to find negative information about them, or by making disclosures aimed at implying that the official was involved in criminal activities despite the agency's knowledge that the official was not involved.[6]

Such charges are not hard to believe for the many Americans of any race who know that J. Edgar Hoover devoted the resources of the FBI to trying to find information to discredit Martin Luther King, Jr., during the Civil Rights era. The perception that the federal government was using its investigatory agencies to try to discredit elected African American officials was not without foundation. In the late 1980s the Congressional Black Caucus conducted its own investigation into the situation and claimed to have found proof that the Justice Department of the Reagan administration was attempting to discredit African American officials. The media helped in the effort by disseminating unsubstantiated allegations, most of which were never proved.[7]

The media seem to have been willing, if perhaps unwitting, accomplices in efforts to damage the credibility of African American elected officials. Just as they did during Senator Joseph McCarthy's witch hunt, journalists seemed to feel they had no obligation to investigate whether charges against a person are accurate, as long as the charges were accurately reported. Such a charge was voiced by Illinois Rep. Mel Reynolds. Nevertheless, he was convicted of having sexual relations with a minor and resigned his position.

In addition, many African Americans, including those in the Congressional Black Caucus, feel the media seem to demand a higher standard of rectitude of African American officials than of Anglo ones. It seems that the higher a person rises in public office, the more negative coverage he or she receives.[8] Certainly Chicago Mayor Harold Washington was subjected to sharp criticism from the media for peccadilloes that seemed insignificant when compared to the rampant venality of Richard Daley's administration.

In a longitudinal study of leading newspapers' coverage of African Americans, it was noticed that many of the stories about prisons, drug use, crime, drug- and alcohol-addicted babies, AIDS patients, the homeless, and ADC mothers and other welfare users were illustrated by photos of African Americans; very few Anglos were shown.[9] Yet statistics indicate that not all—not even most—of the people in the above categories are African American.

Why is there a tendency to choose pictures of African Americans to illustrate social problems that afflict all races of Americans? Perhaps the answer can be found in the fact that such pictures give support to many Anglo media managers' (perhaps unacknowledged) belief that African Americans are inferior. Using such pictures certainly reinforces such beliefs among readers and viewers. The effect of such photos is especially insidious because, as Paul Martin Lester notes, "photographs have the power to immediately impact readers' perception" and many readers gain their first impressions about a story by first looking at the photo that accompanies it.[10]

MORE RECENT STEREOTYPES OF AFRICAN AMERICANS

Recent research has revealed several new images of African Americans turning up frequently in the media. One is the image of the neglectful and abusive African American mother. As is the case with stories about African Americans accused of other kinds of crimes, the media always seem to manage to run at least one photo of the accused between the first accusation and the final disposition of the case. Thus, even though the race label has been dropped from written coverage, readers quickly become aware that the person accused of the crime is African American. Although Anglo Americans also are accused of abusing their children, and their photos also are run, photos of African Americans accused of such crimes seem to appear more frequently than those of Anglos as the case progresses through the courts.

A recent study of 200 local TV newscasts in Chicago found that Anglos who were arrested tended to be photographed with their attorneys, if at all, but suspects from other races were usually shown being handcuffed and taken into custody.[11] The study also revealed that African Americans accused of crimes were portrayed as more threatening than Anglos accused of similar crimes, were less often named in photos, and were less often allowed to present their perspectives. "Prejudice is fed by a tendency to homogenize, to assume there are no significant differences among individual members of the outgroup," the author states. "When blacks are not given a name in a picture, it suggests the visual representation can be assimilated to a larger, undifferentiated group, in this case the stereotype of the dangerous black male."[12]

By far the most familiar and powerful stereotype of African Americans in newspapers today is the photo of an African American youth wrestled to the ground, his hands being handcuffed behind his back by Anglo police officers. This photo is so common that it is almost a cliché. Not only does it reinforce the most frightening stereotype of African American men, but it does so with the most powerful and memorable of images—photographs, rather than words. These pictures are burned indelibly into our brains, not only by the frequency with which they are run, but by their dramatic quality, their message of arrested violence, and of drama. By contrast, photos of Anglo youths wrestled to the ground by police are exceedingly rare. When an uncommon shot of Anglo prisoners being led into court is presented, it lacks the impact, the sheer drama, of the photos of black youths subdued by police.

A 1986 study of local news coverage by mainstream media in Boston in 1986 revealed that 85 percent of the stories about Boston's two predominantly African American neighborhoods showed the inhabitants as drug pushers and users, as thieves, troublemakers, and victims or perpetrators of violence. Although the two neighborhoods accounted for only 7 percent of the crime news during the period studied, 59 percent of all the news about these neighborhoods was about crime. "The tacit message," the author stated, "is that while all criminals may not be black, most inner-city blacks are criminals."[13]

By contrast, in Boston's African American media, 57 percent of the stories about the two neighborhoods showed a community eager for improvement in education and achievement in business, and working to remedy poor living conditions. Most of these stories went unreported in the white media, the author reported. An example was Boston Mayor Raymond Flynn's response to complaints from African American neighborhoods; he funded a cleanup program and came to the neighborhoods to help rake up trash himself. Although it was big news in Boston's African American-owned media, this story was not covered at all by the city's Anglo newspapers and TV stations.[14]

CONCLUSIONS

Newspaper and television executives and reporters who are concerned with avoiding the perpetuation of racism and racial stereotypes have several options for pursuing these goals. They can:

1. Show the everyday life of the black community, and of individual African Americans, just as they do with white Americans. The African American high school choir that performs at the mayor's luncheon should be filmed just as the suburban high school band is pictured in parade coverage.
2. Show the achievements of individual African Americans, just as those of Anglo Americans are covered. The successful African American businessman who wins a state award, the African American woman who starts a local business, or the youth who wins a scholarship to Yale should be covered, and covered as prominently, as their Anglo counterparts.
3. Examine stories and photos about local African Americans accused of crimes with the same standards of judgment used on those about Anglos. Such news should not be played up or returned to more often than it would be if the accused were Anglo.
4. Subject wire stories about charges against African Americans in other parts of the country to the same scrutiny. Would this story be picked up and run if the accused were Anglo? Would the story be played as prominently?
5. Investigate and report on the reality behind stereotypes. The facts rabout the race of welfare mothers, cocaine users, and victims of social problems would be a good starting place for story assignments. Reporters also could frame stories in new ways that would challenge stereotypes, as Chicago *Tribune* reporter George Curry did when he was assigned a story about the public's views on welfare. Among his sources he used an affluent African American woman from a Chicago suburb and an Anglo welfare mother from the inner city.[15]

Some editors and news directors may protest that they already try to be color blind in their news judgments, that they do treat news about African Americans the same as they do news about Anglos. But the point here is that they should not be color blind. Four hundred years of racist messages have produced among all Anglos, even the most egalitarian, a set of unexamined assumptions that exert a subtle effect on news judgments.

When coverage is not race-neutral, it grows out of prejudice—however unconscious—and it reinforces prejudice. Media managers need to scrutinize their news judgments carefully to make sure such coverage does not continue.

5

The Mexican Americans

Ramón Chávez

It would be inaccurate to state that there has been no progress in the portrayal of the Mexican Americans in mass media popular culture, particularly since the 1960s Civil Rights movement. Media progress, as in all social situations, however, has been painfully slow and has been measured in small victories, not in significant trends. And many of the more important changes have come about as a result of the work of Mexican Americans and other Latinos themselves who have risen through the ranks of media professions into positions of management, production, and decision-making. Much, however, remains to be done as these professionals continue their struggle to become a part of the image-making power structure.[1]

Media portrayals of Hispanics in general, be it in popular culture such as television or movies, or in the mainstream press through depictions of the Latino experience in this country in newspapers or magazines, have been stilted at best and racist at worst. It should then come as no surprise that the term "Hispanic" to describe the Latino community comes under fire and causes confusion for the community at large.

The U.S. Census Bureau has historically used "Hispanic" to define a broad range of peoples whose common heritage dates back to their ancestors on the Iberian Peninsula. In the United States, that term has come to encompass three primary groups: Mexican Americans, Cuban Americans, and Puerto Ricans.

According to the revised 1990 Census, the U.S. population of Hispanic origin stands at 23.5 million, constituting slightly more than 9 percent of the total population. The Southwest Voter Research Institute in San Antonio, Texas, later issued a revised count, based on the 1990 Census Bureau original count and from projections of population growth. The figures were adjusted to compensate for an officially estimated undercount. The new figure for the spring of 1993 stood at 26.2 million, constituting 10 percent of the population. For the first time, one out of every

10 U.S. residents is classified as Hispanic.[2]

Mexican Americans are the largest of this subgroup, conservatively estimated at 13.5 million, or about 5 percent of the overall population and 60 percent of the Hispanic/Latino population. Younger, more politically active Mexican Americans prefer to call themselves Chicanos, partially as a result of the 1960s Chicano movement, and partially as a show of defiance of U.S. mainstream "Anglo" culture. They primarily live in the Southwest and West Coast, where in some cities they constitute a numerical majority. Sizable and significant populations also reside in numerous areas of the Midwest, most notably in Chicago.

Cuban Americans, many of whom prefer just to call themselves Cubans, dominate the South Florida region, primarily in Miami, where they constitute about 60 percent of the metropolitan area's Hispanic population. Many are exiles from the island of Cuba, while a considerable number of second-and-third generation Cubanos were born and raised on U.S. soil. However, since the early 1980s, the majority of new Hispanic arrivals in South Florida are from Central and South America.[3]

Puerto Ricans primarily reside in the northern reaches of the East Coast, constituting the majority in many New York City area boroughs and in areas of northern New Jersey. A U.S. territory since 1898, Puerto Rico became a self-governing commonwealth in 1952. Because of the territorial status of the island of Puerto Rico, there is a great deal of travel and intermingling of native Puerto Ricans (those residing on the island) and their relatives now residing on the U.S. mainland, all with full U.S. citizenship. This proximity to the island and the relative closeness of families residing in both the United States and in Puerto Rico lead to social and political factors that make these "Hispanics" different from their Cuban counterparts and their Southwestern cousins.

Add to the mix the latest influx of immigrants from Central America, primarily those from El Salvador and Nicaragua, and South America, the Colombians, Guatemalans, Venezuelans, Chileans, Argentineans, and others. With that influx, the broad term of "Hispanic" comes to define only the narrowest of commonalties. The picture of Hispanics in the United States is in reality a mosaic, composed of an extremely diverse cultural group.

Not only are the Latino cultures and customs diverse, but so are the politics. Mexican Americans are traditionalists (read that as pro-family values and Catholic) who nevertheless lean toward political liberalism. Mexican Americans have been decidedly pro-Democratic Party in elections this century.

The Cubans, slightly more affluent than their Mexican American counterparts and with a decidedly anti-Communist attitude due to their economic, social and political experience with a Communist regime in the homeland, are much more conservative and pro-Republican. The existence, for example, of a Ronald Reagan Boulevard in Miami's "Little Havana" neighborhood is no accident. It is a result of the staunch support of this community for the former president's battle against "the evil empire."

The Puerto Ricans have their politically active "Chicano" counterparts in the form of the Boricua. A lot of political time and effort is still spent on the continuing debate of commonwealth versus statehood status for the island. But many subsequent generations of Puerto Ricans focus more on the inner city politics of their neighborhoods and cities, and their continuing second-class status in the mainstream social and political setting.

This multicultural, multilingual (for example, Brazilians primarily speak Portuguese, not Spanish), multipolitical mix leads many to conclude that the term "Hispanic" is an unfortunate, unreliable label used by the U.S. government and by mainstream Anglo Europeans to define a group they have never quite understood.

This chapter can only touch upon a small aspect of that misunderstanding by mainstream U.S. culture of the Hispanic/Latino experience in this country. In focusing on the Mexican American stereotype, no disrespect is intended for the other Latino subgroups. But in focusing on the Mexican American experience with media stereotyping, one can see the similarities that lead to the negative stereotyping and overall misunderstanding by the mainstream culture.

The stereotyping by the entertainment industry is most blatant among the mass media. But the news media is not without fault and will be discussed in the latter portions of this chapter. Still, the primary guilt remains in television and movie portrayals.

Prior to *The Magnificent Seven*, a movie whose plot was borrowed from a Japanese tale, *The Seven Samurai*, there were a number of other westerns that carried the Mexican stereotype. The Mexican bandits became the staple "bad guys" whenever the script called for a change from the usual bad guys in westerns, the Indians. Rarely was the hero of Hispanic descent, and key roles for Latinos were few and far between. Even when the script called for a Spaniard or a Latino, the Latino actor was not called upon. For example, Tyrone Power won the lead role in his stilted portrayal of the fateful matador in Hollywood's version of *Blood and Sand*.

Even today the trend continues, as if to say that Latino-oriented characters will not sell to a general audience. Hollywood's version of Isabel Allende's popular book, *The House of the Spirits*, was heavily criticized. Although the story focuses on history of a Chilean family, the main characters in the movie are all non-Hispanic.

The changing demographic profile and the emerging Hispanic market have also greatly affected the movie industry. The Motion Picture Association of America's survey data indicates that Hispanics, on average, spend about a third more on the movies than does the general population. Although Hispanics now make up 10 percent of the population, they constitute 13 to 17 percent of all movie admissions. Hispanics spent $633 million at movie theaters in 1992, the overwhelming majority of that on English-language films.[4]

Overall spending habits of Hispanics point to even larger potential. Already established as the largest growing group in the country, the Hispanic population is younger than the national average. Hispanics have more than $192 billion to spend each year.

In 1990, Hispanics spent more than $6 billion in entertainment. This includes spending not just on admission to movie theaters but on audio and video, spectator sports and other events, children's toys, playgrounds, pets, and other related supplies and services.[5]

Because of these changes and the burgeoning Hispanic market, media managers are being careful not to offend their newfound audience. With the recognition of the potential of the Hispanic dollar, managers are gaining a new respect for the sensitivities of this audience—and clearly attempting to avoid the stereotypes of the past.

The working press also would do well to learn from these experiences. The press has established some stereotypical treatment of its own in addressing coverage of the Latino community. First and foremost, Hispanics remain dissatisfied with news coverage of their community.

The Hispanic Link news service conducted a national survey in 1990 of leaders of Latino organizations to get their assessment of newspaper coverage. Hispanic Link found that 79 percent of the Latinos surveyed believed that newspapers in their communities had not made sufficient efforts to improve coverage of and outreach to Latinos. As quoted in the survey, Elsa Nunez-Wormack, chair of New Jersey's Hispanic Association of Higher Education, said, "There's a lot going on in our communities, but we only see the bad–the stereotypes."[6]

In assessing newspaper coverage of their communities on a scale of 1 to 10, with 10 being excellent, respondents gave an average score of 3.4. The Hispanic Link *Weekly Report* said the survey was based on a mailing of questionnaires to 100 opinion makers at local, state, and national levels. Of these, fifty-eight opinion makers in twenty-five cities responded.

In general the low esteem held for newspaper coverage of Hispanics can be attributed to a number of reasons. Primary among them was the opinion voiced by community critics that there simply weren't enough Latino reporters, editors, and media managers on staff to gain the insight necessary for an accurate portrayal of the community. It is an old and continuing problem.

At the beginning of the decade, the National Association of Hispanic Journalists (NAHJ) and the Hispanic News Media Association issued the results of its survey of Hispanic employment in the nation's top newspapers, defined as newspapers with circulations of 100,000 or more. The organizations presented a dismal picture.

The survey found that Hispanics constitute only 2.8 percent of the staff at fifty-six of the top newsrooms in the country. A separate study of minorities in the newsroom, conducted by the American Society of Newspaper Editors, showed Hispanics accounted for 2.1 percent of total newsroom employees nationwide, in 1990.[7]

According to the NAHJ study, 14 of the 56 newsrooms responding reported Hispanic representation at one percent or less. Three of the newspapers had no Hispanics on staff, while 29 of the newspapers reported having no Hispanic managers.

Overall, Latinos comprise 1.5 percent of the management at the 56 newspapers, 2.6 percent of copy editors, 3.4 percent of writers and reporters, and 3.9 percent of photographers and artists.

With such low numbers, it is not surprising that America's newspapers have not fared well in the eyes of the Latino community in portraying the realities of life, issues and concerns of Hispanics.

But what can one expect when the working press only discovered Latinos some 30 years ago, despite the existence of Hispanics on this continent for more than three centuries?

Renowned Chicano media historian Felix Gutierrez said the discovery of the Hispanic community by the mainstream press occurred during the turbulent mid-1960s. He states that when news organizations began to wake up to the existence of what the press termed "the invisible minority," they often rushed to cover the group with simplistic overviews and facile headlines that revealed more of their own biases that the reality of the people they sought to cover.

"Thus," Gutierrez writes, "the *Atlantic* headlined a 1967 overview article on Chicanos as 'The Minority Nobody Knows,' indicating that if the existence of Chicanos was news to the editors of the *Atlantic* it must be news to everyone else who mattered."[8]

Gutierrez cites as another example a *Time* magazine reporter who rode through East Los Angeles in 1967, writing about "tawdry taco joints and rollicking cantinas," the "reek of cheap wine," and "lurid hotrods." Similarly, 1969 Los Angeles TV documentary was titled "The Siesta is Over," implying perhaps that the area's two million Chicanos must have suddenly awakened to their own existence.

"Such simplistic approaches glossed over the reality of Chicano life in the United States and played on the preconceptions and stereotypes of those controlling the media and their predominantly Anglo audience," Gutierrez said.

Another observer of the period, journalist Rubén Salazar, became socially and politically active in the 1960s. In a 1969 speech, Salazar said:

The news media is figuratively taking the serape and sombrero wraps off the Mexican American. What it finds under the serape and sombrero, however, seems to puzzle newspapers, radio and television. The media, having ignored Mexican Americans for so long but now willing to report them, seem impatient about the complexities of the story. It's as if the media, having finally discovered the Mexican American, is not amused that under that serape and sombrero is a complex Chicano—instead of a potential Gringo.[9]

News coverage in the 1960s led to one unintended stereotype that left most of mainstream America confused over the plight of the Mexican American. In the its quest to identify leaders and to rely upon those leaders as quick and easy sources of information, the press painted an inaccurate picture of Hispanic life in the United States. This came with the emergence of Cesar Chávez and his United Farmworkers Union as a symbol of the Chicano Civil Rights movement.

In Chávez, the press found a likable, articulate, and therefore quotable folk hero. In his pursuit of decent working conditions and equitable compensation for farm laborers, Chávez expanded the movement to include issues of Civil Rights. Chávez became more than a union organizer; he became the symbol of the entire movement. In the public mind, Chávez became the Hispanic equivalent of a Martin Luther King, Jr.

Little wonder then that most of America believed that Hispanics were a rural phenomenon. The popular impression was that America's Latinos had arrived via the migrant farmworker stream and that their problems were centered in the rural areas of the nation.

Though many immigrate from rural areas and have ties to the migrant stream, Hispanics in the United States are overwhelmingly an urban population. In excess of 90 percent of them live in cities or suburban towns.[10]

The old, stereotypical images of the Mexican Bracero no longer apply. The Bracero was a short-lived, government-sponsored program of legal importation of laborers from Mexico into the United States to help with a shortage of farm laborers.

To be sure, there are still major problems in the rural areas where migrants experience the worst of living conditions, the poorest attainment of educational levels, and the health hazards of farmworker life. But the problems of the rural Hispanic are not the same as those of the predominant urban dwellers.

The U.S. Census Bureau reports that the real median income of Hispanic households declined 3.4 percent from 1989 to 1990. About 6 million, or 28.1 percent of Latinos, were below the official government poverty level in 1990, an increase of 576,000 persons or 1.9 percent in the poverty rate.[11]

About two-thirds of the nation's poor in 1990 were Anglo, followed by African Americans with 29.3 percent. About 17.9 percent of the poor were Hispanic.

About 92 percent of poor Hispanics lived in metropolitan areas, compared with 78.2 percent of poor African Americans and 70.4 percent of poor Anglos.

The Census also found that 44 percent of Hispanics living in central cities lived in poverty areas, and 61 percent of poor Hispanics living in cities were concentrated in poverty areas.

In the critical area of education, the proportion of Hispanics aged twenty-five and over who had completed four or more years of high school was 51 percent in 1991, compared with 46 percent in 1983.[12]

The variations are not just along the rural versus urban definitions. The Census report also highlighted differences among the three major Hispanic groups.

Among Hispanic subgroups, median family incomes varied from $18,000 for Puerto Ricans and $23,200 for Mexicans to $31,400 for Cubans. Proportionately, more Cuban families had incomes of $50,000 or more than Mexican origin families.

Also among the subgroups, Puerto Rican families were the most likely to be in poverty in 1990. The proportion of Puerto Rican origin families earning less than $10,000 in 1990, or 34 percent, was the most of any Hispanic subgroup.[13]

Two repeating images of the Hispanic emerged out of the 1980s and 1990s news accounts. The old image of vast hordes of "illegal aliens" clamoring at America's gates experienced a revival as a result of the continuing U.S.-Mexico borderland influx of immigrants. The "wetback" image of the Latino immigrant as a parasite on society, feeding off food stamps and living on welfare, enjoyed renewed vigor as politicians looked for someone to blame for economic woes and clamored for a solution. The press insists on using the double negative, "illegal alien," to describe these people who come here to burden the system. Ethnic media groups have made strong recommendations to news organizations that they be more selective in their use of such terms and that they recognize the damage being done by such stereotypes.[14]

Groups have asked for a change in newspaper and television newsroom policies with respect to the term "illegal alien." They have asked that alternative terms such as "illegal immigrant" or "undocumented worker" be used where appropriate in news accounts. The change has been slow to be accepted by news managers.

Media accounts of the immigration problem also tend to be one-sided, giving extensive coverage to the political debate over solutions, while inadequately portraying the image of these individuals who come here in pursuit of the American dream. In that sense, these immigrants are no different from any other previous immigrants; they've come to pursue a better life for themselves and their families. They take jobs no one else will take, work hard and loyally, pay sales taxes disproportionate to their numbers, and are exploited by a number of people they encounter here. Many avoid the welfare lines, either out of personal pride or for fear that they may become more detectable to immigration authorities who will deport them immediately.

The second image that has emerged is that of the urban criminal—the gang member. To be sure, the level of violence has increased in the barrios and ghettos of the nation. But so has violent behavior increased in all aspects of American life. Gangs are not restricted to ethnic neighborhoods. Drugs are not the sole property of the inner cities; they are a fact of life in Anglo suburbia as well. Drugs aren't just sold on the street corners of poor neighborhoods by disadvantaged youth; they are also sold to the lawyers and doctors for their high-priced social parties and "power" get-togethers.

Newspaper accounts avoid the whys and wherefores of these social situations and highlight the who and what of immediate incidents. The faces and soul of the immigrant are nonexistent on the front pages. The humanity of the troubled youth is rarely explained in the stories that follow the initial arrest of yet another juvenile criminal. News organizations are attempting to overcome their inadequacy in focusing on social trends, and their subsequent inability to serve the Latino community. But it will take initiative and innovation to overcome past sins.[15]

In many respects, the "gang banger" has become the bandido of the 1990s. The Hispanic community has become the complacent and weak campesinos of the past, unable to help itself in the face of overwhelming odds against its success. News accounts fail to focus on the community organizations that are fighting the deterioration of their neighborhoods and their families.

The achievements of Chicano youth give way to overdramatized accounts of gang members, complete in their attire of baggy pants or shorts, oversized T-shirts, and baseball caps worn backward. It's the same style worn by the non-ethnic kids at the affluent high school across town. But who can explain youthful whims of fashion— or the whims of selective news coverage and ethnic youth portrayals?

A revised U.S. Census Bureau study has amended a previous estimate on when the Hispanic population will overtake African Americans as this nation's largest minority. The Census study states that it will certainly happen by the 2010 national Census, perhaps as early as 2006.

With such sheer numbers, it is vital that the media accurately reflect the realities of that population rather than rely on the practices and stereotypes of the past. Without such adjustments, the very survival of some of those media entities is at stake.

6

Exotics, Erotics, and Coco-Nuts: Stereotypes of Pacific Islanders

Tom Brislin

"Watch the hands," the tour guide tells literally millions of visitors a year. "The hula is a gentle dance of the hands—and hips." Maybe so at the Hotel Luau. It is, after all, one of the more appealing images that popular media have presented of Pacific Islanders for more than a century: inviting, exotic, and more than a little erotic.

Maybe a few of the tourists will get a taste of more truly traditional hula—active and vibrant, producing a high intensity sweat and some serious slapping of the soles to the surface of the earth. This is a dance of the feet that unites the dancers with the spirits from the earth. The dancers get their power, their *mana*, from the land.

Land is a significant concern of most Pacific Islanders. Throughout the region there have been recent movements to restore indigenous rights, particularly the return of native lands seized through the nineteenth and twentieth centuries by colonial and occupying nations. But rarely in popular media are we presented an image of a proud people wronged or struggling for a return of their land.

From *Bird of Paradise* on the 1932 movie screen to "Byrds of Paradise" on 1994 TV screens, the Pacific Islands and their people have provided a colorful backdrop to the adventures and exploits of visitors from the Western world. Outside of a few documentaries, and fewer but a growing number of locally made Pacific productions, there have been no attempts to portray the rich textures and structures of Pacific societies and cultures. They have existed only as aberrations of, or adopted adjuncts to, a Western world view of life as it should be.

FROM BIRD TO BYRDS

In the 1993-1994 TV season, wunderkind producer Steven Bochco guided viewers through two new perspectives on traditional themes. One worked: "NYPD Blue" a rawer, coarser view of police on the mean streets of New York. One didn't:

"Byrds of Paradise," a sincere but flawed attempt to look at Hawaii from a decidedly more "Hawaiian" perspective. Although wildly popular in Hawaii, the show failed to attract a broad enough following on the mainland. The cast had someone for everyone: adult and teen love interests, comic relief through an almost Rip Van Winkle hippie character, a bit of coming-of-age angst, and a heavy dose of good old-fashioned nuclear family values. And, of course, it had the knockout-spectacular backdrop of Hawaii, the tropical paradise complete with surf, hibiscus, cascading waterfalls, a volcano thrown in for good measure, and a rainbow of Islanders, including Hawaiians, Samoans, Asians, and Filipinos.

What separated "Byrds" from its popular media predecessors was that this time, the background refused to stay put. The people of the islands kept intruding into the spotlight, presenting images that attempted to defy the stereotypical Pacific Islander. Yes, the women were drop-dead gorgeous. And yes, they did have a tendency to fall for the *haole* fresh from the mainland. But they also showed a resilient streak of independence. Rather than abandoning their own culture to become an adjunct to the Westerner, they were quick to tell the *haole* boy to bag it when he insisted they act less "local."

Yes, the local guys were pretty laid back. Yes, more than a few of them surfed and occasionally strummed a ukulele. But dumb they weren't. They weren't looking to become anyone's sidekick or play second banana in an Anglo man's world.

The island social structure, portrayed with fair accuracy on "Byrds," particularly among the youth, was initially closed to these *haole* outsiders who, among other things, couldn't speak pidgin (the local dialect), didn't know sushi from sashimi, and didn't know that prolonged eye contact with a stranger—"stink eye"—is an invitation to fight.

For the first time the "Western" stars of an island show were the outsiders—the aliens, the aberration. The Byrd family couldn't float freely through this new culture and win instant acceptance. It was they who had to fit in, who had to adjust. While other programs have made use of the "fish out of water" theme, it's mostly played for comedy. The "locals" live in a fictional, exaggerated society. When played for drama, it's the star who brings the locals around to his (usually superior) way of thinking, rather than having to change his own value structure to fit in. The Byrds faced entry into a society that was very real and well researched by its producers. It was a society that, quite frankly and openly, got along quite well before the Byrds arrival and, should they choose to leave, would continue just fine without them. As a professor of philosophy, the head of the Byrd family brought no new and improved Western civilized cure for whatever ailed island values.

It's difficult to say why a program with a strong cast, firm writing, and high production values doesn't make it. "Byrds" certainly wasn't the first to fall despite what it had going for it. But the producers admitted they took some risks by playing a more "real Hawaii" so close to the front of the stories, rather than the "typical" Hawaii as a palm-lined backdrop for police or private eye adventures. They worried they may have scripted too much about Hawaii that is unfamiliar to the mainland (and mainstream) audience, too many island "types" might have been confusing. The Filipinos were different from the Japanese, who were different from the Chinese and the Hawaiians. And there were too many accents, too. They all sounded different. There was too much pidgin, which forms the seams of this crazy quilt of ethnicities and cultures. And they worried about presenting too much of the sometimes fierce pride and "insiderism" of local culture that lies behind the facade of the tourism industry's promotion of "gentle breezes and gentler people."

And worry, they should. It was a more realistic, therefore a more uncomfortable image. The tourism industry for decades sold Hawaii and the Pacific Islands as exotic (and not a little erotic) but safe, kind of foreign but familiar. You can drink the water and the natives aren't restless. Now the only comfort audiences were left with was that the water is still safe to drink. The Hawaii on "Byrds" wasn't really the Hawaii they knew. And apparently they didn't particularly like it.

And why should they? The "Byrds" Hawaii cut against the grain of more than a century of "tropical paradise" imagery of the Pacific Islands. Writers such as Robert Louis Stevenson and Mark Twain laid the foundation in the 1800s and early films cemented it for the twentieth century. The title of TV's "Byrds of Paradise" was an ironic throwback to *Bird of Paradise*, a stereotype-setting 1932 film that was remade in the same vein in 1951. Both versions portrayed the heroine—Delores Del Rio in 1932 and Debra Paget in 1951—as promiscuous Polynesians. The story was staple stereotype. Island girl Luana (Kalua in the second version) falls in love with wealthy, worldly *haole* boy (Joel McCrea in the 1930s, Louis Jourdain in the 1950s). But she can't escape the primitive she ultimately is, and must appease the angry volcano by taking the big dive into the hot lava.

Now that's the islands we know!

BROWNFACE AND ANYPLACE

The plot device and characterizations of *Bird of Paradise* were lampooned in 1990's *Joe Versus the Volcano*, where the natives of fictional Waponi Woo are the descendants of intermarriages with Jewish shipwreckees. (They consider orange soda the nectar of the gods.) The wicked high priest of the Waponi Woos is a comic ringer for the played-for-straight "kahuna" of the 1932 *Bird*, Maurice Schwartz in brownface.

Early films about the islands were marked by the fact that in many cases they had no islanders in them and in others, no island. Like Del Rio, Paget, and Schwartz, these early adventures in paradise cast white actors to play in brownface—"coco-nuts," if you will. Long after the deplorable practice of Anglo actors playing minstrel-like in blackface, Hollywood has continued to cast Anglos in yellowface, playing Asians, or brownface, playing islanders. The controversy has touched Broadway, as well, when Asian-American actors recently protested the casting of an Anglo to play a key role in "Miss Saigon." It seems to be almost a rite of passage (like playing Shakespeare) for actors to don facial prosthetics, hairpieces, eyepieces, and heavy makeup to play an Asian or islander character. It is, however, not a reciprocal deal. No Asian or Pacific Islander has been invited to adopt the reverse in prosthetics (lowering cheekbones, sharpening noses, flattening eyes and folding eyelids, light-hued makeup) and take a stab at Rhett Butler and Scarlet O'Hara in a remake of *Gone with the Wind*.

Honolulu's legendary detective, the Chinese-Hawaiian Chang Apana, found his exploits translated to film in the early Charlie Chan series. The locale was later shifted to San Francisco and the acting duties shifted through a succession of players from Warner Oland to Peter Ustinov (whose casting drew a few clouds of protest over the continued stereotype in Honolulu, Los Angeles, Seattle, and San Francisco). But Chan was never played by either a Chinese or Hawaiian. Unlike the screen Chan, the real-life Apana was hardly one to spout fortune-cookie aphorisms while matching criminal wits with his inscrutability. Apana was tough and often two-fisted in his real-life crime solving. He'd still make a good subject for the screen.

Not only were non-island actors substituted for the real thing, but many early films that reflected and reinforced the South Seas stereotype, such as *Wings Over Honolulu* (1937), weren't even filmed in the islands. A few paper leis, potted palms, an ocean backdrop and the stray stock footage of Diamond Head were enough to create the illusion, as far back as Thomas Ince's *Aloha Oe* in 1915. Bing Crosby enjoyed a *Waikiki Wedding* (1937) without the benefit of Waikiki, and Johnny Downs wooed the local beauties in *Hawaiian Nights* (1939) without ever seeing the sun go down over Honolulu. And there was no "Gilligan's Island" apart from an artificial lagoon on the Universal Studio back lot.

FOUR IMAGES THAT INJURE

"Coco-nut" casting—Anglos in brownface—could do little but reinforce stereotypes of island life from a predominantly Anglo male perspective. So, naturally the island women were pliable lovelies, ever willing and ready to serve the visiting *haole*, or Anglo, male needs. The island men were mostly emasculated "heyboys" willing to serve the master, controlled by trinkets, booze, or simply the senior status of being in the shadow of a superior *haole*.

These major stereotypes of Pacific Islanders in popular media can be placed in four categories:

- Pleasant, but basically ignorant natives in subsistence social structures. Even after Western contact they cling to their picturesque but primitive customs and mores.
- Savage cannibals who inevitably are overcome with superior Western firepower.
- Shapely, sexy, uninhibited women ever-willing to take a roll in the taro with a Westerner.
- Self-inflated men who preen and strut, but are easily fooled by superior Western intelligence—often played comically.

The land itself has similarly been portrayed as ripe and ready for the Westerner's picking. The image of the "deserted tropical isle" is alluring as the place that will save, support and nurture the life of the lonely castoff—from *Robinson Crusoe* to the pair coming-of-age in the *Blue Lagoon*. The land, like the people, exists only to give—never expecting to receive anything in return.

THE ELVIS INFLUENCE

Post-war Hawaii focused on two things: Building a tourism economy to replace the boom of the war years and statehood. They were intertwined. Jet travel, that made the islands accessible to every tourist, and statehood came in the same year—1959. Two years later the fledging state and tourist economy got its biggest boost from the "King of Rock-and-Roll" who chose Hawaii as the site for his post-Army hitch film. The 90 minutes of beaches, babes, leis, and luaus was a technicolor travelogue credited with attracting tourists by the 707-load.

Blue Hawaii was not Elvis Presley's first brush with the isles. He had performed in concert in 1957—and starred in a special benefit to raise money for the USS Arizona memorial. Elvis and Hawaii shared a mutual attraction through the remainder of his professional life. He made three films there and performed his worldwide satellite concert from the Honolulu International Center following another benefit to pay the medical expenses of his friend, Hawaiian songwriter and singer Kui Lee. In his final years, Elvis slipped into Hawaii several times to stay at a remote beach house where local residents respected—and helped guard—his privacy.

Although *Blue Hawaii* and *Paradise Hawaiian Style* layered the screen with beautiful scenery, women, and a carefree lifestyle, the Elvis version of Hawaii fell back on many of the same stereotypes and filming conventions of the 1930s. An Anglo actress in brownface played his *Blue Hawaii* girlfriend. Although Islander actors played his beach boy buddies, they were portrayed as not having jobs or ambition. The island social structure was pictured as a dichotomy between the rich, urban, and Anglo bosses and the rural, happy-go-lucky, and musical local folk.

Paradise Hawaiian Style did a little better. This time Elvis' boss was an islander, but his girlfriends remained mostly the saronged and shaky-hipped hula girls with an appetite for Western boys. Strangely, his third Hawaiian film, *Girls, Girls, Girls* had nothing to do with Hawaii. Although shot in the islands, Elvis played a shrimp boat captain (an occupation more likely along the southern U.S. coast) and bunked with a Chinese family. There was a hula-luau scene, but not a mention of Hawaii. His adopted family was given little beyond the Chinese stereotype—kids in pigtails with a father spouting the usual fortune cookie wisdom.

THE TV IMAGE

The "Byrds of Paradise" was a descendent of a Hawaii/Pacific Islands TV tradition begun with "Adventures in Paradise" in the 1960s—a sort of "Route 66" under sail. Although a few family-oriented TV series have been set in Hawaii ("Byrds," "Little People"), the bulk of the shows used the islands as a backdrop for crime adventures, beginning with "Hawaiian Eye," with the sleuths mostly Anglo and the criminals brown. The longest-running and most successful was "Hawaii 5-0," which presented a Hawaii almost entirely in the control of *haoles*, with a few local actors playing lower-level cops. Even when Hawaii had Asian-Americans, Hawaiians, and Filipinos in every top position from governor to chief of police, "5-0" gave audiences the images of an island where good local folk took orders and the bad ones got booked by Danno.

But compared to its successor, "Magnum, P.I.," "5-0" was a cornucopia of ethnicity. "Magnum" starred a Vietnam vet who solved crimes with his in-country buddies, lived in an absent author's estate managed by a British major domo and romanced just about every good-looking damsel in distress who got off a United jet at Honolulu International Airport. Occasionally someone who actually might live or work in Hawaii stumbled onto the set, usually in a bikini on the beach. There was one recurring role for an islander—the police detective who, of course, was always befuddled and a step behind Magnum in solving any case. The show made good use of the scenery, but otherwise could just as successfully been filmed in San Diego as Diamond Head.

The *haole* hero who moves in to solve the island folks' crimes has continued with several spins. "Raven" featured an American trained as a Ninja in Japan who sought out local bad guys and kicked them into submission. "Jake and the Fatman" presented the rotund William Conrad. "One West Waikiki" is the next series in the lineup, featuring a female medical examiner. Another project vying for network attention stars a detective on Maui in tune with the land and spirits who uses his native clairvoyance to solve crimes. A Hawaiian in touch with his heritage? No, a Cherokee transplanted to the islands. With such a steady diet of staple stereotypes, it is little wonder that "Byrds of Paradise" was considered such a foreign entry in the domestic TV market.

LOOKING FORWARD

Finding stereotypical portrayals of Pacific Islanders and Asian Americans is often like shooting fish in a barrel. The challenge, of course, is presenting more realistic images for the future. There are some bright spots. Some are in documentaries, such as Eddie Kamae's *Li'a: The Legacy of a Hawaiian Man*, Stephanie Castillo's *Simple Courage* about Father Damien and the Hansen's Disease (leprosy) colony of Molokai, and Renee Tajima's *Who Killed Vincent Chin?* A number of recent feature films have brought Asian-American images into the mainstream, including *Joy Luck Club*, *Wedding Banquet*, and *Picture Bride*. Even the obvious Japan-bashing of *Rising Sun* attempted to balance its "evil empire" imagery and to present a Japanese character in a richer context.

As film editor Walter Louie has remarked, the important thing is to get more images of the Asian and Pacific Island experience—positive and negative—onto film and TV screens. "The more images you have," he said, "the less the chance that one will become the overriding stereotype."[1]

7

Native American Stereotypes

Lucy A. Ganje

One little, two little, three little . . .
going on the warpath . . .
so circle the wagons.

Stereotypical images of Native people have become part of America's culture, slipping into our lexicons and finding a home as mascots and icons for everything from sports teams to butter, from cars to malt liquor. Most Americans—and others—have preconceived ideas and images of Native people and their cultures. Unfortunately, these ideas are often born of ignorance and old western movies, where Native people either played the role of the noble savage or the bloodthirsty warrior.

Since the first accounts in 1706 of "the skulking Indian enemy,"[1] the media have played a major role in fostering fear and hatred of Native Americans by Anglo people and inciting public opinion against them. Newspapers often fanned the flames of racial hatred by embellishing and sensationalizing the news of "Indian attacks" in order to sell papers. But it wasn't just the newspapers who perpetuated this myth. Movies, comic books, cartoons, novels, music, and textbooks all continue to play a role in what some term "symbolic extermination." They continue to propagate the misconception that the story of America begins in 1492 and that Native people and cultures are dying.

STEREOTYPICAL IMAGES AND CONTEMPORARY ISSUES

The Bloodthirsty Savage Stereotype

Native people are stereotyped in many ways by today's media organizations—some obvious and some more subtle. Many stereotypes, such as those arising from old western movies and books, are easy to recognize. These are usually accompanied by phrases such as "Indian Wars," "hostile Indians," or "Indian uprising." The images are often those of bloodthirsty savages with painted faces descending on the unsuspecting women and children of innocent white settlers. Images such as this were often used to justify inhuman treatment of Native peoples. These stories and images were made popular not only by newspapers, but also by dime novels of the seventeenth and eighteenth centuries. That tradition in contemporary form can be seen by scanning the bookshelves at most supermarkets where there is usually at least one woman collapsed in the arms of a Native warrior on the cover of a "romance novel."

This type of image is also often used to sell sports teams. The "Fighting Sioux" of North Dakota, the Cleveland Indians, and the Atlanta Braves all depend on the idea of Native people as warlike and bloodthirsty in order to sell their image. Fans wave plastic weapons, decorate their faces with "war paint" and whoop and holler as they perform their "war dances." And the Redskins (a term viewed by many Native people with the same disgust as the word "nigger") don't just defeat a team, they "scalp" them, an image that brings with it another violent stereotype. Scalping is a term often accompanied by "Indian" and presents the image of fierceness, savagery and violence. Most people don't know that Europeans, not Native people, were the originators of this practice in America. In the 1700s, Massachusetts was offering bounties of 40 pounds for a male Indian scalp, and 20 pounds for scalps of females or of children under twelve years old.[2] Although some defend the use of Native people as symbols, saying they are meant to honor and not insult Native Americans, others are unwilling to accept as "honorable" these acts, which convey a lack of respect for Native culture and spirituality and which turn a race of people into sports mascots.

The Noble Savage

Although the "savage warrior" image is still used, another visual more often seen in advertising is that of the "noble savage."

Stories of Native people who helped the settlers, often at the risk of their own lives and family relationships, were and are also popular. This stereotypical image portrays America's indigenous population as not only the friend of the "white man," but part of a once-great but now dying culture. This is a very subtle form of racism because it usually implies that indigenous people existed to serve Anglo society and were thankful to be "civilized" by the Anglo Americans. Related to this is the misconception of the "stoical Indian," an image that often translates to a perceived lack of humor. Monty Roessel, a Navajo photojournalist, related a conversation with a Navajo woman who wondered why Native people were never photographed smiling. "People must think we don't have any teeth," she laughed. Roessel explained that the "unsmiling Indian" was usually a "set-up" shot composed by the photographer, usually Anglo American, to conform to a preconceived notion.

Indian as "Spirit Guide"

Many Native people also object to the cultural and spiritual appropriation of their cultures that can be found in almost any "New Age" store or catalog. Native spirituality, which centers around respect for the earth and all its inhabitants, has drawn many non-Native followers. While those seeking, "in a good way," inner knowledge and the sacred in their own lives are usually welcomed, those who try to buy or sell spirituality are not. There are catalogs that sell a variety of tools and fetishes associated with various earth-based religions. Native images are very often used to sell these items. For example, a "sacred medicine pouch" can be purchased for $10, along with ceremonial drums and shields. This marketing of Native American spirituality has recently found its way to electronic bulletin boards, where a "chief" was selling "Indian names" over the America Online (AOL) network. The perpetuated myth, harmful to us all, is that spirituality can be bought. Many Native people view this as "cultural genocide" and the people who contribute to it as "culture vultures" because appropriated ceremonies and ritual elements are not treated with respect and honor. They also point to the fact that many people come to them for help and healing but are unwilling to participate in the fight for land or sovereignty or to join in the hundreds of meaningful ways in which they could offer support for Native rights.

Indians as Protesters

Native people themselves, who continue these struggles, are often viewed in the media as troublemakers or usurpers, outsiders in their own homelands. Besides the obligatory once-a-year powwow story by the news organizations, the most often seen media images of Native people are usually confrontational. Native Americans can often be seen dissenting or politically challenging a generally accepted stereotype: carrying signs and banners outside a Redskins game, questioning a reduction of sovereignty, or fighting for the return of ancestral remains from museums around the world. Dennis Banks, a founder of the American Indian Movement, put it this way, "In the news we're always protesting, protesting—hell, we're surviving!"[3]

When people are always seen in conflict, they're often viewed as troublemakers and a threat to society. This type of confrontation makes for great images on the six o'clock news; however, rarely is any time given to explain the historical and cultural reasons for the protest and why the event being protested is seen as objectionable.

WHAT TO WATCH OUT FOR

Imaging that places Native people only in the past

A constant visual diet of Native people in traditional regalia is problematic. The word "costume" is often used when describing this type of clothing. However, "costume" is objectionable to many Native people because of its associations with the theater. If all the media give us are pictures of Native peoples and cultures taken during annual powwows, it feeds the notion that they do not exist in the present and are not part of a continuum. This denial of Native people as part of today's contemporary world is further fostered when we use them as symbols of the past.

Objectifying Native people by using them as characterizations

Turning people into objects, or dehumanizing them, is often the first step in justifying inhumane treatment toward them. According to sports team owners and fans, names like Redskins, Braves, Warriors, Indians, and Fighting Sioux are signs of respect, meant to honor Native Americans. As one Redskins football fan, adorned with Redskin team symbols, put it after being chased by Native people who were protesting the name, "We support the Indians. We love 'em. To think we're against them is crazy. We're gonna win the championship for 'em."[4] In spite of all this honor, many Native people and organizations continue to decry the use of these racially demeaning stereotypes. Several points are made to support these views:

- Consider the fact that Native people are used as names for teams and mascots in the same way that wild animals such as gophers, badgers and wolves are. This, many people believe, leads to the view that they are less than human.
- The mascots for these teams are often drawn or portrayed in humorous caricatures. The fans, following this lead, often paint their faces, wear feathers and beat drums in complete disregard of the sacred traditions they are mimicking. Some people in the Native community have drawn the following parallel: A sports team called the Christians with a mascot dressed like the Pope, in long robes and miter, brandishing a crucifix and incense. The fans could wave Styrofoam crucifixes in the air and bring buckets of "holy water" to sprinkle on each other.

That portrayal would be unthinkable of course, but the same type of insensitivity and spiritual defilement can still be seen during half-time displays at many sporting events throughout the United States.

Now you see them, now you don't: The problem of invisibility

Many people, with help from the mass media, do not see Native Americans as persons. And some argue that the mass media not only refuse to see Native Americans as persons, but often refuse to see them at all.

When a Native person is in "traditional" dress, the mass media seem to feel no obligation to identify that person. This lack of identifying information perpetuates the idea that it isn't a person at all, but only an "Indian." There are many examples of a front-page, close-up photo of a man dancing at a powwow in which the man is not identified. Although he is well known in many Native communities and is a world champion dancer, no cutline accompanies the image. A postcard of a person dancing is labeled simply "Indian Dancer." The family of a young Lakota child from the Pine Ridge Reservation brings suit against the rock group Cult for using a photo of their son in traditional dress, without their permission, on the cover of a CD. A North Dakota tourist magazine includes a short story on "cowboys and Indians" along with two photos. The photo of a woman in a cowboy hat standing by her horse is accompanied by a caption giving her name, her title, and her hometown. It even gives the name of her horse! The identity of the "Indian," a young man in traditional dress, is not stated.

These subtle forms of racism send the unspoken message that "Indians" are not people, that they have no names or identities. Seeing them only in traditional dress gives media audiences the idea that they are simply historical artifacts without significance in today's modern society. This misconception is often fed by the lack of news coverage of Native communities by the mainstream media. Unfortunately, most of what people know about Native tribes and other cultures is learned through what they read, see, or hear in the media. And if all they see are stories about annual powwows, gambling, or the effects of alcoholism, a reader might assume that such stories are all there is to report. As in other communities, there are well-tended homes, farms, and ranches on the reservation along with modern community centers, clinics, businesses and colleges. The media have a responsibility, not only to Native people, but to all people, to relate all sides of the story. To give a balanced picture, the media must show Native people living in their communities year around—working, laughing, loving, and crying within the context of their existence as active, productive members of today's societies both on and off the reservations.

Giving all sides of the story also means understanding that there are over 300 "sides" to the Native American experience in the United States. Along with this knowledge should come the realization that the terms "American Indian" or "Native American" are generalizations. There are over 300 separate and distinct tribes and nations in the United States alone. Each nation has its own unique language, customs, beliefs, and history. Using the term "American Indian" to identify someone who is Lakota or Chippewa, for example, is like describing someone from Germany or France as European. And by the same token, to say someone speaks "Indian" would be the same as saying someone speaks "European." One of the biggest misconceptions regarding Native people seems to be that they are all alike, that the tribes in the Pacific Northwest are the same as the southwestern nations, who are the same as the Native peoples of the Upper Plains. This misconception fuels the notion that there can be a spokesperson for all Native people, that they all think alike and should all agree on topics ranging from what constitutes a stereotype to school curricula. Often, when Native people or tribes voice opposing views, this is shown as an example of a lack of cooperation. It is a sign of infighting among people who can't even get along with each other. While this presumption of a unified voice is not expected in the broader community, large or small, it is often expected of people in underrepresented groups. Of course the Native community is as diverse as the number of nations, and the nations are as diverse as the number of members.

THE CONSEQUENCES OF MISREPRESENTATION

The consequences of stereotyping in both Native and non-Native communities are far-reaching. According to one Native parent, who filed a legal complaint against the use of school mascots, "By tolerating the use of demeaning stereotypes in our public school systems, we desensitize entire generations of children."[5] Many people feel the issue of stereotyping is an issue of self-esteem, that Native children have the right to grow up believing they're more than mascots for products and sports teams. They have the right to attend a football game without standing next to someone yelling, "Scalp the Indians!"

All people deserve to see themselves reflected with honesty and balance by the media organizations that serve their communities. Children are especially vulnerable and if they're excluded or seen only in a negative way they may begin to wonder if they're okay. Some critics believe the media are, in part, responsible for the high rate of suicide among Native young people, that this high rate reflects low self-esteem based on negative imaging.[6] If we only see ourselves reflected only when there's a crisis or only as part of the past, this raises anger, anxiety, and uncertainty. Misrepresentation should be of great concern to us all and certainly belies the naive argument that there are more important things to worry about than sports mascots or advertising images.

Change is coming from within the Native community where Native people themselves are taking steps to address this imbalance in the media. The Native American Journalists Association (NAJA) recognizes the need for more Native people in the media as writers, anchors, and policymakers. NAJA provides a base from which its over 400 members develop national priorities for Native participation in national media and the Native press. NAJA also supports journalism education for Native students through scholarships, internships, and summer workshops. This organization is also an excellent source of information regarding Native people and the media and can provide a list of Native journalists and publications throughout the United States and Canada. Other organizations, such as the American Indian High Education Consortium (AIHEC) and the Native American Broadcasting Consortium (NABC), provide educational outlets and services enabling Native people to tell their own stories, reporting the news for and about their communities.

Through the efforts of Native people and organizations, changes are being made. Offensive advertising is being challenged and in some cases the negative images are being withdrawn, as in the Nike ad. Newspaper organizations like the *Portland Oregonian* and the *Minneapolis Star Tribune* are involving themselves in their community and refusing to print the names of sports teams considered offensive by Native people. Encouraged by Native activists, enlightened high school and university students and administrators have worked to remove degrading mascots at their schools. Stanford University, over twenty years ago, changed its team name from the "Indians" to the "Cardinals," and more recently, Marquette University dropped the name "Warriors," eliminating a demeaning stereotype from their school. This type of sensitivity is necessary to provide an environment in which all people are comfortable and made welcome.

8

Jewish Images that Injure

Marsha Woodbury

He is the Jewish attorney on the TV program "Picket Fences"—offensive, sleazy, aggressive, obnoxious.[1]   He is short and pushy, hot for a non-Jewish woman (derogatorily known as a *shiksa*). He is the fat kid, the one at the bar mitzvah; on TV he's the one who finishes last in a race. He is the indulging, *nouveau riche* father, telling you what to buy wholesale. He is "my son the doctor" or the smart kid in *Broadcast News*, and after his graduation speech, the other students beat him up.

She is a JAP, a Jewish American Princess—pampered, demanding, loud, and tasteless. She is the JAM, Jewish American Mother, overprotective, can't let go, the "Yiddish mama," loudmouthed and pushy. She is *The Heartbreak Kid*, left on her honeymoon while her newlywed husband pursues the blonde he spies on the beach. She is Rhoda Morgenstern from "The Mary Tyler Moore Show" or Melissa Steadman from "thirty-something," characters who are basically losers—demanding, smart, and neurotic—that is, if she is represented at all.

They talk funny, with a Yiddish accent. They are the money lenders, the Shylocks. They are slave traders of old, who today conspire to take over America's finances and communications. They bravely wrested Israel from Palestine after World War II. They slaughter innocent Palestinians. They went passively into the Nazi gas chambers during World War II. They kidnapped Africans and sold them as slaves.

He, she, and they are Jewish, as portrayed in the media. Those images linger in the mind, creating stereotypes, entering our subconscious, and becoming a part of our culture. In 1994 the CNN broadcasts of hate speeches by Louis Farrakhan spokesmen tended to wipe out more subtle, positive images. Jewish stereotypes were and are serious and deserve explanation and understanding, particularly in this time of political correctness, skinheads, and hate speech.

This chapter begins with what a "Jew" is, what the images of Jews are, and explores the reactions of Jewish people to those portrayals. The Jewish people who provide insight and examples for this chapter felt the lack of positive Jewish role models in the media hurt them while they were growing up in America. The interviewees are from the University of Illinois and Internet community. The chapter includes suggestions to sensitize those who work in the media about ways that they can reduce harmful images.

WHAT IS A JEW?

When we talk about images of those from underrepresented cultures, the basic question of who and what they are does not need to be explained. We can identify a child or a woman or an Asian. Jews are harder to identify. They can have blue eyes, freckles, and blond hair, or be African American, like Sammy Davis, Jr.

Jews are an ancient people who today share some distinctive characteristics such as culture, religion, and language. The word "tribe" describes Jewishness best, but it's not a word that comes to mind when one is speaking of a modern people.[2] They appear to maintain a tribal format, so much so that a gentile (non-Jew) might refer to a group of Jews in a hotel lobby as "a gathering of the tribe." They become Jewish through birth or religious conversion. The definition of Jewishness was widened in Hitler's Germany, where being married to a Jew or being the child of a mixed marriage or even having one Jew in your family tree qualified you for the death camps.

Jews have a long history of being subject to persecution and pogroms (planned elimination) in countries all over the world, which forced them to seek safety in many lands. Because they held to their religion, they have been called a stubborn people for refusing to convert to Christianity. Only in the last part of this century did the pope recognize Judaism. Medieval Christianity portrayed Jews as grotesque individuals, ever-ready to steal consecrated wafers, murder innocent children, and mock the rituals and the beliefs of the "true" faith.[3] The stereotype of the Jew as an avaricious money-lender was born after Jews were forbidden from doing any business other than lending money for a profit in medieval times.[4]

The only certain way that you can tell a Jew from any other person is if she or he wears special clothing. A stereotype often seen in the media is the Hassid. Hassidism is a "family" in the tribe, a group that springs from Polish roots and holds to very strict observance and worship. They are easily identified by their appearance, for they wear black clothes, with yarmulkes (little black hats), long beards, and long curly sidelocks. Mainstream Jews often feel uncomfortable about Hassidism. In one of Woody Allen's films, *Annie Hall*, Allen spoofs his own caricature. When he goes to visit Annie's straight-laced, Midwestern family, he thinks that they are looking at him and seeing a Hassidic with sidelocks and a black hat.[5]

IMAGES THAT INJURE

In today's media we don't encounter the more devastating images of the past. In the 1930s, the Nazis widely spread grotesque caricatures of Jews, featuring protruding noses and mouths salivating at the sight of money. These images laid the groundwork for the mass extermination that followed. Because of the horrific history of Jewish stereotyping and persecution, Jewish people are extremely sensitive to hateful portrayals. The Jewish Anti-Defamation League has fought anti-Semitism (hatred of Jews) for eighty years. In these days of politically correct speech, the word "Jew" can offend some people, who prefer "Jewish person." Reporters are urged to use the word "Jew" as a noun, never a verb, and not as a synonym for stingy.[6]

Some common stereotypes of Jewish people are accurate generalizations. Yes, they have been high achievers in America. They stress education seriously, and their representation in the professions is out of proportion to their numbers. By 1970, 60 percent of all employed Jews were professionals, technical managers, or administrators. By 1988, Jews were twice as likely as non-Jewish Anglos to report annual household incomes of more than $50,000. They have been called "the richest ethnic group in the richest country in history."[7] Sometimes the role models weren't clear, as when Albert Einstein was labeled as German in a Chicago public school textbook.[8]

Yes, Jews are humorous. Mild stereotyping is combated with their humor, for which Jews are rightly famous: "There is a unique tendency—cultural, religious, and ethnic—for the Jew to pick up on the terrible miseries of his life, as well as its absurdities, to make jokes and laugh at them."[9] However, if the joke is generated or repeated to derogate Jews, to spread anti-Semitism, then the purpose is lost.

COMMON STEREOTYPES

In spite of, or perhaps because of, their success, Jews are "typed." As one Jew defined media portrayal, "He is the smart (but lacking in social skills) Jew who isn't a good lover because he is too focused on making money and cheating the rest of the world while falling in love with the forbidden fruit of a non-Jew, since we all know that Jewish women just whine and shop while daddy supports them. Yuck!"[10]

Holidays

Due to a lack of understanding and education, the media errs in reporting simple things like religious holidays. As one Jew said, "I mostly get angry when someone who is doing the 'politically correct' thing actually shows off his or her ignorance. For example, I heard on the radio, on the second of April, 'Have a nice Easter or Passover weekend.' Passover was over by then. Or when someone refers to Chanukah as a 'major holiday,' or 'your Christmas.'"[11] Apparently, Christian reporters commonly put other religions into a Christian context.

Reporters need to be mindful of the photos they run. One Jew noted:

As a child I recall the *Chicago Tribune* running pictures to depict the coming of the winter holidays. Christmas was symbolized by an attractive blonde cherub with twinkling eyes, colorful clothes, and so on. Chanukah was portrayed either by a decrepit old man (often overweight), or a wizened little boy who looked like he hadn't slept in weeks (he always had black circles under his eyes).[12]

Advertisements

Ads seldom show obviously Jewish characters. One successful campaign used a catchy phrase for Levy's rye bread: "You don't have to be Jewish to eat Levy's rye." An unspoken interpretation might be, "Thank God, you don't have to be Jewish . . . ." The ads were everywhere: "I'm from New York City, and I remember the ads in the subway when I was a kid."[13] Funny, effective, memorable, and possibly hurtful.

POLITICAL CARTOONS

Jews and Arabs in cartoons often have huge noses. The caricature stereotypes are not merely reflections of bigotry but are often weapons used to consciously isolate and persecute targeted populations. They remind Jews of Nazi propaganda. "Suburbanites have learned to live without lawn statuettes of servile Black stable hands. Cartoonists can certainly survive without their pictorial counterparts."[14] Out of approximately 150 full-time cartoonists working for daily papers, only two are women, none are African American, and fewer than five are Latino or Asian. The caricatures should be biting and revealing, but there is a difference between exaggerating the observable features of an identifiable public figure (Barbra Streisand's nose, for example) and putting nasty, hate-inducing features on all members of an ethnic group (casting Jews as Shylocks).[15]

Weight and Health

Jewish children are often portrayed as overweight. In "Big Brother Jake" and "Mighty Ducks" on TV, the Jewish identity of the fat children is revealed through their names or additional references or pictures of the child being bar mitzvahed.[16]

Jewish women strive to avoid the stereotype of being unattractive and overweight, sometimes becoming anorexic in the process. They worry about their children's weight, and with good reason. Public health workers are also concerned about the image of the fat Jewish child. Among groups of children, the overweight child is the one most rejected. Compared with children with other handicaps, including facial disfigurement, the overweight child is seen as responsible for his or her condition, and almost deserving of victimization.[17]

JAPs

JAP stands for Jewish American princess, which began as a fairly gentle stereotype of an overindulged daughter of a newly prosperous suburban Jew. As with any *nouveau riche*, the immigrant Jewish family would lack the social skills to go with its new wealth. The JAP jokes caused mirth, spreading to T-shirts, greeting cards, books, and cartoons. Today, JAP stands for a whining, materialistic, small-minded woman averse to sex, obsessed with shopping, and generally repugnant. The image brought on a wave of JAP-bashing.[18]

At Cornell and other colleges, students wear T-shirts reading SLAP-A-JAP! and BACK OFF BITCH, I'M A JAP-BUSTER! "Anti-Semitism masked as sexism is more socially acceptable," says Rabbi Laura Geller, director of the Hillel Jewish Center at the University of Southern California, "because, unfortunately, sexism is still an accepted form of bigotry."[19]

Graffiti at Syracuse University read, "A Solution to the JAP Problem: When they go to get nose jobs, tie their tubes as well." This sort of hatred is a short step from the Nazi images of the 1930s.

The media could help by highlighting women like Ruth Bader Ginsburg, President Clinton's appointee to the U.S. Supreme Court, whose opinions have consistently leaned toward religious tolerance. Singer Paula Abdul's mother is a Canadian Jew, and her father was born of Syrian Jewish parents.[20] One person remarked, "See the beautiful things Arabs and Jews can make when they work together."[21]

Typical Jewish Family

The most common media stereotype depicts Jews as wealthy, grasping, and acquisitive, and Jewish culture as mainly materialistic. For example, the movie *Dirty Dancing* shows nearly all the Jewish characters as lacking social grace, and all the women, except the leading lady, as unpleasant JAP stereotypes. "Frankly, I'm surprised that all the anti-Jewish stereotyping in this film didn't get more attention at the time, since it struck me right away," said one respondent.[22]

Jewish Mother

The Jewish mother has been fairly well carved out by novelists like Philip Roth. Part of the stereotype comes from the historical roots of Judaism, the closeness of the family, and the struggle for survival in a new country. The Jewish woman had to manage the family while her husband pursued religion, and consequently developed the strong personality and sharp business skills that perpetuate the stereotype. In the process, she also sacrificed herself for the well-being of her children.[23] Other cultures have the same familial bond. Sons and mothers are very close in Asian families, and often after marriage, the children move into the family home. In America, children move out at eighteen. The dominant U.S. culture has difficulty understanding foreign relationships and sees them as tainted.

A few years ago, the sitcom called "Chicken Soup," about a Jewish mother and her family, seemed appealing but didn't last. One problem was scheduling—the show was shown on a Friday night, when devout Jews would not be watching TV.[24]

Passive Victims

Films have been criticized for showing Jews as passive, helpless, and childlike. In *Schindler's List*, a war profiteer fooled the Nazis into letting him use Jews as cheap labor, rescuing more than 1,100 from death camps. In the film, only one main character is Jewish, the accountant, yet the number of Jews is large and amorphous. All are portrayed as victims. Some Jews complain that films have not told the whole story by excluding the Jews who fought fiercely and that the movies perpetuate a theme of "Ooh, look at the helpless victims about to be butchered by Nazis."[25]

Holocaust museums in Washington, D.C. and Los Angeles attempt to tell the full story of those who died in the camps.

Seeking the Non-Jewish Woman

The popular TV formula in which male Jews are married or romantically involved with a blonde denigrates Jewish women, because it makes them appear undesirable, and because almost never is the reverse true. In fact, some Jewish people use the word *shiksa* as a slur to imply that non-Jewish women are sex objects. In the popular media, few Jewish women are lusted after by gentile men, save Barbra Streisand by

Robert Redford in the film *The Way We Were*, and in the film, the two lovers separate at the end. Jewish interviewees mentioned TV programs as being the common vehicles for the Jew/non-Jew image, including "Bridget Loves Bernie," "Sisters," "Brooklyn Bridge," "Love and War," "L.A. Law," "Northern Exposure," "Seinfeld," and "thirty-something." Any Woody Allen film has the same theme. "I have never, ever, seen a major show where the central couple is a male Jew with a Jewish love interest," said one respondent.[26]

"Woody Allen" Types

Allen's movie persona is a true stereotype, a male with morose introspection, a fixation upon persecution and the Holocaust, with a restless, questing Jewish intellectuality. His relationships with non-Jewish women are always doomed to fail.[27] Philip Roth's characters are equally insecure and unsure of their identity. In a strange way, even the children's show "Sesame Street" contributed to the stereotyping of Jews. Mr. Hooper, the identified Jewish character, was an old man who died in the course of the show (the actor, Will Lee, actually did die). Jews are often portrayed as old (symbolic of a dying culture?).[28]

The best way to portray Jewish people is as unmistakably Jewish, yet possessing a common humanity, and experiencing the joys and sorrows of all people. In the film *Bugsy*, the Jewish character Meyer Lansky controlled the money for the Las Vegas mobsters, but it's a historical fact that he did so because he was universally trusted by the Italian mob.[29]

Programming is changing. The "Northern Exposure" creators were careful not to make Dr. Fleischman just another nebbish Jewish guy. He's athletic, not the clumsy stereotype, and open to others, not haughty. "Joel's a strong guy. And he knows how to fix things. That runs counter to the stereotype," said the producer.[30]

Alienated Jew

In plays and movies, Jews have been depicted as alienated from society, persecuted, isolated by their Jewish identity, and more recently, isolated from the identity. Steven Spielberg said he made the film *Schindler's List* for himself, to retake his roots. His relatives were Polish and Ukrainian victims of the Nazis. As a boy in Ohio, "I was embarrassed because of my Jewishness." He was "smacked and kicked around" at high school: "Two bloody noses. It was horrible."[31] The alienation of the Jew has led to serious suffering and the survival tactic of "going undercover."

CONCLUSION

They are the largest contributors (per capita) to all charities, including the NAACP. They went to the South during the Civil Rights Movement. Some died there.

He or she might save your life in the operating room, defend you adroitly in court, fight for your civil rights in the ACLU.

There's more to them than meets the eye.

NOTE

The material for this article came from the popular press, books, and face-to-face, telephone, and E-mail interviews, along with posts to Internet news groups such as "soc.culture.jewish." My thanks to the interviewees: Seth Adelson, Alan Asper, Jessica Bernhardt, Eleanor Blum, David R. Brill, Ava Brody, Bonnie Jean Chakravorty, Spencer Cox, Sheree R. Curry, Karen Ford, Andy Goldfinger, Thomas Hamilton, Steven Jon Haruch, Jerry Hirsch, Joerg von Kirschbaum, Andrew G. Kriger, Eugene Kushnirsky, Michael A. Leeds, Rendi Mann-Stadt, Steve Mayer, Lee Parpart, Naomi Rivkis, Dan Vitale, and Claire Ellen Weinstein.

9

The Emotional, Irascible Irish

Susan Dente Ross

Although America had been and would continue to be peopled by a steady stream of immigrants, the Irish embodied the first great wave of immigrants to work America's burgeoning industry and to build and inhabit its urban slums.[1] Irish Americans were, in one sense, a byproduct of industrialization's demand for cheap labor. The massive Irish influx served the needs of a growing American economy, but it presented a social problem.

Irish immigrants inhabited the most rundown parts of the Eastern cities to which they gravitated. They built shanty towns behind the warehouses and alongside the railroad tracks, where, amid poor sanitation and overcrowding, they raised cows, goats, and pigs. They had no choice but to live amid poverty, squalor, and disease. Their low social status caused personal feelings of inferiority and depression. Many escaped through alcohol and were arrested by the police for public drunkenness and fighting, thus creating the foundation of the stereotype of the lazy, drunken Irish person.

The negative image of the Irish in nineteenth-century America flourished outside the media. Until the mid-nineteenth century, the great annual Irish celebration of St. Patrick's Day gave rise to physical effigies of the Irish stereotype. The eve of St. Patrick's Day was marked by "Paddy making," in which a life-size image of an Irishman "dressed in rags, its mouth smeared with molasses, sometimes wearing a string of potatoes around its neck or a codfish to mock the Friday fasting and with a whiskey bottle stuck out of one pocket" was erected in a public place.[2]

Cartoons, many penned by Thomas Nast, of Irish cops and Tammany Hall politicians on the take became so much a part of the culture that the traditional Irish symbols could be omitted without losing meaning. Cartoons derisive of the Irish featured their employment, their housing and cleanliness, their social habits, their sexual promiscuity, their proclivity to take bribes and more. They ran regularly in

Harper's Weekly and other media. The Irish were caricatured as "ignorant, shiftless, credulous, impulsive, mechanically inept and boastful" peasants with an "inclination toward drinking and related crimes."[3]

A representative cartoon in *Harper's Weekly* in September 1852 portrayed an Irishman beating a balking mule, which he resembles closely, while two gentlewomen look on in horror. Other drawings throughout the period display Irishmen brawling in the streets during an election; a buxom young Irish woman surrounded by leering, drinking men who look on as she tells her employer that they are all her "cousins"; and ragged, filthy, violent men, women, and children crowded into a slum above the label, "A Court for King Cholera."

Albert Memmi, Jean Paul Sartre, and others said such colonial stereotypes are "self-fulfilling and self-justifying images,"[4] and Richard Lebow suggested that the stereotype "had a profound effect on later policy" and on the Irish self-image.[5]

By the turn of the century, concurrent with the arrival of new ethnic groups to America, the cartoon image of the Irish would soften and become more comic. The Irishman of the early twentieth century is portrayed as a "good-natured, fun-loving, imaginative" fellow,[6] a jolly leprechaun busily consuming hard liquor.[7] At the same time, Finley Peter Dunne's narrative sketches of *Mr. Dooley*, a bachelor bartender who proffered one-sided conversations to the slow-witted, heavy-drinking Hennessy, presented a less caustic and more romanticized version of lower-class Irish immigrant life to American newspaper readers.

For more than twenty years beginning in 1893, character Martin Dooley satirized the Irish community, which included the policeman who "drinks his beat" and the alderman who does "no work or worry." While Dunne's sketches often addressed the deeper human reality of Irish immigrants, they also continued to portray and to reinforce the stereotype of the Irish American as a "happy drunk."[8] The Irish themselves contributed to this portrayal with literally "dozens of [popular] Irish songs [that] represent the Irish as good-natured, roistering, and brawling individuals who get drunk, meet their friend, and for love knock him down."[9]

The stereotyped image of Irish Americans lost credence as the Irish escaped poverty in the 1930s and after. Empowered by the positive moral values of the Catholic church, they worked through their powerful government and labor organizations to improve the living conditions of all citizens. Better jobs improved their economic position and status. Education aided their assimilation as more Irish had better knowledge of English and were able to mix more successfully with mainstream culture.

In his 1981 apology to all Irish Americans, Andrew Greeley noted that while the harsh nineteenth-century stereotype of the Irish had largely disappeared, it had been replaced in the late twentieth century by the plaint of Irish American writers lamenting the economic failure of the Irish in America.[10] Greeley said neither portrait is accurate. He contended that the Irish had been both successful and had retained their ethnic identity in America.[11] In similar vein, historian Marjorie Fallows noted that "[i]f any immigrant group can be said to have merged into the American social structure to the point where neither they nor the host society any longer cares to dwell on presumed ethnic differences or to limit participation in any area of life because of them, this may well be true of the Irish American."[12] Others disagree.[13]

As Richard Stivers noted in 1976, "[t]o the non-Irish world perhaps no behavior is more associated with the Irish than drinking."[14] Authors Margaret Fitzgerald, Joseph King, and Andrew Greeley among others have condemned the tendency of some historians to repeat and reinforce this popular image that a disproportionate weakness for alcohol is one of the few surviving residues of Irish heritage.[15] "It is distressing that historians . . . are still parroting nonsense"[16] that drink is the principal fact of being Irish that they have not been able to shake.[17] Historians who have said the Irish possessed more than a mere reputation for drink can cite numerous studies showing that the Irish are the ethnic group of Anglo Americans with the greatest tendency toward drunkenness and alcoholism.[18]

A pair of newer studies have found otherwise. A study published in 1993 by the Economic and Social Research Institute in Dublin found that alcohol consumption by adults in Ireland is half that of France or Spain. Another study published in London found that Irish immigrants to Britain drank no more heavily than their British counterparts. Fitzgerald and King also noted in 1990 that omissions and distortions in modern textbooks about the historic role of Irish immigrants to America contribute to the persistence of stereotypical images of the Irish.

An abundance of modern media accounts also continues to reinforce the stereotype of Irish drinkers. A database search of major U.S. newspaper stories on the Irish between Jan. 1, 1992, and April 30, 1994, found that a preponderance of the stories dealt with drinking and/or St. Patrick's Day. One story said that "aside from the focus on violence in news stories, the other most common source of the Irish persona is entertainment; movies and television, both prone to leaving viewers with fast easy labels of the Irish . . . 'either as warring factions or as leprechaun stereotypes.'"[19]

In a representative example, on the eve of St. Patrick's Day, March 16, 1994, the *New York Times* ran a story reminiscent of media stereotyping of more than a century earlier focused on the role of the pub. The story, titled "The Pub: A Center of Ireland in Exile," concentrated on a women's dart championship after which the "women got rowdy, . . . shook bottles of beer, covering the tops with their thumbs, and sprayed each other until their faces and blouses were soaked and sticky . . . . They climbed up on the bar and ran up and down, shimmying and screaming for joy."[20]

The Irish in this news account said their social life centered on the pub, but "the new immigrants resent the stereotype that portrays the Irish as heavy drinkers."[21] Yet, the article noted, the number of new New York pubs increased alongside rising Irish immigration to the city.[22]

Violence, cunning, and graft also continue to dominate media coverage of the Irish Americans. A 1984 "Frontline" documentary, "The Old Man and the Gun," focused on Michael Flannery, who had been acquitted of conspiring to ship guns to the Irish Republican Army. The rather unsympathetic portrait showed Flannery comparing himself to George Washington and boasting that he "got away" with pulling the wool over the eyes of the jury.

A 1993 *Newsday* column opens with an Irish American man explaining that as a boy his family duty had been to close all the windows in the family's Brooklyn apartment when a family fight broke out to prevent the neighbors from hearing.[23] Then the man told of family gatherings with hours of drinking, the eventual fistfights, and the visit from the police.[24] The author acknowledged the stereotyping of Irish and said it was not "politically correct" but concluded that as an Irish American she could use it to help other Irish Americans face "the truth" and challenge them to meet a "higher standard of behavior and responsibility."[25]

Coverage of St. Patrick's Day in the 1990s has focused heavily on conflict over the exclusion of gay marchers from several historic parades. Some of the early stories included a 1991 column in which Anna Quindlen said sponsors of the New York parade had helped confirm the stereotype of the Irish as "antediluvian bigots" by trying to keep the homosexual contingent from marching.[26] That same day, a column by Pete Hamill called opponents of the gay marchers "terminal Donkey[s]" who had "barely risen from the primeval bogs of Ireland" and who epitomized Irish cruelty, stupidity, and hypocrisy.[27] Jimmy Breslin weighed in against Irish Catholicism, as contrasted with Italian Catholicism, and said the former was filled with "hate and meanness."[28]

Thus, it seems clear that although more than one-sixth of the U.S. population, as measured by the 1990 Census, is Irish, negative stereotypes abound. Nearly a century and a half after the arrival of large numbers of Irish immigrants, the American media continue to reinforce presumed ethnic differences of the Irish.

10

Anglo American Stereotypes

Charles N. Davis

The mass media stand accused of perpetuating stereotypes of many American multicultural groups. But ignored in most analyses of visual stereotypes is the Anglo-Saxon.[1] This is unfortunate, for stereotypes in the mass media begin and end with the Anglo-Saxon or white person (defined for purposes of this chapter as Anglo), the group held largely responsible for all other stereotypical presentations.

The inclusion of Anglo Americans in a discussion of visual stereotypes may offend those from other cultural groups whose stereotypes constitute the bulk of this book. The question arises whether Anglos, as owners and operators of the press that perpetuated so many of the stereotypes discussed in this book, are capable of feeling the sting of stereotypical portrayal in the mass media. Upon deeper reflection, however, it becomes clear that just as Native Americans, Irish Americans, women, and children have fought stereotypical presentation in popular culture, the Anglo's contradictory position in American society has generated its fair share of stereotypes.

Indeed, the Anglo's stereotypical portrayal as the preferred class in American society is a mixture of truth and fairy tale. Throughout North American history, the Anglo male and, to a lesser degree, the Anglo female, are portrayed as the fortunate class to whom the spoils of democracy fell as if by divine birthright. The earliest visual presentations of Anglos in colonial America were uniformly powerful and aristocratic in nature.[2] The colonials were portrayed through the actions of their leaders: They were men of substance off on adventure.

That colonial newspapers generated some of the nation's first media stereotypes was more a product of the times than a deliberate attempt to isolate certain segments of society. Outside New England, literacy rates were low and potential readers were scattered too widely to justify many publications.[3] Indeed, the early colonial newspaper was the province of the educated Anglo male. *The New England*

Courant, the *Boston Gazette*, the *American Weekly Mercury*, and the other colonial publications that sprang from the political debates of the day certainly fostered their share of stereotypical narrative. As the seeds of the American Revolution were sown, foreign nations were treated with uniform contempt.[4] The state religion—be it Calvinism, Lutheranism or Anglican—was closely linked to editorial coverage while other religions were rarely tolerated and usually ignored.[5]

Printers, publishers, and editors were important influences in preparing the public for revolution and maintaining morale during the War of Independence. Isaiah Thomas' *Massachusetts Spy*, Thomas Paine's *Common Sense*, and other revolutionary editors concentrated on weighty political debates, serving their largely Anglo, largely male readers a dose of politics, commerce, and daily events that can best be described as propaganda.[6] Patriotism and nationalism were perhaps the first stereotypical attributes created by the American press. The newspapers of the day portrayed a united front struggling for independence, ignoring the vast political schisms that dominated the drafting of the Articles of Confederation and later of the Constitution. The patriot was the embodiment of Anglo-Saxon power, risking life and limb against royal oppression. This was the Patriot Ideology,[7] a stereotypical warlike image that still appears frequently.

By the end of the American Revolution, the newspaper had grown in sophistication but had not broadened its scope from political debate to encompass the day-to-day journalism which typifies the mass media today. One simple observation about the early press may help explain why the media today still are struggling to incorporate the disenfranchised. Put bluntly, the early newspaper was not created to serve a mass audience. This means that as the United States grew into an industrialized nation, newspapers that wished to survive were forced to change their basic editorial mission. This was accomplished by covering the masses–a task for which the newspaper was ill-prepared. As a result, the media presented non-Anglo groups through their own belief systems. Their own preconceived notions about Africans, Native Americans, women, and countless other groups can be reviewed in the accompanying discussions of media stereotypes.

Under-represented groups, however, were not the only victims of this myopic presentation. It is important to remember that until the 1960s, the newsroom, like the newspaper, was the product of educated Anglo males—not at all highly educated or wealthy, but nevertheless products of newsroom owned and operated by a single socioeconomic class. By the end of the 1800s, entry into big-city journalism was prohibited to all but the rich. Henry Raymond started the *New York Times* in 1851 with $100,000; by 1883, Joseph Pulitzer had to pay $346,000 for the financially troubled *New York World*.[8] In short, the news media had become big business. Newspapers reflected their ownership, creating the stereotypes lamented today. Yet the stereotype of the Anglo fostered during the development of the American press created what we shall describe as the Anglo stereotype: the image of the Anglo as ruler of his world, as rich, fat, and happy and at all times in charge of his destiny.

Stereotypical visual presentations of Anglo Americans can be traced to the earliest graphical illustrations in American newspapers, and continue today in television, newspapers, and magazines. Today it is called "male-bashing" or "reverse discrimination," but in its infancy stereotypical portrayals of Anglos was little more than a fantastical presentation of the status quo. Regardless of form or motivation, any media portrayal of Anglos that subjugates the individual to racial generalizations may be described as stereotypical. More often than not, no ill will is intended; in fact, the most persistent stereotypes of Anglos are perpetuated by themselves!

THE ANGLO AS POWER BROKER

The most enduring visual stereotype of the Anglo is as power broker or decision-maker. This stereotypical presentation, like so many other generalities attributed to Anglos, began as historical fact before turning into a stereotype. In politics, finance, and religion, to name but a few, our first decisions were made by Anglos whose images even today are associated with power. For example, think about the visual contacts you have had with George Washington, Abraham Lincoln or, for that matter, Donald Trump. The unmistakable image is power, whether manifested in desirable actions or tasteless greed. Now think about the images that dominate the daily makeup of the news: the mayor talking with reporters, the city council meeting, an attorney presenting evidence, or two bank presidents signing a merger agreement. The racial and gender component of these images has finally begun to change, but the theme underlying the image itself has not.

THE ANGLO AS RICH

Of course, the stereotypical image of the Anglo was created by Anglos themselves, but only by the smallest minority of a large and diverse class of people. The "typical" Anglo American in 1957 enjoyed less than eight years of formal education, worked for an hourly wage, and did not own an automobile.[9] These figures far exceeded the African American population, but America in the 1950s was far from the economic Shangri-La depicted by the mass media. In many sections of the country, Anglos and African Americans alike had suffered from crushing poverty since the Civil War, yet distinctions grew between the "ignorant, uneducated" African American and the "unfortunate" Anglo American.

Today, when Anglo financial giants fall upon misfortune or draw the wrath of government regulators, the media unwittingly contribute to the stereotype of the rich but corrupt business tycoon. A photograph of bond traders led away in handcuffs following an insider trading investigation is merely the stuff of news—albeit exciting news—but the reader surely connects the picture with the message that these are men not to be trusted, men who all happen to be Anglo. In a way, the financial community's historical unwillingness to diversify its work force has resulted in the types of visual stereotypes inevitable through news coverage.

THE ANGLO AS RACIST

In the late 1960s, as the United States continued to struggle with its racial identity, television executives discovered a new market. Surveys told them that the most voracious consumers were now affluent, urban, educated people under the age of thirty-five.[10] In an attempt to reach this audience, CBS (which by 1971 had lost much of the thirty-five-year-old market) launched "All In The Family," Norman Lear's situation comedy about a middle-American antihero who bullied his wife, tyrannized the rest of his family, and vented the most bigoted opinions imaginable. From the start, Archie Bunker became the object of controversy. Did the depiction of Archie Bunker have the therapeutic effect of forcing viewers to confront their own prejudices? Or did it merely reinforce prejudice by making it respectable?

Researchers continue to debate the show's impact on popular culture, but throughout the literature one theme resurfaces: Archie Bunker was, at least on some level, an accurate visual portrayal of middle-class Anglo American values and beliefs.[11] What "All In The Family" most definitely accomplished, however, was the perpetuation of a decades-old stereotype—the Anglo as inherently racist—that is furthered by countless visual messages presented every day.

CONCLUSION

One scholar described stereotypes as nothing more than "oversimplifications whose creation and form vary with different media but commonly invoke simplistic mental reactions."[12] When visual messages produce stereotypes, they encourage the recipient of the message to judge the image through predetermined values instead of asking the viewer to judge the information accompanying the image in the context in which it is presented. In other words, the viewer uses the image as confirmation of internal beliefs rather than as information to refine or change beliefs.[13] This thought process means that stereotypes are analogous to trademarks: When we see a trademark, we think of the product.

If that fact is true, Anglos face their fair share of stereotypical presentations. Anglo Americans are commonly referred to as a group, ignoring the regional, political, religious, philosophical, and other differences between each individual. The press, which gives the favored class ability to control and produce stereotypes, still is largely owned and operated by Anglos. Curiously, however, ownership has never stopped the Anglos from stereotyping themselves when it was in their interest.

Many of the historical stereotypes of the Anglo are crumbling, thanks in large part to the changes in American society since they were fostered. Our politicians, businesspeople, and soldiers no longer share a single socioeconomic background and the media no longer service an Anglo readership. Yet many stereotypes persist, posing troubling issues for visual communicators.

Visual stereotypes cannot be eradicated, for they often arise as a result of legitimate news coverage. If hundreds of Anglo bond traders are arrested for white-collar crimes, the news value of the image is not lessened by the lack of racial diversity. The same goes for the African American juvenile criminal whose photograph gives the editor pause. Visual messages in journalism deliver important news and information to the viewer. Stereotypes are an unfortunate, sometimes unavoidable consequence.

11

Arab Americans: Middle East Conflicts Hit Home

Nancy Beth Jackson

Terrorism invaded the American heartland on the morning of April 19, 1995, when a bomb in a rental van destroyed the federal building in Oklahoma City, leaving 169 dead and more than 500 others injured. As TV crews and emergency workers raced to the scene of the worst terrorist act on American soil, the media reported that the FBI had issued an alert for a pickup truck containing three male passengers, two of them said to be "Middle Eastern with dark hair and beards." In the end, Anglo American males were arrested for the crime.

The initial report, however, reflected an all-too-familiar stereotype—the Arab as terrorist. Shaped by international events, the stereotype was reinforced in February, 1993 when a 1,200-pound bound exploded in another rental van in the World Trade Center parking garage, killing six and injuring more than 1,000. Middle East terrorism became a local story as the suspects arrested turned out to be not members of an elite hit squad out of a Le Carré novel, but Arab immigrants.

The images on television and in the press of the Trade Center bombing played up the intrigue and drama as a blind sheik with diabetes, taxi drivers, hospital technicians, a chemical engineer, and grocery store clerks stood accused of carrying out the attack on the world's second tallest building and laying plans to blow up tunnels and other New York landmarks.[1] Shortly later, more Arabs made headlines in St. Louis when investigators discovered that a Palestinian immigrant and his wife had brutally knifed their teenage daughter to death, not for dating a black youth, as originally reported, but because her father's cell of plotters feared she would betray them.

By July 1993, *Time* was warning against "The Terror Within" and trumpeting that "the low-rent, loosely organized plot to bomb New York City demonstrates a deadly new threat to America's public safety."[2] The cover of the Oct. 4, 1993, national edition identified "a new breed of militant zealot" in "Mahmoud the Red," playing on Mahmoud's red hair, Danny the Red who led the 1968 student demonstrations in Paris, and fears symbolized by the color. The bold red block-lettered teaser invited readers "On the Trail of Terror" as a red-haired man, relaxed in an open-collared shirt, grinned from the cover. The eleven-page spread promised to explain "how an immigrant cabdriver from Egypt became an alleged ringleader of the gang that planted the powerful bomb at the World Trade Center."[3] Only after the reader was four inches into the text was the immigrant named in full as Mahmoud Abouhamlima, shown in an accompanying full-page snapshot wearing a baseball cap backward when he took his children to a Newark, New Jersey park.

He could have been any new immigrant looking for a better life in America, but Abouhamlima was "the epitome of the modern terrorist, a self-made commando pursuing a homemade agenda to disrupt Western civilization."[4] He was a "Teflon Terrorist" who left few tracks as he moved his family around predominantly Arab neighborhoods in Brooklyn and Jersey City. More disquieting was the almost full page of mug shots of other bearded Arab immigrants who were among the twenty-two alleged conspirators. Clearly, Mahmoud Abouhamlima was not the only Arab immigrant in America dedicated to destruction in his new homeland.

The bombing and the investigation that followed only confirmed the stereotype held by many Americans of "dirty Arabs" at home and abroad, a stereotype fed by international politics, sustained by the media both visually and in text and encouraged in literature and film by Americans from Mark Twain to Walt Disney. The Arabs themselves contribute to the negative image, believes David Lamb. "Public relations, I was to learn, was a concept the Israelis understood and the Arabs didn't and during my stay in the Middle East, I was constantly struck by the Arabs' inability to present to the world a favorable or accurate image of either themselves or their causes," he wrote after a four-year tour as *Los Angeles Times* correspondent based in Cairo.[5] Academics, too, have recognized the difficulties Arabs have had in securing such coverage. Because of the electronic media, conflicts in the Middle East have entered American living rooms just as Vietnam did and are perhaps accompanied by even less understanding despite the intimacy. "It is only a slight overstatement to say that Muslims and Arabs are essentially covered, discussed, apprehended, either as oil suppliers or as potential terrorists. Very little of the detail, the human density, the passion of Arab-Muslim life has entered the awareness of even those people whose profession it is to report the Islamic world," Edward W. Said, a Columbia University scholar, charged in 1981, "What we have instead is a limited series of crude, essentialized caricatures of the Islamic world presented in such a way as to make that world vulnerable to military aggression."[6] In an interview with the author in Cairo in May 1994, Said said he would make the same statement nearly 15 years later.

Yet the caricatures have changed. Although the Gulf War suggests that the Middle East is still "vulnerable" to intervention from the West, a new image has surfaced following the demise of the Soviet Union. Islam—or at least a militant Islam—has been cast as a stand-in for Communism. Once again the forces of Islam threaten to rush out of the Arabian deserts into the civilized world of the West, this time including a fifth column of immigrants in the growing Muslim populations of countries like the United States and France. The cover of the international edition of *Time* on June 15, 1992, posed the question, "Islam: Should the World Be Afraid?" The question appeared at the lower right hand corner of a dramatic photo of a minaret paralleled by a semi-automatic machine gun held aloft by a robed arm.

Viewed as monolithic and militant, Islam has become a favorite bogeyman among pundits. An *International Herald Tribune* editorial page column, reprinted from The *New York Times,* compared the threat to Nazism and fascism in the 1930s and Communism in 1950s. The author suggested that "Muslim fundamentalism is fast becoming the chief threat to global peace and security as well as a cause of national and local disturbance through terrorism." In case the reader had any doubts about the danger, the headline declared: "Another Despotic Creed Seeks to Infiltrate the West."[7] To add historical perspective, the top of the page featured a MacNeely editorial cartoon showing "crude weapons of the Crusades of the late 20th century": the Tomahawk and "the high accurate, mobile, stealth car cruise missile," a car loaded down with TNT. Even scholars like John L. Esposito, director of the Center for Muslim-Christian Understanding and author of a number of books about Muslims, inadvertently contribute to the scare campaign. Esposito wrote *The Islamic Threat: Myth or Reality?* to counter exaggerated views of Islam, yet anyone who went no further than the paperback cover might assume that Esposito saw more threat than reality. The cover photo was the ominous black outline of dome and minarets against the red sky of a setting sun.

Barbarism and cruelty are the most common traits associated with Arabs in recent films, which tend to lump Arabs, Muslim, Middle East into one highly negative image of violence and danger, if not death for anyone from the West. *Lawrence of Arabia* with its scenes of cruelty and torture, *Indiana Jones* films with snake pits in Egypt, and *Midnight Express* exposing the horrors of a Turkish (but not Arab) jail with Billy Hayes's courtroom indictment of the whole society are some of the most popular films that have reinforced negative images of peoples of the region.

The Arab actor best known in the West has been Omar Sharif, a Muslim convert born Michael Shalboub, son of a wealthy Alexandrian merchant of Lebanese descent. He won an Academy Award nomination for his portrayal of Ali, the handsome but seemingly cruel tribesman in *Lawrence of Arabia.* Dressed in black, Ali comes riding up as if out of a mirage. Even before he is within shouting distance, he shoots and kills Lawrence's guide for breaking tribal taboos and drinking at his desert well. Sharif's subsequent international fame as a leading man came not as an Arab lover but as a sort of generic exotic heartthrob. Cast as Dr. Zhivago and the Jewish gambler loved by Fanny Brice in *Funny Girl,* he played a sheik only once in *The Fabulous Adventures of Marco Polo.*

Media coverage of the Gulf War including Peter Arnett's dramatic live-from-Baghdad reports, computer-generated graphics on the networks and efforts of newspapers like The *Detroit Free Press* to present the news in language and design that would help everyone understand the war have replaced the Biblical maps as an introduction to the Middle East. High-tech coverage brought the Middle East into American homes but in the end did little to deepen understanding of the Arab World or its people. Later when another media blitz focused on two old foes, meeting not at Armageddon but on the White House lawn, the handshake image overshadowed the peace process itself as though one handshake solved it all.

Arabs remain the fall guys of editorial page cartoons. Arafat in a *Newsweek* cartoon reprinted by the *Egyptian Mail* on May 21, 1994, wears his familiar *hata* but his battle fatigues have been replaced by a striped shirt, tie and suspenders. He sits behind a desk bearing the sign "Palestinian Gov't." Five phones ring off the hook, stacks of paper crowd desk and floor. Behind him a chart shows a confused diagram of taxes, mail, police and sewers. His machine gun has been discarded, barrel down, into the waste basket. Bug-eyed, big-nosed and five-o'clock-shadowed, he thinks: "This may be a tad more complicated than pulling a trigger." Just as in *Lawrence of Arabia,* in which Arabs could win a savage battle for Damascus but fail to run the power plant or keep the water flowing from the taps, Arafat is portrayed as another quarrelsome, disorganized Arab.

Handshakes aside, images of the Arab world and Arab Americans have changed little in recent years, believes Edward Said, who rejects attempts to hyphenate his identity by religion, language, or national origin. Such a label "disqualifies" rather than qualifies an Arab American. "There is something already suspicious about you," he said in the Cairo interview. The image is not of diversity and success, of owners of professional football teams or Princeton scholars or impresarios, but of terrorists, militants, and extremists.

Even language, so important in Arab identity, is suspect. Said recalls his publisher asking him a decade ago to suggest Arabic literature to be translated for American audiences. Some months later when they met, Said discovered that his suggestions had been ignored. No Arabic texts were scheduled. When he asked why, the publisher replied, "The problem is that Arabic is such a controversial language."

In recent years, Arabic literature has been translated, including the works of Nobel Prize-winner Naguib Mahfouz, yet Said notes ruefully that such books "uniformly are never reviewed" simply, he says, because editors don't know what kind of people to pick as reviewers. Not only are politics a factor but knowledge of Arabic and its literature is rare. Arabic is still an "other" in America. It doesn't even make the Scholastic Aptitude Test's lengthy list of languages studied in high school. It can be indicated at the bottom of the list by checking "Other," more subtle than an editorial cartoon but perhaps a more damaging image.

In this era of multiculturalism, in which ethnic origin often translates into job opportunity as employees seek cultural diversity in the workplace, Arab Americans no longer are classified as "Turks" or "Turkos." But Arab Americans today find themselves equally ignored and misunderstood, victims of numbers or international and domestic events or an early success in assimilation. Said explains, "We're always 'other.' There are African Americans and Asian Americans and all that stuff, but we haven't made the list."[8]

PART III

GENDER STEREOTYPES

12

Women in the Work Force in Non-Traditional Jobs

Patsy G. Watkins

It's an undeniable fact that we rely on appearances to communicate something about who we are and how others should regard us. As more women move into work force positions of power, authority, and responsibility, the importance of appearance becomes increasingly clear. As women learn to compete successfully, they become aware of a not-so-subtle fact of life: Appearance is an essential external display of their authority—vis-à-vis male counterparts, the people they supervise and the world in general.

In the 1970s, women adhered to a carefully constructed appearance that more often than not involved a three-piece, dark-toned suit, patterned after the "power suit" worn by men in positions of authority. Now the "dress-for-success" guidelines have evolved to a different level as women have become more established in those same positions. Consider, for example, Glenn Close in the recent movie *The Paper,* as a powerful and ambitious New York City newspaper editor. She wore draping pants suits in soft, rich fabrics and light-colored silk blouses—clothes that certainly distinguished her from the female reporters on the paper.

These visual guidelines come about through an undefined process of communication carried on largely at the unconscious level. As women in challenging work force positions discover which appearance cues seem to be associated with professional respect, this information is conveyed to other women who hope to follow in their shoes—whether high or medium-to-low heels. The mass media play a critical role in the transfer of this information. The process itself is an example of how members of a certain cultural group—in this case, women who hold or seek positions of power and authority—develop agreement on ideas, values, and beliefs and how they should be expressed.

Like movies, magazines also offer excellent sources for searching out these visual cues. Although advertising photos would yield rich information, it would be more useful to consider photos of "real" women—the ones who are the subjects of magazine articles and who have to deal with real-world clothing budgets and executive culture. Therefore, this chapter focuses specifically on non-advertising photos in a sample of high-circulation magazines considered general interest, general business, and women's. By looking at these publications, perhaps we can determine what visual appearance cues signify female power and authority in the workplace. Do women seen as holding power and authority in the workplace share a certain "look"? If so, what are the features of that "look"? This chapter identifies such women and analyzes their appearances to determine the visual cues women use to establish their power and authority.

The appearance of members of a certain group is part of the cultural expression of that group, and such a group can be thought of as a subculture with its own values and beliefs. Theories about how cultural expression evolves among the members of a group have been offered by several observers of society, among them Emile Durkheim, the late nineteenth-century, early twentieth-century social scientist. Durkheim viewed culture as a social product. The culture of a particular society, he wrote, is the collective representation of the values, beliefs, activities, and rituals of that group. His work suggested that all cultural expressions are representations of a collective agreement and understanding: "They represent not just a particular society but social experience itself. . . . Groups and societies need collective representations of themselves to inspire sentiments of unity and mutual support."[1]

Consider the "subculture" of women in a New York City secretarial pool in the movie *Working Girl*—how they look, of course, but also how they act, how they talk, and the men they date. They represent a certain kind of social experience, and thus they have a "collective representation."

Wendy Griswold, discussing Durkheim, states that in the attempt to understand a certain group of people, one looks for these expressive forms "through which they represent themselves to themselves." She offers the example of Bessie Smith's blues songs, which are very expressive in relating the sorrow of an individual with a particular problem. But because they also resonate with something fundamental about the culture from which Smith came, the songs become a cultural expression of or association with that group, a specific representation of the difficulties of sustained relationships among poor blacks in the rural South.[2]

But how do members of a culture go about "agreeing" on these expressions— songs, dances, works of art, stories—as reflecting something about what they share? Durkheim labeled the process "collective production," and said that it involved the generation of art, ideas, beliefs, and culture through the interaction, cooperation, and organization of a group.[3] In collective production theory, then, cultural expressions are a consequence of the interactions of the members of a group.

Social psychologists call these interactions or dealings, "symbolic interactionism," which is concerned with how people develop and portray their roles in society. This means, for example, how we are socialized, how we learn to act in socially appropriate ways and present ourselves in socially acceptable "formats," such as appropriate clothing, hairstyles, cars, or the decoration of our homes.[4] It is a process through which an individual develops a sense of her identity in relation to the larger culture through reinforcement by approval or rejection by members of the group.

Stuart Ewen, another observer, calls this expressiveness "style," and suggests that "style provides us with ways of understanding societies." Personal style is a significant aspect of how people express themselves as individuals. Style also shows how groups express themselves in order to achieve self-identification and recognition. Personal and/or group style therefore becomes a means of communicating a variety of social values and ideas. For example, Ewen notes that in American culture, style has developed as a significant "qualification" for social and political leadership. Social relations of power are "refracted through the prism of style."[5] To assume the role, one must look the part. Thus, one's membership in different groups may be achieved by manipulating visual messages.

The idealization of female body shape and the meanings attached to its variations are included in the language of style and have changed dramatically in the past forty years. For example, the image of Marilyn Monroe published in the 1953 issues of *Playboy* magazine would seem plump by today's standards. The current preference in today's mass media images is for slenderness: "Thinness is a by-product of modernity," says Ewen. In fact, our culture associates class meaning and social value with certain body shapes.[6] Ewen calls it the middle-class bodily rhetoric of the 1980s. Certain advertisements, he says, "mark a culture in which self-absorbed careerism, conspicuous consumption, and a conception of *self* as an object of competitive display have fused to become the preponderant symbols of achievement."[7]

By becoming consciously aware of the underlying modes of style communication, any woman potentially can communicate immediately through those visual cues to a variety of social groups that she is a powerful and important person. Through social interactionism, she learns which groups are desirable and the visual cues associated with belonging to them. So, she can pierce her ears five times and shave her head, or wear sweats with Greek letters and pull back her hair with fluffy bows to indicate not only group membership, but even her status within that group.

The socialization process is accomplished in a variety of ways, but one of the most significant is through the mass media. As an example, consider magazines and how extremely specialized they are in the audiences they serve. Calvin, of the comic strip "Calvin and Hobbes," once proposed the idea of a magazine for gum-chewers because, he argued, there is a magazine for everybody. One important source of information for a woman who wants to learn how to present herself as powerful and authoritative would be magazines that carry pictures of women in such roles.

In looking for these images, however, a potential member of such a group would first have to be able to identify the women as powerful and authoritative before noting their visual appearance cues. Erving Goffman, in his 1976 book *Gender Advertisements*, analyzed how viewers of magazine ads could visually determine power and authority relationships among people pictured in the ads. He focused on gender roles in these ads and how they indicated dominance and subordination in the presentation of men and women. His framework has been used before in analyses of images, for example, by Klassen, Jasper, and Schwartz.[8]

In his study Goffman examined selected advertisements, asserting that the poses of women and men were contrived by the photographer to project a certain message for an ad. These messages, he said, were scenarios that reflected gender relationships in a society; the power or dominance dynamics of the relationships could be determined by certain poses, looks, or actions.

Goffman suggested that members of a society use a "common idiom" of wordless postures, positions, and glances to establish their relationships with others in social situations. Therefore, he says, because of the general acceptance and usage of such idioms, images that catch these behaviors can be interpreted.[9] Goffman identified several such idioms and defined them as categories. His classification system included five types of subtle messages that can convey dominance or subordination in a relationship; four of those classifications are relevant to this study and are used for determining whether or not a woman can be seen as powerful and authoritative. These are relative size, function ranking, ritualization of subordination, and licensed withdrawal.

If it is the case that postures and glances can establish social relationships, women looking for tips on how to dress to look powerful and authoritative will be able to spot role models, because they will understand the posture signals of power. It's an easy step from that to draw conclusions about the appearance cues associated with female power and authority.

In a recent study of sixty-six popular magazines, a total of seventy-nine women were identified as pictured in positions of authority and responsibility in the workplace. Of the periodicals sampled, two (*Ladies Home Journal* and *Lears*) included no photographs that fit this study, and one (*Seventeen*) included only one such photograph. Most of the images of women sought in this project were found in *Good Housekeeping, Time, Newsweek, Forbes,* and *Fortune.*

Mug shots (head shots) were avoided because they left too many questions either open to subjective judgment or completely unanswerable. Most photos used here pictured women from the waist or hips upward; therefore, information about skirt length, the wearing of pants versus skirts, and shoe styles was unavailable. Such information could be important because of its implications for suggesting a more reserved or provocative approach to dressing that is, long skirts versus short skirts, or medium-to-low heels versus high heels. The discussion of the individual categories examined will include more specifics about the subjects' appearance.

Hair

There was no overwhelming distinction in this sample among women with short hair and long hair. Exactly 50 percent of the women wore their hair long—shoulder length or below—whereas 42.5 percent wore their hair at eartip length or shorter. The remaining 7.5 percent wore their hair at a moderate chin length. Hair length as a style or appearance factor, therefore, does not seem too critical as a visual cue associated with power and authority.

Clothes

The clothing categories were "formal," "informal," and "casual." Examination of the sample led to the addition of another category, "uniforms." The category "casual" was dropped as inappropriate as the distinction between informal and casual was too vague. More than half of the women pictured (55.6 percent) wore formal office attire: carefully matched suits or suit jackets, all in a variety of colors—in fact, some very bright colors. There were no three-piece suits in pinstripes.

The number of women shown in uniforms was surprising—nearly 23 percent. These uniforms included laboratory coats as well as military attire. It should be noted that uniforms can both denote rank as well as cover up differences in rank. In most of these examples, however, the uniforms also confirmed the power and authority of the women pictured.

Figure

As mentioned earlier, Ewen noted that certain advertisements become symbols for achievement within society.[10]

This sampling of powerful and authoritative—*achieving*—women fit that expectation. The categories used here covered body shapes from the slenderness seen in models in magazine and television advertisements, to body shapes estimated to be somewhat heavier (ten to twenty pounds), and to body shapes estimated as much heavier (thirty pounds and more). Sixty-five percent were judged as ten to twenty pounds over the typical slender model body shape. Not quite one-third (28.75 percent) were model-slender and only 6.25 percent appeared to be thirty pounds or more over model-slenderness (see Chapter 22).

Facial Expression

The choices here were smiling, frowning, or neutral (no particularly discernible expression). Just over half (51.9 percent) of the women in this project smiled. Thirty-nine percent, however, were neutral. Less than 10 percent (8.86 percent) were frowning.

Apparent Age

The age categories were fixed in ten-year groups: twenties, thirties, fourties, fifties, sixties, and seventies. Often, the perceived age of a subject could be confirmed through the text of accompanying captions or articles; this checking of text was used only to pin down age estimates.

The women in these photos primarily appeared to be in their thirties and fourties (62.9 percent). Slightly more women seemed to be in their twenties (18.5 percent) than their fifties (16 percent). The remaining 4.93 percent represents the fraction of women in their sixties and seventies.

This same pattern is roughly reflected in the figures gathered by the U.S. Department of Labor (DOL) in 1993. That is, the age groups with the highest percentages of labor force participation were twenty-five to thirty-four (74.1 percent of women) and thirty-five to forty-four (76.8 percent). The age group forty-five to fifty-four dropped off only slightly (72.7 percent).[11] The DOL figures, of course, refer to women in all areas of the work force, not only managerial/administrative, so women in sales, for example, are also included. In all, by 1990 the proportion of women in the labor force in the U.S. was 57 percent of all women aged sixteen and over.[12]

CONCLUSION

The purpose of this project was to identify a visual profile of powerful women in the workplace. Two questions were posed: Are there visual cues associated with women pictured as powerful and authoritative? And, if so, what are those visual cues?

The research suggests there are certain features of physical appearance that are associated with women perceived as powerful. The profile developed here shows that length of hair is not an issue; women were seen with short, medium, and long styles. The two main factors were style of clothing and figure. Women definitely dressed the part; they wore formal office attire, such as suits or color-coordinated jackets and blouses. They did not confine themselves to dark colors, but wore very bright yellows and pinks as well. If they were not in formal office attire, they were more likely to be in uniform, whether the uniform was U.S. military, scientist's lab coat, or judge's robes.

In terms of a woman's figure, these subjects were not fashion-model thin, but they certainly were not overweight by any standards. Although the shape of their figures was never made apparent by their clothes, they appeared to be of medium weight. Only a small percentage of this sample could be considered overweight by mid-1990s standards.

Facial expression also seemed to be a moot point. Although many more subjects smiled or had neutral expressions, rather than frowning, the general impression from looking through these magazines was that these were standard expressions for both men and women.

Achieving women tend to be fairly young, in their thirties and forties. The relatively few images of women in their fifties, sixties or seventies can be attributed to the fact that fewer women of that generation were able or encouraged to get professional training. Women began to enter professional schools in large numbers in the 1970s, and those women would be in leadership positions today.

The research also suggests the following:

- The mass media carry relatively few images of professionally achieving women; in this study, only seventy-nine images were found in sixty-six issues of magazines. The "women's" magazines used in this study included very few such images, and, in fact, issues of some magazines in this sample had none. The general interest and general business magazines tended to have more pictures of powerful women. However, looking through these magazines, one gains the distinct impression that pictures of achieving men far outnumber those of women.
  This could simply reflect the fact that there are fewer women in roles of power and authority. U.S. government research shows that even though women have made progress in entering occupations held predominantly by men in the past, especially managerial and professional specialty occupations, the majority of women are still in traditional "female" occupations.
  Of all women in the workforce in 1990, 42.2 percent were in "administrative and managerial" positions.[13]
- This research was not concerned with whether women of power and authority dressed in sexually provocative ways. However, it was noted informally that their clothing was definitely conservative and professional. Suits and dresses did not cling to their bodies or emphasize figures; there was no cleavage. Since there were almost no full-body photos, length of skirt could not be determined. Their clothing only slightly echoed the structure of the male business suit, but with more feminine touches such as bright colors and softer fabrics.

The meaning of this research is that in the culture of women in professionally powerful and authoritative positions—and those who would like to be—there is a "common idiom" of visual appearance cues that signify their status. Through their appearance they confirm their self-identity as well as identify themselves and their roles to colleagues and subordinates. These factors of appearance serve as visual cues to the world that they are to be taken seriously and are communicated by the media.

As Coco Chanel would say, "Dress shabbily, they notice the dress; dress impeccably, they notice the woman."

13

Women as Mothers

Dona Schwartz

At the conclusion of my first prenatal checkup twelve years ago, the obstetrician's receptionist offered me copies of two magazines for expectant mothers, *American Baby* and *Expecting*. Each time I came in for a checkup I would pick up the new issue, free of charge. Reading these publications produced a mixed response: I was eager to read whatever I could find that promised to prepare me for the upcoming birth of my first child, yet at the same time, reading *American Baby* and *Expecting* was somewhat unsettling, rather like morning sickness. The smiling faces of happy women, men, and babies overwhelmed me. I resolved to save my growing collection for future research so that I might examine the image of mothering they presented.

For years my mommy magazines lay untouched, awaiting the analysis I'd promised. They moved with me from house to house. In the intervening years the academic literature devoted to the subject of mothering has grown[1] and at the same time, the number of publications targeting the so-called "childbirth market" has mushroomed, coincident with the "echo boom" of the late 1980s. These changes and another pregnancy provided me with the impetus to collect a new set of magazines and investigate the images they offer parents, especially women, the majority of their readership.

My discussion here focuses on childbirth and parenting magazines available on the newsstand: *Parents, Working Mother, Child,* and *Parenting* and several magazines distributed free to expectant and new parents. Among the subscription-based magazines, *Parents* is the oldest and most traditional of the magazines, emerging in 1926. *Working Mother* first appeared in 1977 to capitalize upon the increasing presence of mothers in the labor force. *Child* in 1986 and *Parenting* in 1987 were positioned to exploit nesting baby boomers.

Cahners Publishing Company, a division of Reed Publishing USA, produces

American Baby (in publication since 1938), one of the complimentary magazines available in the waiting rooms of obstetricians. At childbirth education classes Cahners distributes *Childbirth* as part of a prenatal "sampling and couponing package" called the *American Baby Basket for Expectant Parents*. And *American Baby's First Year of Life* arrives via the *American Baby Basket for New Mothers*, delivered to the hospital room.

In 1991 Time Warner purchased *Baby Talk*, a magazine published since 1935. The recently formed Parenting Group of Time Publishing Ventures includes its free publications, *Baby Talk* and *Baby on the Way*, along with *Parenting*, mentioned above. *Baby Talk* appears monthly, making its way to new and expectant mothers at doctors' offices, in diaper service bundles, and in the baby departments of stores like Sears, Macy's, JCPenney, Best, Target, Walmart, Nordstrom, Bloomingdales, and Marshall Fields.

Baby on the Way, an annual, also appears in a version called *Baby on the Way: Basics*, targeting women who "read at a grade school level or are just learning English." The editorial content of the two magazines is similar even though *Basics* is written at a fifth-grade level.[2] Although the editorial copy is not updated, *Baby on the Way* is issued in March and September to allow for the insertion of new advertising. The *Basics* edition is slimmer, with shorter, less detailed articles, and significantly fewer ads. *Baby on the Way* is available in doctors' offices, while *Basics* is primarily distributed through clinics, state health departments, WIC programs, schools, and literacy programs.

The sample described here (with the exception of *Baby on the Way: Basics*) represents the range of childbirth and parenting magazines middle-class women typically encounter in their doctors' waiting rooms. These publications provide an authoritative resource for contemporary mothers seeking reliable information. While female kin may once have served this function, industrialization's dispersal of the extended family makes such expertise inaccessible to many women. Even when such first-hand knowledge is available, it is often devalued and treated as lore or "old wives' tales," inferior to the printed word or the wisdom of the medical establishment.

Stuart Ewen traces the displacement of familial authority during the early twentieth century.[3] He argues that the growth of consumer capitalism in the 1920s and 1930s depended on investing patriarchal authority in industrialists, enabling them to instruct families in "proper living," including appropriate patterns of consumption. Thus, consumer capitalism transformed the family from a unit of production into a unit of consumption. This transfer of authority created a need for new sources of information, a role that could be assumed in part by mass circulation magazines. Magazines still serve this function while they simultaneously tie the family to consumer culture. As Time Warner explains to potential advertisers: "New mothers rely on a host of information resources—pediatricians, friends and relatives, childcare books and childcare magazines. Magazines play a vital role in their passionate search for information."

Childbirth and parenting magazines exemplify corporate capitalism's penetration of the domestic sphere. Their pages affirm a consumerist view of family life. The range of topics covered varies little from publication to publication, although a distinctive style may create an illusion of difference among them. The annuals, *Childbirth*, *Baby on the Way*, and *First Year of Life*, focus on pregnancy and prenatal care, labor and delivery, and infants' growth, development, care and feeding, along with articles advising prospective and new parents on "essential" purchases:

maternity clothes, the layette, furnishings, toys, car safety seats, and the like.

The remaining magazines present the same topics as the annuals with these additions to the mix: fashions for mothers and babies; exercise; home management advice, including recipes, laundry tips, housework strategies, activities to keep kids (and their mothers) busy; childcare options; marital relations; fathers and fathering; child discipline; infant, child, and maternal health; employment and employment-related issues. *Working Mother*, targeting women who work both inside and outside the home, presents a nearly identical lineup, complete with articles on such topics as bathroom cleaning. Only its heavier emphasis on employment-related issues distinguishes *Working Mother* from the rest.

Magazines compete for their share of readers by offering an impressive slate of expert consultants and columnists representing the medical establishment. *Baby on the Way* takes this strategy furthest, placing the seal of the American College of Obstetricians and Gynecologists on the cover. The smiling face of its president greets the reader on page one and his message to the "mother-to-be," placed where the editor's column typically appears, suggests he plays an important role in the magazine's production.

While the editorial copy found in these magazines acknowledges, at least superficially, the changes affecting contemporary mothering, the visual messages present hollow stereotypes. The images of mothers illustrating both editorial and advertising copy evoke a world of blissful, predominantly Anglo, dual-parent childrearing. On these pages everyone smiles broad toothy grins (except for the infants). With remarkable uniformity women appear well rested, well dressed, well groomed, and in control of both baby and domestic surround. Even in childbirth, women maintain their composure and their polish. They are shown at each stage of labor and delivery, absorbed in the task at hand, exerting genuine effort while keeping every hair in place.

The babies and children who appear solo or with their mothers (or, on occasion, with their fathers) reflect the same well being and contentment. Nestled in their mothers' arms, they offer no resistance to being fed; they show no evidence of colic or fussiness of any kind. They attentively listen to the books their loving mothers read. Their faces beam as they sit in their swings and strollers or play with their toys. Their cute clothes never suggest that babies regularly spit up and mash food on themselves. These kids don't get dirty.

Despite claims that they address contemporary "parents," the magazines show mothers almost exclusively. Fathers occasionally join mothers in the admiration of their offspring, play with them, or tenderly administer to their needs. But more often men appear in illustrations accompanying articles about pregnancy, childbirth, or postpartum sexual relations. In this way, men are primarily shown as husbands and not fathers, associated with their wives instead of their children. Men fade from view altogether as magazines embrace such topics as childrearing practices, household maintenance, and self preservation (that is, articles about fashion, exercise, cosmetics, or domestic survival skills).

The world of childbirth and parenting magazines is overwhelmingly white. Fair-haired Anglo babies gambol across the pages of article after article, ad after ad. A sprinkling of Asian, African American, and Latino children signals the existence of a non-Anglo middle-class population. When children of color do appear, they symbolize multiple races and ethnicities simultaneously through their ambiguous identity. All of the babies and children on these pages have extremely light skin; they can interchangeably represent African American, Latino, Mediterranean,

Native American, or Middle Eastern populations. This polysemy accomplishes two tasks: First, magazines require fewer images of children of color to simultaneously represent a variety of communities, and second, the light-skinned children presented in these pages more easily blend into the white terrain, diminishing their claim on the reader's attention. Non-Anglo mothers are seldom seen. When they do appear, in almost all cases they too have light brown skin; non-Anglo fathers are virtually nonexistent.

In these pages, mothers and children pose and do little more. Pictures that show women working rarely appear. Articles instructing women on bathing their infants or breast-feeding show them engaged in a task. Ads for strollers may show women pushing them (or they may simply stand alongside them, posing like a man with his new car, a genre found in many family photo albums). Women occasionally appear reading to their children or playing with them. Women themselves are depicted reading while their infants sit pacified in a mechanical swing. No one tires, no one sweats, no one frets. Motherhood is presented as a series of appealing snapshots.

Images of pregnancy, childbirth, and mothering presented to women through mass circulation magazines offer a mythological representation far removed from everyday life. They depict a narrowly circumscribed world of Anglo nuclear families aglow with happiness and plenty. Framed as informative resources for women, they serve most effectively as training manuals in the practice of purchasing goods and services. Heeded well, they offer the promise of fulfillment they so relentlessly represent.

Ewen persuasively argues that industrialization wrested the wife's productive role from her and transformed her into a domestic manager whose primary responsibility was to marshal family consumption of mass-produced goods.[4] This trend extended to her performance as a mother.

Ewen explains, "Even in the area of motherhood, women were told to rely on the guidance provided by ads and other corporate agencies of information. Motherhood had become a profession sustained by industrial production. Women were told of dangers in their homes and to their children, and were given commodity solutions."[5]

Contemporary publications continue to provide that guidance. Through advertising and editorial copy, mothering magazines help to inculcate an approach to domestic life that perpetuates industrial capitalism by simultaneously promoting consumerism and offering solutions to the problems it creates.

Examining the media kits publishers prepare for potential advertisers corroborates the motivations suggested by these representations. For example, the Time Warner kit for publications in its Parenting Group trumpets:

More than 1.7 million women receive *Baby on the Way* early in their pregnancies, before all the many purchases required for baby have been made.

Baby Talk reaches expectant and new mothers every month through a targeted circulation system that ensures that readers receive *Baby Talk* just as they're seeking information, forming brand loyalties, deciding on purchases. 52% of the magazine's circulation is via point-of-sale newsstand-type displays in the baby departments of nearly 5,000 leading retail stores . . . . This means your audience is getting your message in the right place and at the perfect time—when they're ready to buy.

PARENTING READERS ARE AS RESPONSIVE TO
ADVERTISERS AS THEY ARE TO THEIR CHILDREN!

Everyone knows that parenting is a demanding job. It's also inspiring, challenging, enlightening, emotional, and rewarding. Because of all those things and more, today's parents need products and services that respond to their changing needs. As their family grows, so does their need for new products and services. And those needs are growing by leaps and bounds.

That these and many other magazines targeting women (and men) promote consumption seems unremarkable. Yet several points merit further note. The strategy evinced in these representations underscores John Berger's arguments regarding the methods and consequences of advertising.[6] These depictions of mothers suggest very little of the actual labor involved, or the context in which that labor takes place. They present static idealizations that fail to encompass the challenges contemporary mothers face. Berger suggests that publicity tends to be "retrospective and traditional" because it "cannot itself supply the standards of its own claims."[7] The images in childbirth and parenting magazines evoke the world inhabited by Donna Reed or June Cleaver, images of perfection familiar to baby boom mothers.

Berger argues further that "the purpose of publicity is to make the spectator marginally dissatisfied with his present way of life—not with the way of life of society, but with his own within it. It suggests that if he buys what it is offering, his life will become better. It offers him an improved alternative to what he is."[8]

Both publicity images and editorial illustrations in mothering magazines offer readers fantasy. Images of dual-parent families, unhurried and without want fail to ring true yet hold out the promise of fulfillment achieved through appropriate consumption. The regular introduction of newer and better products to improve women's lives continually defers satisfaction and ensures perpetual inadequacy, thus renewing the cycle.

Publicity performs an important social function, according to Berger, and my analysis leads to a similar conclusion. He writes, "Publicity turns consumption into a substitute for democracy. The choice of what one eats (or wears or drives) takes the place of significant political choice. Publicity helps to mask and compensate for all that is undemocratic within society. And it also masks what is happening in the rest of the world."[9]

Magazine images of motherhood mask the everyday realities of women's lives. A brief survey of recent U.S. statistics makes the fissure between image and reality clear. Magazine media kits emphasize the existence of an "echo boom" that has produced, according to Time Warner, a "new mother market."

From Time Warner's media kit, "Every twenty-one months, this market totally recycles itself, with a whole new crop of expectant and new mothers to step in and purchase more and more products, year after year. And since the birthrate is projected to remain high well into the first decade of the twenty-first century, the new mother market will remain a powerful and sizable purchasing force."

Census data provide detail lacking in this pitch. Fertility rates reported for underrepresented groups were 95.2 per 1,000 Latina women and 69.2 for African American women, compared with 61.6 for Anglo women. While Latina women ages fifteen to forty-four represent 9 percent of all women in the United States, they accounted for 14.3 percent of all births. Of the 35 million families with children in 1992, nearly 30 percent were headed by a single parent; 86 percent of those single parents were mothers. In 1990, 45 percent of female-headed families with children lived in poverty. In 1989, only 26 percent of custodial mothers who were awarded child support received the full amount. In 1993, 57.9 percent of mothers with children under six worked outside the home, an increase of about 50 percent since 1975. Of 59.8 million owner-occupied housing units listed in the 1991 Census, just under 90 percent were owned by Anglos, 8 percent by African Americans, and 4 percent by Latinos. Among the homeless population, families with children are estimated to constitute 36 percent. The 1992 median state AFDC grant for a family of three fell short of the monthly poverty threshold by more than $500. Reports of child abuse and child neglect have nearly tripled since 1980.[10]

Some of these same statistics can be found in media kits, but the magazine images presented to women readers are unresponsive to the data. Rather than deal with the real circumstances of women's lives, the publications promote allegiance to a false, if appealing ideal. Except for *Baby on the Way: Basics*, these magazines target a middle-class readership primed and ready to make the purchases considered necessary to childrearing. The socialization middle-class women undergo shapes the experience of poor women as well, as the undifferentiated imagery of *Basics* demonstrates. For poor women, domestic management and the consumption it dictates present greater challenges; poor women's perceptions of their own inadequacy may be more profound.

Social statistics make it clear that capitalism has failed to ensure the well-being of women and children. The family wage system engendered by industrialization maintained the supremacy of the husband within the nuclear family, while cementing the wife's dependency.[11] That social and economic contract no longer holds, and we have witnessed the "feminization of poverty." Today, the gap between those who can sufficiently provide for their families and those who cannot continues to widen. Most needy of all are women and their children. Childbirth and parenting magazines obscure these statistics and the social consequences they portend.

As a representative of the primary audience for whom these messages are intended, I can testify to their seduction. Like the first time I discovered them in the obstetrician's waiting room, I eagerly paged through all of the magazines I encountered during my recent pregnancy. I marveled at the improvements in products manufactured since my first child's birth. I bought some new stuff. But the unsettling feeling I experienced twelve years ago has grown to full blown nausea. The more I have learned about motherhood, the less these messages charm. The problems they mask have multiplied, their reach has extended, and I know fantasy cannot expunge reality. As the emptiness of these images becomes increasingly salient, they may provoke unexpected responses from the women whose interests they undermine.

14

Women as Sex Partners

Kim Walsh-Childers

What is sexy?

Learning the answers to that question and ways to incorporate those answers into one's psychological, social, emotional, and behavioral identity is one of the central tasks of adolescence and one of the continuing tasks of adulthood. It also may be one of the most difficult tasks, at least in the United States, because our society is reluctant to answer, in any systematic way, the question of "What is sexy?" and all of the related questions that follow from it: "How can I be sexy?" "Should I be sexy?" "To whom should I appear sexy?" and "Once I've learned how to be sexy, what should I do with that knowledge?" As a society, we're uncomfortable with questions about sexuality, and we pass that discomfort on to our children through our failure, in most cases, to discuss sexuality openly and honestly.

The research on sex education among American teenagers, for instance, shows that about two-thirds have talked with their parents about sex and pregnancy, although only half of those talks included discussion about birth control. About 60 percent of teens polled in a Planned Parenthood survey had taken a sex education class at school, but only 35 percent had taken "comprehensive" courses that included information about such topics as how contraceptives work and where to get them, how to cope with sexual development and how to prevent sexual abuse. Most school sex education courses focus on "mechanics"—the biological facts about reproduction.[1]

The teens in that same poll ranked television fourth, behind parents, peers, and school, as a source of information about birth control. Large minorities of the teens believed television programs present realistic portrayals of pregnancy and the consequences of sex, sexually transmitted diseases, family planning, and people making love. The potential problem is compounded by the fact that the teens most in need of reliable information—young teens, those who have not taken sex education classes and those whose parents are not college graduates and therefore are least likely to have talked to them about sex—are most likely to perceive TV portrayals of sexuality as realistic.[2]

Of course, it isn't only teenagers who may be influenced by media images of sexuality. Among adults as well as teens, the media certainly can reinforce existing attitudes and at times even change attitudes and beliefs about a variety of groups and phenomena. This chapter focuses on the ways the media may affect teenagers' and young adults' perceptions of women as sexual partners because attitudes formed during the teen years are highly likely to carry over into adulthood. Thus, it seems important that we consider what "injury" media images may do to teenagers' developing sexual belief systems, through their presentation of unrealistic and often unhealthy messages about women's sexuality.

SEXUAL ATTRACTIVENESS

One of the most consistently repeated images, particularly in magazine advertising, is that the sexy woman has large breasts. From the covers of the annual *Sports Illustrated* swimsuit issue to the covers of most issues of *Cosmopolitan* to ads for dozens of different kinds of women's clothing and cosmetic products, big breasts are the models' most compelling features. Often the photographs seem to be placed so that the woman's breasts are in the visual center of the page, the point just above the true center where the eye naturally lands first. The cover of *Sports Illustrated*'s twentieth anniversary swimsuit issue, for instance, shows a deeply tanned Kathy Ireland wearing a canary yellow strapless bikini. She's seated near a tropical-looking pool, knees about shoulder-width apart, and her arms are crossed so that she's holding the top of each shin with her opposite-side hand. The effect is to create the maximum possible cleavage below the model's "come hither" smile.

What effect does this emphasis on large breasts have on the developing teenager's views about women as sexual partners? It's very difficult to pinpoint how teenage girls or boys are affected by these portrayals, but it's easy to imagine the types of effects the images might have. Certainly most women can remember what it means to the self-esteem of the average girl as she develops, particularly if she doesn't develop a bustline to match those of the models. Clearer evidence of the potential effect comes from plastic surgeons' reports that they now see girls as young as 14 seeking surgery to enlarge their breasts.[3]

But large breasts aren't the only answer to the question of "What is sexy?" According to the media, another very important qualification for sexiness is thinness. A slender build seems very nearly required for a character to be presented as sexually attractive in the mediated world, and this is particularly true for women. Kaufman found that an average of 12 percent of television characters—15 percent of men and only 8 percent of women—were obese; in the real world, 25 percent of adults are considered obese.[4] Other researchers have found that the current standard of attractiveness portrayed on television and in magazines is slimmer for women than for men; the standard character in magazines and movies now is thinner than she has been since the last epidemic of eating disorders occurred in the mid-1920s.[5]

Some media images of sexual attractiveness are disturbing not so much for their messages about standards of beauty as for what they imply about who should be considered sexy. These images, most often but not always found in advertising, display young children, usually girls, in the same sexualized light in which adult women are presented. For instance, one magazine advertisement for Bain de Soleil sun tan products shows a woman and a young girl, presumably mother and daughter, lounging together in the sun. They wear identical strapless black bikinis, and the headline above the ad explains: "To the women of St. Tropez, protection is a delicate matter." The common understanding of the word "protection" as a euphemism for "birth control" seems to make this headline all the more provocative, as does the inclusion of the little girl as one of the "women" of St. Tropez. Similarly, some of the ads in Revlon's "most unforgettable women" campaign included a girl about five to seven years old in their photographs of beautiful models. These ads seem problematic for two reasons. First, they suggest to young girls that they should begin trying to make themselves sexually attractive as early as possible, and second, they may suggest to some audiences that children can be viewed as appropriate sex partners.

Do these images affect society's perceptions of who is and isn't sexy? It seems they do. For instance, one study demonstrated that male college students who watched an episode of "Charlie's Angels"—which featured three beautiful women— were more critical in their subsequent evaluation of pictures of potential dates than were men who had not watched the show.[6]

SEXUAL RELATIONSHIPS

Media images present messages about more than attractiveness, however. Even single-frame print advertisements often tell or imply a story of sorts, and these stories often include messages about what men and women should expect in sexual relationships. Many of these images portray women as being subservient to the men with whom they have relationships, either explicitly or implicitly. For instance, a Christmas season Macy's ad for Red Door perfume and Elizabeth Arden products shows a beaming blonde model, who appears to be wearing only a long strand of pearls, seated among a collection of red and gold boxes of various sizes, festooned with gold ribbon. The ad urges the reader to "Have a Red Door holiday. Open it!" The woman, it seems, is to be a Christmas present for someone.

Media images also may help to perpetuate the sexual double-standard that tells women and men that "good" girls may say no to sex when they really mean yes. For instance, in one Nuance perfume ad, a woman in an evening dress stands in front of a full-length mirror, apparently dressing for a date with the man who waits behind her, his hand resting on the small of her back. The ad copy tells the reader that: "Nuance always says yes. You can always say no." A teen magazine ad for Champion-brand clothes uses the same mixed-messages theme. It features a young woman leaning back against a jukebox in a restaurant, while a young man watches her from the background. The ad copy lets us know what the young woman is thinking: "Yes is easy. No drives 'em crazy. Maybe drives 'em . . . Yeah. Maybe." The copy, unfortunately, not only reinforces the "no sometimes means yes" message but also teaches audiences that the focus of a woman's concern should be how the man reacts to what she wants, not what she wants herself. Regardless of what she wants, she cannot say "yes" without appearing easy or loose, but she dare not say "no" for fear of losing the man's attention.

SEXUAL VIOLENCE

Given the "no-means-yes" messages that appear in some media images, it's perhaps not surprising that rape myths and portrayals of sexual violence are not uncommon. Some images, for instance, seem to advance the notion that women are easily aroused sexually and sexually available for any man who comes along. In advertising, the message of availability seems to be communicated through the positions in which the models appear. For instance, an ad for Tecate, a Mexican beer, shows a model wearing a minuscule diaper-wrap-style swimsuit of black leather or vinyl. She's kneeling on one knee and has her other knee propped up on a large wooden beam. She's holding the beer can at about hip level, which serves to direct the eye to her barely covered pubic area. Her facial expression, of course, is one of invitation. Another example, perhaps even clearer, is an Ipanema swimwear ad that shows the model, wearing a jungle-print bikini, seated on a straight-backed wooden chair. She's straddling the front of the chair so that her knees are spread apart, and her hands are resting on the top of her knees. The image of availability is quite clear.

In fact, some images suggest that women may be available as sex partners even for animals other than men. In an ad for Crocojelly shoes, the lower half of a woman is lying half on, half off a bed, one foot resting on the bed and the other on the floor. She's wearing hose and shoes and appears to be having sex with a crocodile; its long tail curves down from between her legs and onto the floor.

But such images appear not only in advertising but in other forms of media as well. For instance, Jhally has argued that one of the most common themes in music videos is that women are sexually provocative, easily aroused and non-discriminating in their choice of partners.[7]

Another type of image seems to suggest that fear is sexy in women. For instance, a Penaljo shoe ad shows a busty, lingerie-clad woman grimacing as she uses her shoe to smash a spider. Another ad, for Smalto cologne, shows a woman in an evening dress, apparently recoiling from something she sees. Her arms are up, one of them in front of her face, in a defensive posture, and her facial expression is one of uncertainty if not anguish. The headline reads, "Smalto. You make me weak."

Other images present behaviors some would classify as sexual harassment as being just good, clean fun. An ad for Esprit clothing, for instance, shows a woman with a man on each side of her. Each of them is pulling up one side of her skirt, while she tries to hold down the front of it. Her expression is startled and perhaps embarrassed, but everyone seems to be having a good time.

The woman in the Georges Marciano ad, however, does not appear to be having a good time. In this controversial ad, the first frame shows a woman seated next to the door of a car. Her shirt is unbuttoned below her breasts but is held together in the front by the arm she has across her waist. There's a man sitting behind her, holding her shoulder, but her expression is not a happy one. In the second frame, the same man is carrying the woman off over his shoulder. Sexual violence also is implied in an Obsession perfume ad, which shows a nude woman involved in sexual contact with two men. The images are deliberately grainy and shadowed, but again, the expression on the woman's face appears more anguished than ecstatic.

Music videos, too, at least sometimes contain images that suggest an acceptance of sexual violence. Perhaps one of the best known or most controversial of these videos was Michael Jackson's "The Way You Make Me Feel." In this video, Jackson's character becomes infatuated with a beautiful young woman he sees walking alone on a dark, inner-city street. He follows her, becoming increasingly insistent and aggressive in his efforts to gain her attention. The woman initially ignores and rejects him but eventually accepts his advances after she is accosted by a group of men in a scene that at least suggests the threat of a gang rape.

Do these images make their viewers more accepting of sexual violence against women? That, of course, is almost impossible to prove conclusively. However, there is some evidence that exposure to images of sexual violence can lead to acceptance of sexual violence. Malamuth and Briere and Zillman and Bryant have concluded that exposure to certain types of violent pornography may make male viewers more willing to condone sexual violence and sexual aggression and less sympathetic toward rape victims.[8]

What seems, in a way, more disturbing is the ways in which media's portrayal of women as sex partners may affect women's views of themselves. Although the audience for music videos is primarily male adolescents and young adults, most advertising that contains such stereotyped and negative images of women seems to be promoting women's products—women's clothing, women's perfumes, women's magazines. Are women really attracted to these images of themselves? Do women really want to see themselves portrayed as, at best, sexy clothes horses and, at worst, as willing participants in their own sexual victimization?

Finally, it's important to note that this discussion has focused almost exclusively on images to be found in mainstream media. Given that much more damaging images of women as sex partners are available in violent pornography, such as Malamuth, Zillman, and others have studied, why should we even be concerned about the far milder images found in mainstream media? The answer, I believe, is threefold:

1. Far more people are exposed to mainstream media images than are exposed to pornography, and the former type of exposure is much more frequent. For example, a spring 1990 survey of high school and college age youth indicated that about one-fourth of the men and only 2 percent of the women viewed hard-core pornography from "adult" bookstores at least once or twice a year. About 20 percent of males and 7 percent of females saw X-rated films at least once or twice a year. But at least 95 percent of men and 96 percent of women watched R-rated movies, and nearly three-quarters of the males saw slasher films, which very often link sex and gory violence either implicitly or explicitly, at least a couple of times a year. Stereotypical images are most likely to have an effect on viewers' attitudes if the exposure to those images is repeated frequently. With mainstream media, that repetition is occurring.
2. Mainstream media may be at least as important, if not more important, than pornography because mainstream media are less likely to be labeled as deviant. Mainstream media, by definition, are those that contain images and messages the society finds acceptable, and that makes those accepted images and messages even more insidious.
3. Mainstream media images discussed in this chapter will likely seem tame by the standards for mainstream media in the year 2000. In *Media, Sex and the Adolescent*, Greenberg argues that sexual content will become "more prevalent and more diffuse in a media era characterized by unyielding and increasing competition for audience and reader segments."[9]

Sexual images are likely to become not only more prevalent but also more graphic. It seems crucial, then, that we prepare for the increased frequency and explicitness of sexual images in the mainstream media by doing what we can now to understand the effects those images may have and what injuries they may produce among both teenagers and adults.

15

Super Bowl Commercials: The Best a Man Can Get (Or Is It?)

Bonnie Drewniany

Each January, half of America gathers around television sets to participate in the ritual of Super Bowl Sunday. According to Nielsen Media Research, Super Bowls account for five of the top ten shows in the history of American television, reaching approximately 40 million households each year.[1] Unlike a typical football event that caters to male viewers, the Super Bowl attracts viewers of both sexes as well as all age groups, income levels and regions of the country.[2]

In order to reach half of America, advertisers are willing to pay a super price. In 1994, each second of air time cost advertisers $30,000, or $1.8 million for a sixty-second spot.[3] While skeptics are quick to point out the many things one could buy with that kind of money, many companies, including Budweiser, Pepsi, and Master Lock, seem sold on the idea. Marketers use the Super Bowl to introduce new products, such as the Dodge Neon in 1994, the Subaru Impreza, and Crystal Pepsi in 1993, the Nicoderm patch in 1992, the L.A. Gear Catapult in 1991, the Gillette Sensor in 1990, and perhaps the most famous introduction of all, the Apple Macintosh in 1984.

Before the game airs, previews of the commercials are shown on national television and highlights of the best spots appear in national newspapers and magazines. People are primed to expect great commercials and therefore don't leave their television sets when a Super Bowl commercial comes on the air. Instead, they wait until the game gets boring to make a run to the refrigerator or restroom. Many people watch the game at parties and discuss the commercials after they air. In 1993, for example, 35 percent of Super Bowl viewers watched the game at a party.[4] As a result, product recall for Super Bowl commercials is far above average. Next-day recall of the 1993 commercials was 66 percent, or nearly triple the national prime time ad recall of 23 percent.[5]

If half of America watches the game each year, and product recall is three times higher than average, one cannot deny the impact of Super Bowl commercials. Therefore, I found it important to study the way various groups are portrayed in the commercials.

BACKGROUND OF THE STUDY

The 1989 to 1994 Super Bowls were recorded, the games removed and the commercials were coded. Local commercials were eliminated to avoid regional bias. (The *USA Today* Annual Ad Meter Poll was used to identify the national buys.) Commercials for movies and television programs were eliminated because this type of advertising often includes scenes from the shows that could unfairly skew this study. Repeats of commercials were also eliminated. A total of 248 commercials were coded.

Two coders recorded the product advertised, as well as the sex, age, race and role of the person shown in the commercial. In cases where animated characters could be identified as male or female, as in the case of the Bud Bowl bottles and cans, they were included in the figures.

A major role was assigned if the person was a spokesperson, was on camera throughout the commercial, or played a character critical to the theme of the commercial. A minor role was assigned if the person was on camera for less than half of the ad or played a supporting role. A background role was assigned if the person did not speak and was seen only briefly, such as in a crowd scene.

Portrayals of people under eighteen, those eighteen to forty-nine, and those fifty and older were coded to see if there were any differences in the way different age groups were treated. Coders agreed 100 percent on those under eighteen. Determining who was fifty and older was more difficult. Research on the aging body was used to define physical characteristics of a person over fifty, such as pronounced laugh lines, crow's feet, and sagging cheeks.[6] Additionally, references to a grandparent role or being retired were factors used in coding the people over fifty. Any coding differences were resolved by watching the commercial together and discussing the factors used to determine how to code the individual.

RESULTS

Men scored the most points

They appeared in 198 commercials, or 80 percent of the time. Women, on the other hand, were shown in only 112, or 45 percent of the commercials. More alarming, however, is the fact that men had major roles in 135 (54 percent) commercials, compared with women who had major roles in only twenty-eight, or 11 percent of the commercials.

Male stars outshine female stars

Sixty-one commercials featured male celebrities, while only nine commercials featured female celebrities. (People who have become celebrities solely because of their appearances on commercials, such as Pepsi's Uh Huh Girls, are not included here.) These figures are even more dramatic when one considers the commercials that feature more than one celebrity. To illustrate, let's look at the star lineup for 1994. Female stars were limited to Kathie Lee Gifford and Cindy Crawford (actresses Christine Lahti and Linda Hunt provided voice-overs, but were not seen). Male stars included basketball players Charles Barkley, Larry Bird, Larry Johnson, Michael Jordan (for McDonald's and Nike), and Shaquille O'Neal (for Pepsi and Reebok); comedians Chevy Chase, Rodney Dangerfield, Steve Martin, and Michael Richards; former football coaches Mike Ditka and Bum Phillips; sportscaster Marv Albert (for Anheuser-Busch and Nike); actor David Carradine; musicians John Sebastian, Country Joe McDonald, and the Jefferson Airplane; Bo Jackson, and talk show host Regis Philbin. (Dan Quayle's appearance with child actor Elijah Wood and Dallas quarterback Troy Aikman in the Wavy Lays "potatoe" chip spot isn't included in the official listing because the commercial aired during the half-time, not during the game.)

While Bo Jackson, Michael Jordan, Joe Montanta, Shaquille O'Neal, and other male stars appear in multiple Super Bowl commercials, only Cindy Crawford stars more than one time. The male stars are shown bouncing basketballs off Mount Rushmore, racing up the stairs of skyscrapers and doing other super hero feats, while Cindy is a mere sex object. In her 1992 Pepsi debut, Cindy, dressed in high-cut shorts and a low-cut top, slithers past two awestruck boys and slowly drinks a Pepsi. As one of the boy's jaw almost drops to his knees, he utters the punch line, "Is that a great new Pepsi can, or what?" It's a clever ending, but one must question if the average viewer even noticed Pepsi's new can.

A glamorous Cindy returned in a 1994 spot, wearing a skimpy red sequin dress and dangling earrings. As she goes into a Pepsi deprivation tank, she announces, "I'll do anything for science" (which is about as believable as the boy's line in the previous spot). After she's deprived of Pepsi for one month, she comes out of the tank as Rodney Dangerfield. What's the message? Is it, "Drink Pepsi, get respect." Or is it, "Drink Pepsi, look sexy?" I'll leave it to the reader to determine which message Pepsi intended.

Men are the voices of authority

Now let's take a look at the announcers, the voices of authority who are out of sight but are very much in your mind. One would hope to hear an equal number of male and female voice-overs, but the power of the male voice came across loud and strong 167 times, while the female voice was heard a mere sixteen times. The good news, if there is any, is that ten of the sixteen spots ran in 1993 and 1994. We may be seeing progress. The disappointing news is that five of the spots were for the 1993 Subaru Impreza, which received the lowest ratings in the history of the *USA Today* Ad Meter Poll. If the advertising industry wants to find an excuse not to hire more women voice-overs, they could refer to this campaign.

Women are portrayed as sexual aggressors

Women are shown in scene after scene in Gillette commercials stroking men's faces, throwing their arms around men's necks, running up to them, surprising them with kisses and hugs, jumping into their arms. As the Gillette commercials state, it's "the best a man can get."

Career women aren't taken very seriously

Women in minor roles and background shots play a variety of career roles, including fire fighters, researchers, assembly line workers, office managers, teachers, and so on. Only three spots featured a career woman in a major role. One of these spots, which ran in 1991 for Panasonic, opens with a woman as she picks up her mail from her box outside of her home. She walks into her home, turns on her answering machine (which sounds very official, with the message, "Hegleman, Hanrahan and Zangrillo Worldwide"), pats her son on the head, turns on the computer, sends a fax, and answers the phone. On line one she says, "Hegleman, here." On line two, she answers, "Hanrahan." When she answers line three with, "Zangrillo speaking," her son rolls his eyes. Even a child can figure she's a fake.

Moms are comforters, dads are companions

Fathers are portrayed in twenty-five commercials, while moms appear less than half the time, in only twelve spots. With the exception of Coca-Cola's 1990 "Hilltop Reunion," moms are shown mainly in the home or in a background setting. In several commercials, they are shown consoling their children. In a 1991 spot for Tylenol, for example, a mom is shown wrapping a raincoat over a disappointed boy as he leaves a soccer game in the pouring rain. One genuinely feels sorry for the kid as his friends run by him.

Dads, on the other hand, are shown sharing their children's fun, whether it's sailing a toy boat, playing ball, coaching a game, or showing their sons how to shave. In a 1992 spot for McDonald's, for example, over a dozen dads are shown coaching pee-wee football. In this spot, we see a dad giving the boys lessons in life, "A great man once said, 'Winning, gentlemen, isn't everything. It's the only thing,'" another dad offering coaching tips, "Give Mike the ball and tell him to run towards his Dad," and two dads being genuine good sports as they form a human goal post. Where were the moms in this spot? Only one was shown as she was leaving the game, giving a consoling hug to a son. Where were the dads after the game? Celebrating with their sons at McDonald's, of course.

Older men have power, older women are shown as weak

Older men were authority figures in several Super Bowl commercials. For example, an unidentified older chairman was shown preparing to give a speech to stockholders in a commercial for Coopers & Lybrand in 1993. A real chairman, Lee Iacocca, pitched Chrysler in 1990. Another commercial in 1990 featured an older New York Life insurance agent and his long-time customer chatting about the importance of having an agent who is a trusted family friend.

Being an older woman is not quite so glamorous, however. If an older woman is not portrayed as a loving grandmother, there is a good chance she will act senile or persnickety in a Super Bowl commercial. In a 1994 spot, the audience was led to believe that justice is being served as a feisty old lady grabs a bag of Doritos back from Chevy Chase. However, Chevy gets the last word, saying, "Tough year. Good chip," as he bites into a Doritos chip (see Chapter 19).

Old age is not all the rage

In several commercials, a know-it-all kid has the final word. For example, in the 1994 Wavy Lays half-time commercial, a boy challenged adults, "Betcha can't eat just one," for their seats at the Bowl game. The boy gets better and better seats, even taking over Dan Quayle's spot. Finally, he gets the ultimate spot at the game, Troy Aikman's.

Boys have all the fun

Boys are shown twenty-eight times and star nine times in major roles. Girls are shown eighteen times and have a starring role only once. However, even that one time, when a girl receives a love letter from a boy, the girl is overshadowed by the boy. In this 1990 Pepsi spot, Fred Savage writes a letter to his girlfriend. His inspiration? A bottle of Pepsi, of course. Fred's letter reads, "Dear Jenny, I don't usually pour my heart out like this . . . I'm mesmerized . . . your effervescent charm . . . . My passion for you will never be quenched. I will thirst for the exhilaration of your companionship." Jenny's giggling friend says, "You must feel so special." Jenny squeals with delight, 'I feel like . . . a Pepsi."

While boys often have things to say in commercials, girls are rarely heard. For example, in the 1994 Pepsi "Woodstock reunion" spot, three boys and a girl watch as an overweight man dances. One of the boys asks, "Do you think they'll go skinny dipping again?" and another boy responds, "I hope not." The girl says nothing. In fact, girls speak in only four Super Bowl commercials, including the Pepsi "love letter" spot described above.

Boys will be boys and men will be . . . women??

The year 1993 featured two spots in which a male pretended to be a female. In a Federal Express commercial, a male boss pretends to be a female secretary on the telephone as he tries to check on the status of a package. In a Nike commercial, Bugs Bunny dons sexy women's clothing and a blonde wig to distract four thugs from scoring points in a basketball game. As the players turn their heads and whistle, Bugs flashes a sign to the viewers that reads, "Silly, aren't they?"

African Americans are shown as athletes and musicians

African American male sports stars Bo Jackson, Michael Jordan, and Shaquille O'Neal seem to dominate the airwaves. Singer Ray Charles was a fixture for three years, singing with his Uh Huh girls. But what about the average person? If they were from an underrepresented group, they were in the background. Minor roles and background scenes showed a variety of African American men as fathers, executives, factory workers, waiters, and so on. However, only one commercial featured an "average" African American male in a starring role. In a 1989 commercial for Delta, an African American ticket agent realizes a customer has left his briefcase at the counter. Using the skills he learned when he was a first string halfback, he leaps over the counter, runs through the terminal and catches the man just in time. Note that even the "average" African American male is portrayed as athletic.

People with disabilities play a disappearing act

While many commercials featured athletes doing feats even Superman would envy, few showed people with disabilities. Ray Charles endorsed Diet Pepsi from

1991 to 1993, but his blindness wasn't an issue. However, in a 1990 spot that aired before the Super Bowl, Ray Charles starred in "the ultimate blind taste test" in which Diet Coke and Diet Pepsi were switched.[7]

A SAD CONCLUSION

Super Bowl commercials do not paint a very pretty (or realistic) picture for women, older people, those from diverse ethnic cultures, or those with disabilities. While advertisers spend millions of dollars to deliver their most persuasive messages to half of America, they ignore and insult the majority of their audience. Is this the best advertisers can do? No. It's just the best a man can get. Or should I say, the best a healthy, young Anglo male can get?

16

Rambos and Himbos: Stereotypical Images of Men in Advertising

Philip Patterson

In the middle of the most politically correct decade in history, sex is still being used to sell beverages. It's all there—lots of flesh, objectification, ogling—all to increase market share of a popular drink. But wait. . . this isn't the Swedish Bikini Team and that isn't Joe Sixpack doing the looking. And the sex object on the screen looks more beefy than busty. It's a Diet Coke ad so hot some critics say it needs to be followed by a cigarette ad. In the commercial three women take their daily Diet Coke break at precisely the moment the muscular construction worker across the way discards his shirt. In the words of a 1970s commercial for Virginia Slims, "you've come a long way, baby." But who? The women doing the ogling or the male doing the stripping?

The blurring of gender roles is a popular recent trend. At the same time Diet Coke was airing the "Diet Coke Break" campaign, Hyundai Elantra's "Parking Lot" campaign took the idea of women as full participants in the war between the sexes a step further. In the commercial, two women are ridiculing men as they get out of their fancy sports cars. "Must be compensating for a shortcoming," one says as a man emerges from a hot car. But when a hunk arrives in the sensible Elantra, the ridicule turns to admiration: "I wonder what he's got under his hood?" The ads were conceived out of desperation, co-creator Jim Jolliffe told an interviewer for *Entertainment* magazine: "Let's face it, Hyundai isn't known for making the sexiest cars in the world."[1] The strategy worked: Hyundai's awareness rate for its commercials doubled.

The Diet Coke and Hyundai ads are a part of a new genre of "power babe" commercials in which women enjoy the upper hand over men.[2] However, the flip side of the "power babe" movement is a diminution of male power in commercials. Power is essentially a "zero-sum" game. When one side gets power, it comes at the expense of another side. No new power can be added to the game, and none can be lost; it can only be redistributed. Therefore, the new rash of "power babe" ads is interesting since that newly acquired power comes at the expense of men who long held the upper hand in print and television commercials.

Even when men still have the position of power, the power babe commercials make that advantage look quite temporary. A Federal Express ad shows a demanding boss being tamed by a wiser, calmer female underling who proves that he signed for the package he is fuming over. A commercial for K-Mart clothing depicts a woman in a secretarial position buying clothing not with her current job in mind, but with her eye on her boss's job. Campbell's Soup shows skater Nancy Kerrigan bowling over burly hockey players on the ice, while Saturn featured a female jet pilot test-driving a sports car.

Some media observers put a darker face on the power babe trend, claiming that ads depicting the new confrontational woman are just thinly disguised male bashing. "Marketers are starting to tap into women's growing in-your-face attitude by portraying men in the same negative ways women have been featured for decades," claims *Ad Week*.[3] One ad for Bodyslimmers one-piece undergarment had this headline that epitomizes the trend: "While you don't necessarily dress for men, it doesn't hurt, on occasion, to see one drool like the pathetic dog that he is." Bill Halladay, art director of the Hyundai "Parking Lot" commercial, sees male bashing as an acceptable message in advertising in the mid-1990s. "If a guy slaps a woman on TV, people get pissed off. But if a woman knees a guy in the groin, everyone applauds."[4]

STEREOTYPES OF MEN IN ADVERTISING

In the film project "Stale Roles and Tight Buns: Images of Men in Advertising," a collective of men called the Organized Against Sexism and Institutionalized Stereotypes (OASIS), provides anecdotal evidence of these stereotypes of men prevalent in advertising:

1. The cowboy who is tough, unemotional, and alone;
2. The superman who conquers the world and women around him;
3. Mr. Universe, a muscleman analogous to a Playboy Bunny.[5]

The image of men in advertising is either that of a "Rambo," solo conqueror of all he sees, or a "Himbo," a male bimbo. In an echo of what feminists have been saying for years about women's images in advertising, OASIS criticizes products that are selling a stereotypical ideal of the male body by displaying more of the ideal body in the ad than the product being advertised. A 1993 Calvin Klein print ad campaign featuring rapper Marky Mark is an example of the type of ads that are increasing in such venues as *GQ* or *Esquire*. These ads sell the body as much or more than the product in much the same way that women's bodies have been used for thirty years or more.

Other media critics have attempted to find clusters of male images in ads as well. In an essay in *Adbusters*, "The Advertiser's Man," Jennifer Nicholson finds these stereotypes of men in advertising:

1. Sex object to be pawed and ogled by another new stereotype, the liberated aggressive woman
2. Sensitive new age guy (SNAG) politically correct and even eligible to be called a feminist
3. Domestic man who does his own cooking and shopping and is as at ease in the kitchen

as his female companion for whom he often cooks
4. Superman, the 1990s version of the woman who can do it all, who juggles wife, children, career and hobbies
5. New masculinist (out of Robert Bly's book, *Iron John*, which gave rise to the 1990s men's movement) who challenges the traditional stereotypes of what a man is supposed to be
6. Rugged individualist, who began with the Marlboro man and has now evolved into a "go your own way" guy for a variety of products
7. Self-actualized man who worries less about his hairline or waistline than the traditional man, who could be driven to purchasing frenzy by the slightest introduction of insecurity
8. Self-obsessed man, the backlash to self-actualized man who is wrapped up in himself and his toys.[6]

"INVISIBLE" SEXISM

In addition to relying on a repertoire of new, non-traditional stereotypes of males, advertisers have kept the old stereotypes alive in a covert way as well. While advertising agencies and advertisers have made conscious efforts in the 1990s not to offend large categories of their readers and viewers by what they show, this silent or invisible sexism remains. This sexism cannot be categorized or coded by what is on the page or the screen, but by what is not—namely female consumers. For a number of products that are not innately men's products, men still seem to be the sole target audience. And while the messages do not openly put women down, the imagery of the ads continues to convey the idea that this is a "man's" product.

AN INEVITABLE CHANGE

The role of men in advertising has changed in the last few decades, as has the role of men in society. The most interesting research question becomes not whether the images of men in advertising have changed or even how they have changed, but when. The when question gets at the heart of the more than $100 billion-a-year advertising industry. Do the changes in male images in advertising come after changes in society or do they come before and help to create change in society? Are the media our mirror or our molder? Have men conformed to the roles delegated to them by the media or are the media accurately reflecting the dynamic roles than men already hold in society?

These questions are important in mass communication research. There is no doubt that commercials have selling power. The billions spent on advertising attest to the fact that advertisers accept the premise that the media can sell their products. Is it also possible that commercials can "sell" other commodities besides the product sponsoring the ad? Can television also "sell" an image that helps to define the perfect body? The perfect kitchen? The supermom or superdad? The ideal child? Is it possible that some of our ideas of roles and images comes from buying what the commercial messages are selling in addition to the products?

CONCLUSION

If there is a conclusion to be reached on the image of men in advertising in the 1990s, it is that there is none. Rather than being a point on a line from wimp to macho, boor to sensitive, the image of men in advertising is as varied as the companies that use images to sell their product.

What we are left with, instead, are trends. And the trend for men in advertising, like men in society, is toward what men's advocates have called their feminine qualities—nurturing, caring, sensitivity. Along the way, the softening of the American male in advertising will lend itself to some stereotypes that are sometimes ugly—men as sex objects, men as dumb, and so on. And it will have interesting "poster children" as well, for example O. J. Simpson's former house guest, Kato Kaelin, romance novel cover model Fabio, and *Speed* movie star, Keanu Reeves emerging as the unofficial spokespersons for the Himbo stereotype. Nevertheless, if the final result of this softening is a trend that gets the aloof Marlboro man off his horse and into the human race, the direction is a healthy one.

17

The Disposable Sex: Men in the News

Lee Jolliffe

As a society, we still cling to the myth that all Anglo men are part of a "dominant" group, with ready access to wealth and power. When radical feminists began to identify the harm done by stereotypical treatment of women, it was men who were treated as the oppressors. "*All men* receive economic, sexual and psychological benefits from male supremacy. *All men* have oppressed women," said the *Redstocking Manifesto*.[1]

But the stereotypical roles of men and women in American mainstream society, which reached their apex in the 1950s, have had costs and benefits for both genders. And if men were dominant in the world of work, they were shut out of the world of home. A man without a paying job was a freeloader, as much to be scorned as a woman without a husband.

We have heard much from the feminist movement about the perceived costs to women and benefits to men of the old roles of women. On marriage, the man gained a household drudge, a baby-maker, an on-site mistress, and free childcare. A woman was some combination of mannequin and incubator.

Now we are beginning to hear more about the cost to men and benefits to women of *men's* stereotypical roles in our society. On marriage, women gained a wage slave, a protector, and, after the kids were in school, an endless vacation, while the men died young fighting in foreign countries or worked their way to heart attacks and an early death.

Where the feminist movement has helped create great changes in women's lives and at least some liberation from old stereotypes, men have not enjoyed the same release from their traditional roles. A men's rights movement is only now beginning to gain members.

In this chapter, we will examine stereotypes of men and look closely at how these harmful male roles have been made to seem "natural" to us through pictorial images in the media.

THE ROLES

Early gender studies tended to hold up men's roles as ideals to which women should have equal access. Men were seen as permitted to be more authoritative, powerful, active, rational, intelligent, decisive, and qualified than women, when it came to the activities that "matter,"—like work and politics.

Gradually, though, a few researchers (myself included) began to notice some odd trends in portrayals of men and women in the media. While women were beginning to be shown as active and powerful in the work force and thus multifaceted people, men were shown only as workers, losing their personal identities almost entirely.

In a study for the Ohio State University Women's Studies Center, Turner Bond and I learned that in 1885, men were at least occasionally referred to in terms of family lives, personality, and appearance. But by 1985, media coverage of men virtually ignored these aspects of men's lives. The modern newspaper has further reduced men's importance as people by referring to them using their job titles in place of their given names, calling them "Lawyer Jones" or "Bricklayer Smith."[2]

Still more disturbing are the modern newspaper headlines. In reality, men appear most often in news headlines as the victims of violence. Crime statistics bear this out. Men are far more often the victims of crime than women. Yet through photographs, the media still foster our stereotype of men as strong and powerful. When men are the victims, we rarely see their pictures.

Sam Keen, in his book *Fire in the Belly*, writes powerfully of the damage done by society's stereotypes of men as warriors, workers, and stoics.[3] He sees Marine boot camp as a quintessential example of American society's depersonalization of men. At the Parris Island Marine Base in South Carolina, the dogface learns quickly that his opinions and conscience do not matter. During boot camp, he may wear no rings or personally identifying jewelry except his dogtags. He is given none of his letters from home. With shaved head, ugly uniform, and daily physical ordeals, he is quickly reduced to a non-individual, ready to endure pain, kill other human beings, or die, if given the orders. Should he survive his initiation into warriorhood, he will later reap the "benefit" of joining the ranks of wage-earners, providing a haven and spending money for a wife and children by working long hours outside the home.

Most men will not become president of the United States, or even president of their own companies. But our stereotypes of men create many more opportunities for failure than this perception. Says one friend of his "failures" as a husband, "You make a bookend in high school shop class, and then if you can't build your wife an addition to the kitchen, you're not a man."

Men are not expected to show emotion, yet must somehow be the initiators of dating and the proposers of marriage. A man with close male friends is suspected of being homosexual. A man who sees a doctor about physical pain is being a sissy. And a man out pushing a baby stroller must surely have a sick wife at home.

Think of the many stereotypes we have of men. Almost any scene from the film *Three Men and a Baby* will conjure up a stereotype. Men are sloppy, helpless at changing diapers, riveted to the television for Monday night football, motivated by uncontrollable lust, and so on.

MEN IN THE NEWS

While we know very few men have any real opportunity to become Fortune 500 CEOs, we could never tell that from the newspaper photographs we see. The news, business, and sports pages are filled with photos of men, most of them shown alone.

To get an accurate overview of how men are reported on and pictured in the news, a random sample of news stories from the 1985 *New York Times* was used. To compare the coverage of men with the coverage of women, forty-five stories were selected at random that had a man as the main character and another forty-five stories were selected at random that had a woman as the central figure.

While this sampling will provide us with information about the differences between news stories and photos of men and women, selecting equal numbers of stories about each gender does tend to camouflage one trait: Men appear in news photographs as much as twenty times more often than women do. The U.S. media make it clear that activities outside the home, whether local or international, are generally carried out by men.

But in spite of this dominance, there are strong stereotypes of men, mostly occurring in the photographs.

According to the texts of the news stories, men are most often workers. We are taught that men are primarily valuable for their wage-earning work through the names they are called in the press. In our sample, the men were referred to by their job titles instead of their names 50 percent of the time. Only 15 percent of the time were men called by their own names in these news stories. Women are also shown as workers, but only about 12 percent of the time. And women are named by their job titles only 1 percent of the time.

According to the headlines of these stories, men are primarily victims of crimes. In 53 percent of the headlines, editors placed men in a passive position, being acted upon by others, usually in crime stories.

Notice that "man as worker" does fit our sex-role stereotypes, but "man as crime victim" doesn't. A close examination of the pictures that were selected for these stories will show that picture editing is highly supportive of our stereotypes. The photographs that do support stereotypes of men will be chosen, but where a story contradicts these stereotypes, photographs will not be included.

HOW NEWS PICTURES DISTORT MEN'S REALITY

News pictures of men present a different "reality" than news stories. Men are pictured as violent criminals, loners, and anonymous workers who are expendable and valueless.

Men as Violent

Most important of all, in this sample of news stories, none of the men who were victims were pictured. Such a depiction would run counter to our stereotype that men are strong, powerful, and violent. In fact, the many stories about men as victims were buried on inside pages of the newspaper, as if the editors were embarrassed to mention the male victim. For example, a story of a U.S. Drug Enforcement agent being kidnapped was buried on inside pages between two jewelry ads. Although the story notes that the U.S. Embassy offered a $50,000 reward for information and provided the victim's name and age, no photograph appeared. Other faceless male victims included a "Fort Worth man shot dead by gang" and "off-duty officer shot 5 times at social club."

Men as Criminals

Although male victims were slighted pictorially, most of the men suspected or convicted of crimes were pictured. The *Times'* editors frequently selected photos of convicted murderers on death row or white-collar criminals on the courthouse steps. "Condemned killer of 4 electrocuted in Louisiana" and "Man executed in killing" merited photographic coverage. So did "Seven indicted for drugs are said to sell to players."

From this regular parade of photographs of men as criminals, and given the lack of pictures of murdered or injured men, the viewer could be excused for thinking men are mostly criminals, prone to violence, just as the photographs of women victims teach us that women are helpless and weak.

Another part of our lesson on women's weakness arises when we examine this sample for pictures of women criminals. None of the women who committed crimes were pictured. Headlines such as "Woman is shot after taking hostages on jet," "Brink's suspect held without bail," and "Nurses suspended in morphine death" ran without photos. Even the women who commit misdemeanors are able to remain anonymous. Surely the woman who hired a clown to toss a cream pie at a school official offered a great photo opportunity!

Men as Expendable

While men appeared most often in face-only or "headshot" photos, women were often depicted in three-quarters or full-length photographs.

The use of full-body shots of women has been interpreted as expressing society's view that women are sex objects. Certainly the scantily clad women in advertisements are being hired for their physical attraction. In our sample of news stories and pictures, more women did appear in full body shots than men, but all were fully dressed and none of their clothes were remotely provocative. However, the frequent use of disembodied heads as pictures of men is just as destructive a gender stereotype as the half-dressed women in some advertisements. Here, about a third of the men pictured were depicted in headshots, while less than a fifth of the women were shown without their bodies. The message of the headshot is that men's bodies are unimportant and therefore disposable. The needs of society make it imperative that we take no notice of men as whole people. If we did, we would be far less likely to send them off to distant wars to be maimed or killed and we would raise an outcry at the number of men who die in our communities as crime victims.

Men as Loners

Except for harsh photographs of policemen with suspects or body bags, most men in our sample were alone. Women, on the other hand, were often shown with other people, especially with other women. Several times, women were portrayed using affectionate gestures such as embraces and hand-holding. Men are thus shown to us as cold loners with few attachments to others.

Along with the detachment and loss of physical self in the classic headshot, there is a loss of environment and activity. Nearly a third of the men photographed were portrayed in headshots that showed minimal backgrounds. This creates a sense of sterility and lack of place, adding to the alienation these photographs attribute to men.

Women were more often shown with environments visible in the background. Women were pictured enjoying country gardens and pleasant home settings, complete with pets, women friends, and even birthday cakes.

This distinction in settings between the genders is very important, given the significance of "home" in our society. Although women are shown at home—that is, secure, off-guard, and self-expressive, men are typically shown without environments—alienated, on guard, and carefully in control of themselves or others.

Men as Emotionless

The men in these news photographs tended to be frowning or expressionless and rarely looked directly into the camera. Angry men looked out from stories on Nicaragua's "divine poet," New Jersey campaign chiefs, and radical South African religious leaders. Police, convicted killers, a screenwriter, and a minister all lacked facial expression in these news photos. One foundry worker was actually photographed without his face! He was bent over from the waist to pick up casting molds. As viewers, we see the top of his bill cap.

While feminists complain that a women's gaze into the camera makes them appear available, the men in these pictures are very clearly not available for exchanges of emotion with others. Of the twenty-nine men photographed, only three were visibly smiling: the Rev. Jesse Jackson, the Pope, and a philanthropist visiting toddlers in Central Park. And while women were photographed embracing and affectionately touching one another, men were shown deliberately touching anyone only in two photos: the philanthropist patting the toddler's head and a photo depicting the arrest of a criminal. Even in a photograph showing the Pope and Rev. Jesse Jackson smiling, the men were partly turned away from one another.

Thus, the predominant visual message of men in the news is a stoic male, friendless, uncaring, serious, easily angered, and unable to share emotions.

Men as Anonymous

"To wear a uniform is to give up your right to free speech in the language of clothes . . . . You become part of a mass of identical persons," says Alison Lurie in *The Language of Clothes.*[4]

Men appeared in uniforms of one sort or another in most news pictures in our sample. A third of the men were in a suit and tie, surely the most restrictive, uncomfortable, and dullest form of clothing since women sprouted the Victorian bustle! While the *New York Times* has yet to adopt color photographs on the front page, we are probably safe in assuming these suits to be gray, charcoal, or navy blue. Since the publication of *Dress for Success*, the brown suit has been virtually banned as "too midwestern" and the checked jacket has been relegated to the Florida retiree. Such a uniformity of dress implies that most men are anonymous, one readily exchangeable for another.

A number of real uniforms were also depicted in photographs of men, including the zip-up jumpsuit of the convict, police and paramedic's uniforms, a billcap and work pants, and one sports team outfit.

Women's dress is far less constrained. Women appeared in everything from tanktops and running shorts to full-skirted country tweeds to exotic evening gowns to suits with ruffled shirts. No women wore uniforms and only two wore suits.

The men's uniform clothing contributes further to the stereotypes that men are not individuals and that men's bodies are unimportant. Along with the frequent use of headshots, the appearance in business or work clothing depersonalizes the man.

Men as Workers

Uniformed or not, men appeared frequently as workers in our sample of photos. If a uniform was not in evidence, some other cue to the man's occupation was often part of the photograph. Even in the tight close-ups of men's faces, job cues were given to the viewer. One man wore a radio headset, for example. Another close-up showed segments of a campaign sign just behind the subject. In another, a clerical collar was evident.

Such job cues were rarely used in photographs of women. There is very little difference between the photograph of the woman kidnap victim and that of the woman politician. Only two photos of women contained internal cues to jobs: one of a woman crossing the finish line in a race and another with a woman at a microphone. In general, news photographs of women rely on cutlines to depict the woman as a worker, while news photos of men clearly depict employment without the need for words.

CONCLUSIONS

News photographs present a skewed view of men's reality. If we were to build our mental images of men strictly from news photographs, we would picture a man who worked twenty-four hours a day, alone, and making sure not to express his emotions as he worked. Any man could be replaced by any other, since they would all be anonymous and expendable. The deviant men–those who weren't working– would be criminals, murdering pretty women when not too busy hijacking boats, shooting up convenience stores, spying on the Navy, or smuggling aircraft parts to Iran.

How can we move from these injurious images of men toward images that are healing?

We can free men from constant coverage of their work and give them coverage of their real lives, their families, their pastimes, their hopes, dreams, and needs.

We can institute photographic coverage of all male victims, showing who they were before they were injured.

We can back up and show a man in his environment.

We can center some of our photographic stories about men on their relationships with other men, as we already do with women.

We can picture the many men in the helping professions, tenderly helping the kindergartner onto the schoolbus or weeping over the war refugee.

We can picture a world in which individual men count for something, taking a stand against the warmongers who benefit from the expendability of the common man.

The Berkeley Men's Center Manifesto sums up the new, non-stereotypical values that men's activists hope to achieve:

We, as men, want to take back our full humanity. We no longer want to strain to compete to live up to an impossible oppressive masculine image–strong, silent, cool, handsome, unemotional, successful, master of women, leader of men, wealthy, brilliant, athletic, and "heavy." . . . We want to relate to both women and men in more human ways–with warmth, sensitivity, emotion, and honesty. We want to share our feelings with one another to break down the walls and grow closer. We want to be equal with women and end destructive competitive relationships between men.[5]

PART IV

AGE STEREOTYPES

18

The Child as Image: Photographic Stereotypes of Children

Kathy Brittain McKee

An obligation of any image gatherer—photographer, illustrator, or videographer—is to remember that pervasive images portrayed in print and broadcast media foster stereotypes. Whether it is news footage or advertising photographs, images on a page or screen become images in a viewer's mind.

Because of the power of these images, viewers need to understand that each camera lens sees and defines truth differently, that each photo is, at best, one statement of what may be multiple truths, and that a photo may be an idealized vision held by the one with the lens. Adults can be taught to discount photos in advertisements, to look at different networks' videotapes, and to look at how different photographers shot the same story. But children come to photography without learned skepticism. Consequently, the images of children carried within those media geared primarily for children have a great deal of power to define reality. And certainly the images of children carried by those media have the ability to establish the "truth image" for children as they see themselves as they see images of themselves on screen, on billboards, or on the page. Those depictions may also establish the "truth image" of children for others who look acceptingly without discernment or skepticism.

"HOME ALONE, AND I LOVE IT"—THE CHILD AS ADULT

A child left behind by his parents, forgotten in the bustle of getting luggage, family members and tickets together and bound for the airport. A child who while frightened a bit by the circumstance suddenly finds himself perfectly able to cope in the adult world—all it takes is a little imagination, according to these films. This is a child that really needs no adult supervision or protection; from what he's learned on television and films, he's ready to face the world on his own, even though he's not yet a teenager. He can outwit skeptical adults who don't quite believe his self-sufficient act or burglars intent on harming him and taking his possessions. He is comfortable with modern technologies. He can manipulate audio tape to acquire a usable adult voice and can rig numerous weapons using electricity and household items. He has a thorough understanding of adult patterns; he can check into an upscale New York hotel, order room service, and hail a cab without a problem. Buying groceries on his own or attending a midnight Christmas Eve church service is no challenge. He even overcomes his fear of the frightening next-door neighbor after exercising some adult recognition of the importance of relationships when he's cut off from his traditional family members. Of course, this is all made easier by the upper-class surroundings in which he and his family live.

The child featured in the original *Home Alone* and its sequel offered viewers an opportunity to laugh at the idea of a child alone. But these portrayals just echoed an emerging theme: the self-sufficient child who is in charge of his (or much less frequently, her) world, who while he/she may live with adults actually functions as the adult-in-charge by manipulating the unwary and unwise adults into doing his or her bidding. Take the children's roles in the films *Problem Child I and II*. Their activities are self-chosen and self-determined. In each film, the adult caregivers are shown as powerless while the children rule the family. Within this video environment, the stereotypic portrayal of students again shows them functioning alone as the power-brokers in the adult environment. The children, not the parents, run the home, and apparently the adults are unable to establish boundaries. At home or at school, these children operate within self-defined boundaries, supported by the best in material possessions and technology but not supported by adult caretaking. They, too, like the child in *Home Alone*, show a world of childhood in which no harm comes to the children left alone because they are presented as more clever, wise, and inventive than the few adults pictured in their worlds.

This scenario of child-in-charge is certainly not new to American audiences, but the absence of adults who offer some limits is somewhat new and somewhat disturbing. The world of the "Dennis the Menace" cartoon—not the movie—was bounded by parents who could sit the child in the corner for "time out" and reflection on obedience. The "Beaver," in "Leave it to Beaver," although a mischievous character, was always portrayed within the environment of dependency on adults. He lived within a secure world that was stereotypical of traditional Anglo families, but it was a world with clear divisions between adult and child responsibilities. Imagine portraying the "Beav" left behind twice by the Cleavers as they left for expensive vacations, and the contrast between the new image of child-as-adult and the former image of child-as-child becomes clear.

What's the impact of the new portrayals? Certainly, it is too simplistic to point to a direct relationship between the child-neglect cases painted by the media as *Home Alone* cases and such video images. Yet the fact that the media chose to paint their portrayals of these cases with that stereotype offers evidence that a distinctive stereotype of child-left-to-function-as-adult has been created and accepted as a distinct image within our popular culture. Equating real-life unsafe situations for children with the comic mayhem of the movies illustrates the kind of mental impact such a stereotype can have.

The fallacy of this stereotype is apparent. Children who are left home alone are at risk; children who are expected to act like adults are at risk. Children may believe they can or should be able to manipulate the environments of their home or school in the ways their video counterparts may. And some adults may excuse their lack of nurturing of children through caretaking and boundary-establishing by arguing that such nurturing is obsolete and unnecessary. The "Home Alone, and I Love It" stereotype can then become more than comic relief; it can provide tragic excuse.

"ALL THOSE SMURFS AND ONLY ONE SMURFETTE"— THE CHILD AS GENDER STEREOTYPE

Imagine a world where all the beings are male. Then a sorcerer lays a trap to ensnare the men by creating one lone female. The plot fails, and the female becomes a part of the community—but only somewhat. The males endure her presence or ignore her presence, but only seldom is she allowed to act with power in their presence. Imagine watching such a world as a three- or four-year-old—or even as a twelve- or thirteen-year old. What messages would such a world depiction offer?

Such a world was the setting for the network cartoon series "The Smurfs," a cartoon depiction that without apology or pretense placed males at the center of the universe. The blue inhabitants of this world were all male, given all types of jobs and chores, until an evil plot caused the creation of the only female in their universe. This character, Smurfette, spends the rest of her cartoon life as a foil for the male action, either creating problems for them to solve or by offering fawning cheers for their heroic actions. Females are unnecessary in the Smurf world, and when one does appear, the blue-and-blond "trap" can be trivialized and separated.

Yet such a gender-stratified world is not unusual within children's entertainment, educational and advertising media. Nancy Signorielli's *A Sourcebook on Children and Television* (1991, Greenwood Press) and F. Earle Barcus' *Images of Life on Children's Television* (1983, Praeger) offer comprehensive surveys of the ways children are depicted on television programs and commercials. Their studies suggest that the world of children on television is primarily a male world. More male than females characters appear (Barcus reported that only 16 percent of major characters were female), and the males depicted carry the action as female characters offer support. An earlier study of the world within children's books was described similarly by a 1972 analysis of characters in Caldecott Medal and Newberry Award winners and Little Golden Books top sellers. The study, "Sex-Role Socialization in Picture Books of Preschool Children," reported in *The American Journal of Sociology*, found that males were consistently overrepresented in illustrations, titles, and content of these books.

Certainly, things may have changed within the contexts of certain media and certain programs. Elementary textbooks and "Sesame Street" show a greater diversity of sexual roles and empowerment. However, the older stereotypes persist. In advertisements, little girls play with dolls or bake in their ovens. Little boys play with trucks or run in the yard. Little girls want fashion accessories for their doll-models to wear in their three-story town-homes; little boys want action accessories to use with their action figures as they conquer villains. Little girls want to dress like mommy. Little boys want to dress like their sports heroes. Female students sit in neat rows and listen while males play on educational computers.

What do these images of male and female children suggest? First, children who watch or view such images learn early the physical and emotional traits traditionally associated with their genders; the packaging of such traits into a thirty-second spot or a full-page magazine advertisement merely accentuates the overall message. Having a boy at the computer keyboard while a girl points to the screen tells a different story than if the poses were reversed. Showing boys playing baseball or soccer and girls cooking perpetuates traditional boundaries for gender-linked behaviors, boundaries that have been expanded in society but that apparently have not frequently been stretched within the world of advertising images. However, even the ads that show less gender-specific behavior are viewed within the context of the other advertising, which may mute their impact.

Second, the prevalence of male characters or models is troubling in light of the untrue representation of reality it presents. In reality, females outnumber males in the U.S. population, unlike the character world of children's media. In reality, females are not necessarily passive; neither are males necessarily active. Males do not always solve the problems, or females always cause them. The self-image and self-esteem of both male and female children may be affected by the disparity between the pictorial representation and the real world. The stereotype of a world of male Smurfs happily living without a female may represent some writer's view of idyllic life, but the real world has both genders—and neither of them is painted a masculine blue.

"IF YOU'VE SEEN ONE, YOU'VE SEEN THEM ALL"— THE CHILD AS VICTIM

The advertisements are always centered around the images: large, dark eyes peering wistfully at the camera, ragged clothing, skinny limbs, swollen bellies, skin of all hues. The text or voice-overs speak of malnourishment, neglect, and war. These are the children of want, used as promotional devices for various charitable groups seeking to raise money for aid projects. They may come from South America, Africa, Southeast Asia, or Appalachia. They somehow represent a vast horde not photographed who also stand in need.

The photographic images offer some truth: Some children are victims. Yet the distortion occurs and the stereotype is created when only children are represented and when it is the only way children of some world regions are photographed. Repeating the pictorial stereotype of the child as war or poverty victim enables audiences to ignore the problems either because they have become desensitized to the horror of the image or too overwhelmed by the frequency of its appearance to believe anything can change. Finding different, even jarring, ways to portray the truth visually may help overcome the problems of stereotyping, and audiences must be willing to respond to the new images with more active viewing, looking beyond the surface visuals to prevent the response of turning the page or flipping the channel to avoid dealing with the real issues.

PRETTY BABY—THE CHILD AS SEXUAL OBJECT

The film and film star have grown older now, and the impact has lessened. But the image of a young girl's life as a prostitute shown by the 1978 film *Pretty Baby* presents an easy reference point for those concerned about the sexualization of children within media. In the film, the preteen girl lives in a bordello in 1917 New Orleans. When she matures, she is ceremoniously sold at auction, and her initiation into the life of a prostitute begins. The film, by Louis Malle, raised serious questions about the treatment of children as sexual objects, questions that continue to be raised about the depiction of children in mainstream media as well as the underground media of pornography.

Little ethical discussion about the involvement of children in soft- and hard-core pornography is necessary. Although the Supreme Court continues to grapple with the issue of how much is too much, it's difficult to ethically justify including children in the depiction of sexual acts in any capacity, whether they are clothed or unclothed. Yet the depictions of children in sexual ways in the mainstream media are much less certain. The *Pretty Baby* image of the prepubescent female waiting on her sexual awakening is not restricted to that film. The Barbie generation learns early that *real* dolls have boyfriends. Commercial viewers learn that boys on the playground dream of super-models and X-ray glasses that allow them to see through clothing; their female classmates aren't quite good enough to satisfy their preadolescent urges. Perfume shoppers are sold the sexual fantasies of young schoolboys dreaming about sexual affairs with adults in commercials as well. Even the trend toward thin, waifish fashion models dressed to resemble children indicates the juxtaposition of adult and child sexual attraction. But as Calvin Klein learned when a controversial 1995 advertising campaign was pulled because of public condemnation over images of minors in sexually alluring poses, such advertisements can attract the wrong kind of publicity.

Linking the sale of goods or the promotion of attendance through a sexual motif does not solely rely on the use of children's images, certainly. Yet when it does, there is potential for great harm. Elementary-age children are not developmentally ready for sexual involvement, and misleading media images may unwittingly prompt such activity. Sexual exploitation of children reduces them to objects. The features and benefits that combine to make up a marketing plan for a product or service should not have to include the sexualizing of a child in order for the plan to work. Abandoning the stereotype of child-as-sex-object will allow room for more creativity from marketers, advertisers, and writers as well as from photographers, illustrators, and videographers.

The pictures of children carry a special power when they are geared toward an audience of other children, who may lack the training or ability to make critical judgments about manifest or latent meanings. They also affect the adults who view the images passively, apathetically, or non-critically. For that reason, those who capture the images and plan their use must be mindful of the "truth images" they are creating, and they must exercise critical judgment about the impacts of those images and the stereotypes they create in light of the inherent values represented by the children within the images. Audience members must also learn to look critically at the images of children, to see behind the stereotypes in order to find more of the reality present, and to offer appropriate responses to the stories told by the pictures.[1]

19

Growing Old in Commercials: A Joke Not Shared

Ted Curtis Smythe

One advertiser learned the boundaries to acceptable portrayals of older adults the hard way in 1994 when Chevy Chase appeared in a Doritos Tortilla Thins television commercial.

Kevin Goldman, advertising columnist for the *Wall Street Journal,* summarized the scene as well as it can be done when he wrote: "A gray-haired woman shuffles along munching on chips, oblivious to the runaway steamroller barreling down on her. Comedian Chevy Chase climbs aboard a wrecking ball to rescue—and here is the joke—the chips. The woman is [left to be] plowed into wet cement."[1]

A spokesperson for the company said there was no intention to "offend anyone." But the company got heavy flak from agencies as well as people identified with the over-fifty audience. The "contrite manufacturer delivered cases of free chips to a food bank."[2]

The company and ad agency went a step further by creating a new commercial giving the woman the upper hand. The commercial starts out the same, with the little old lady threatened by the steamroller, but just as Chase starts to "rescue" her, the scene is changed and we see that a commercial is being shot. The agency guy interrupts the production to fire Chase from his position as spokesman. Chase takes the chips as consolation. As he walks from the scene, a gate closes behind him and he stands outside the walls with a bemused look and the bag of chips. But even the pleasure of the chips is denied him as the little old lady, astride a wrecking ball, swoops down and swipes the chips from *him.*

It's a cute attempt to make amends for the first flub. But notice that the advertiser doesn't threaten Chase with being pounded into freshly poured cement. He walks away, munching on a chip.

The chips commercial is just one among several that cut when they attempt to be cute. Goldman claims, "All too many commercials fall back on stereotypes, showing the aged as feeble, foolish or inept, passing their time aimlessly in rocking chairs."[3]

Others weigh in with a more positive outlook. A 1993 survey Roper conducted for *Advertising Age* concluded: "Advertisers are getting better at portraying older consumers positively in advertising, and in the right numbers."[4] Generally the industry got better marks than it did in a similar survey conducted in 1989.

Whatever "improvement" has occurred is marginal. Joseph M. Winski of *Ad Age* gives a positive spin to the figures, but they are subject to a quite different interpretation. While 38 percent of the respondents to the Roper poll reported in *Ad Age* said seniors "are portrayed in a more positive way"—which is what Winski emphasized—47 percent said they were portrayed more negatively *or* there had been no change. In addition, two personal attributes of advertising stuck in the craw of a large number of people: 27 percent said there was too much advertising showing the elderly as frail and unhealthy, and 24 percent said there was too much advertising showing the "older Americans" as forgetful and mentally slow.[5] This survey occurred a year before the Doritos flap.

If there has been improvement in the portrayal of seniors in advertising, it is marginal at best. And this is short sighted on the part of advertisers and the advertising community.

Because seniors are a large and increasingly affluent market—one destined to grow even larger as the 1950s baby boomers mature—advertisers should reflect a sensitivity to this group, or some seniors will take out their anger and frustration toward images in advertising by ignoring or actively boycotting a product.

There are three major reasons that advertisers and their agencies should respond to concerns among seniors: (1) The demographics are in favor of the seniors; (2) marketers should promote their own self-interest in appealing to or attempting to avoid offending this group; and (3) seniors and children are personally affected by the portrayal of seniors in advertising and the media.

DEMOGRAPHICS AND PERCEPTIONS

There were an estimated three million people in America eighty-five or older in the 1990 Census. That's the extreme end of the "elderly," but it is rapidly enlarging under lengthening life spans. The 1990 group was 35 percent larger than in the 1980 Census. Others among the seniors are extending their lifespans, too. Jennifer Day, a specialist for the U.S. Census Bureau, reported that a sixty-five-year-old in 1990 had a life expectancy of 17.2 years. As a result of further study in 1993, the life expectancy of a sixty-five-year-old is 17.6 years. This appears to be but a minor increase on the surface, but a five-month increase in life expectancy in only three years is a "huge jump demographically," as she reported to a *Wall Street Journal* columnist.[6]

Baby boomers are on the edge of joining the "mature market." The proportion of the population over fifty will increase nearly 21 percent in this decade, reaching 76.7 million by 2000. During the next decade, to 2010, it will grow 27 percent to reach 97.3 million. This is a staggering number. For instance, the under-fifty population will be "only" 203.9 million in the year 2010. There already are more people age sixty or older than there are children under fourteen years.[7]

Numbers of seniors are just one indicator of the changing seniors group. Their financial resources also are important. Accurate figures are difficult to get, but one estimate has it that Americans fifty and over hold 50 percent of the country's discretionary income and more than 75 percent of its financial assets.[8] Average household income actually declines in those groups fifty-five and over, but discretionary income rises. Several studies report this phenomenon, which has been summarized in Christy Fisher's *Ad Age* article.[9] The significance should not be lost on advertisers.

Advertisers also should be aware that the mature audience, however one defines it, increasingly has good health and generally is satisfied with its position in life. A study by Dorothy Field, a gerontologist at the University of Georgia, concluded that old age is far from a depressing time for most people; rather, it is the most satisfying period of their lives. The least satisfying period was adolescence. Field said: "It really shatters the old stereotypes. We tend to think of old age as a time where everybody is lonely and in poor health and unhappy—but that's just not true."[10]

Betty Friedan, while researching her book *The Fountain of Age*, found that her own stereotypes of aging were fallacious. "I remember how surprised I was," she said, when revealing the results of her research and interviews, to discover "that only five percent of Americans over 65 will be in nursing homes at any one time. Less than five percent will have any kind of senility, including Alzheimer's. You think from the image that that is what awaits all of us in old age."[11]

ADVERTISER SELF-INTEREST

One advertising executive looked at the senior market and concluded that she "couldn't be bothered with targeting older people because they would all die soon."[12] This stereotype, as we've shown, is so pervasive that normally intelligent ad executives won't even consider what value the senior market is to their product. Not only do they lose, their clients lose.

Not all products appeal to the senior market, of course. But advertisers should be aware that seniors also are grandparents, and during the recent recession gift buying increased "partly because more [Americans] are grandparents."[13] Advertisers tick off this age group at their peril.

STEREOTYPES/IMAGES AFFECT SENIORS AND CHILDREN

Betty Friedan was surprised because what she found out about seniors was different from the stereotype she herself had of seniors. That stereotype is pervasive in America and in Western countries. One writer took her father to the doctor for a check-up. "Afterward, the doctor turned to me and began reporting his prognosis, completely ignoring my father, an alert and lively 70-year-old who spoke up after a few minutes. 'Hey, Doc, I'm the patient, how about talking to me?'"[14] This anecdote would be humorous, perhaps, if it weren't so pervasive and dangerous. The Centers for Disease Control and Prevention has revealed that 10 percent of reported AIDS cases are people fifty or older, or more than 31,000 persons. Doctors are simply not prepared for this situation, as the head of a geriatric unit in New York City admitted. Lack of experience with older AIDS patients is dangerous for the elderly because the "dementia" caused by AIDS can be alleviated; Alzheimer's, which it mimics, cannot. But successful treatment requires early diagnosis. Age stereotypes work against a correct diagnosis.[15]

Stereotypes engender fear among the elderly, too. A study of those who lost jobs but wished to work revealed that they often are "limited by their own identification with the stereotypes of age (i.e. as being useless, sick or too old for certain things)."

The warning was that "the vocational counselor," to whom the results of the study were targeted, "may have to address the worker's own negative self-image."[16]

Young people also have stereotypes of the elderly and a fear of growing old. These beliefs may not have much to do with the media, although both the young and the old are frequently "victims" in television programs. Fear of growing old may have to do with the experience we've all had: Our parents, when we were young, always seemed "old" to us. Nevertheless, "old" is relative and doesn't mean decrepit, as one second-grader had learned to expect. The first thing he blurted out, when he entered a senior center, was, "Where are your beds?" Stereotypes abound among children. A study in Ireland among teenagers showed half of them had a predominantly negative image of old age and of elderly people, while all of the boys and two out of three girls "felt some fear or anxiety about growing old."[17] Stereotypes have a truly negative impact on children.

WHAT CAN BE DONE?

Awareness helps. Advertisers and advertising agencies employee young people to write advertising copy and to prepare commercials. Most recent writers on this subject conclude that the age of the advertising producers is an important factor in the creation of images that injure. The average age of "creatives" working on the senior housing account in the Anderson Fischel Thompson office, Dallas, which is a J. Walter Thompson Co., was twenty-six in December 1993. Cyndee Miller, who interviewed several agency executives, found that "everyone . . . interviewed for this story . . . pointed a finger at the young creatives working on campaigns targeting the 50-plus market."[18]

It's true that the young creatives working on senior accounts can be a problem because they don't share the seniors' perspective. But at least they can overcome this problem by consulting the large amount of research now available on seniors and by using focus groups composed of seniors. Some agencies are even hiring older writers or are using them as consultants.[19]

The major problem with stereotypes of seniors, however, lies in advertising prepared to reach other demographic groups. The elderly are used as foils, as in the Doritos commercial. If the advertiser had been trying to reach seniors the commercial would never have been made. Sensitivity on the part of creative directors to commercials directed to seniors must be used in all commercials, making sure that young producers are sensitive to what they are producing.

PART V

PHYSICAL STEREOTYPES

20

The Invisible Cultural Group: Images of Disability

Jack A. Nelson

Any television viewer knows that when a maimed or hook-armed character shows up on the screen, it's a good bet that he will end up one of the bad guys. At least that's the way it often works out in movies and on the small screen, with villains like Dr. Strangelove and Dr. No both sporting hands and forearms of black leather. In fact, such evil characters join a long line of media portrayals that show those with disabilities as someone to be feared or pitied—and avoided.

These stigmatizing stereotypes that have persevered through the centuries are only now coming to be questioned and replaced by more realistic representations in the media. Sociologists have pondered the effects of such negative representation on television and in feature films. Yet it seems obvious that inappropriate and inaccurate presentations of persons with disabilities tend to stigmatize them in the public mind. Usually they are characterized as victims who possess undesirable social skills and personal qualities. In addition, J. Donaldson found there is a conspicuous absence of persons with disabilities even in incidental roles on television, thus giving the impression that disability is not an important part of mainstream society. Even when depictions of disability are present, they are usually accompanied by what Donaldson calls "some sort of stress, trauma, overcompensation, character flaw, or bizarre behavioral tendencies."[1]

Villainy has long been associated with abnormality. Fictional villains of the last century were often marked by physical disfigurement, and we must remind ourselves that even into the last decade one of the most-watched television programs of all time was the final episode of "The Fugitive." It was in this finale of the long-running series that the innocent doctor who had been hounded week after week as a suspect in the murder of his wife was able to prove that the real murderer was a one-armed man he had been pursuing the whole time. Such stereotypes are burned deep into the public consciousness by centuries of portrayals of those with disabilities as tainted, with deformity of body usually associated with deformity of spirit.

A PATTERN OF STEREOTYPES

The electronic media, of course, are even more powerful than written literature in shaping our views of others. It is perhaps not comforting that the power of television to mold attitudes was shown convincingly by Mankiewicz and Swerdlow in 1978.[2] Indeed, the persuasiveness and efficiency of television commercials are by themselves strong evidence that the medium is the most powerful institution in our society today. Observers have noted that the handicap stereotypes in film and television fit a pattern. These major stereotypes are listed below.

The Disabled Person As Victim: Telethon

One of the pervasive events on television are fund-raising telethons that on a particular weekend may fill more than fifty hours of appeals for funds to benefit "victims" of some disease or other. These programs feature tearful appeals from Hollywood stars, along with a mix of heart-rending requests from those with the targeted disability. Most common are wide-eyed children asking for money to be given for further research of their particular disease or condition.

These telethons are popular, probably because of the star appeal. But disability activist groups have opposed them because they perpetuate the image of those with disabilities as objects of pity. Those featured are usually shown as childlike, incompetent, needing total care, as non-productive, and as a drain on taxpayers.

It is rare that such telethons feature those who manage to live happy and productive lives in spite of having the featured disease. They rarely point out the accomplishments of such people. "Disabled people are not characterized [in telethons] as a social minority with civil rights but as victims of a tragic fate," writes sociologist Paul Longmore.[3]

Perhaps the most famous of these telethons is that sponsored by actor Jerry Lewis, the annual Labor Day Muscular Dystrophy Telethon. In 1992 disability groups around the country protested the telethon's portrayals of the disabled as degrading, demeaning, and dehumanizing. Disability advocates were particularly angered that Lewis had said that if he had muscular dystrophy, he would feel like only half a person.[4] Nevertheless, such portrayals continue in those forums, probably because they are successful at raising large amounts of money by playing on the audience's sympathy.

Newspapers are guilty of much the same fault. When Mary Johnson, then editor of *The Disability Rag*, a disability advocacy publication from Louisville, Kentucky, visited a journalism class at the University of Minnesota, she reminded journalism students there that reporters who solicit pity for people with disabilities do more harm than good. When shown a text that recommended stories showing the disabled triumphing over great odds, she moaned at one of the examples, "One of the most god-awful 'heartwarming cripple' stories I've ever read." Her point was that maudlin news stories reinforce passive images that some disabled people have of themselves, and they reinforce that image in the public mind.[5]

For years Mary Johnson has cajoled and badgered editors about their coverage of those with disabilities. She has had some success in persuading editors to eliminate such demeaning and stereotypical phrases as "victim," "cripple," and "confined to a wheelchair" from their newspapers' coverage.

The Disabled Person As a Hero: Supercrip

Triumphing over great odds is the theme of one of the mainstays of all the media in portraying those with disabilities. The heartwarming story is common of someone who faces the trauma of a disability and through courage and stamina rises above it or succumbs heroically. Television especially thrives on this fare–which on the face of it seems favorable to anyone with a disability. The battles of these people seem heroic, such as *The Terry Fox Story*, the account of a young Canadian who lost a leg to cancer and hopped on one leg across his huge country to raise money for cancer research.

In the disabled community, however, such dramas are regarded as "supercrip" stories that take away from real disability issues. The focusing of public attention on the heroic struggles of a few—the "Disability Chic" approach—diminishes the attention needed to access, transportation, jobs, and housing, and the movement to improve the status of all those with disabilities.

"Sure, Fox's story raised money for cancer and sure, it showed the human capacity for achievement," says actor Alan Toy, who walks with a brace and has appeared in television shows ranging from "Airwolf" to "Trauma Center," "But a lot of ordinary disabled people are made to feel like failures if they haven't done something extraordinary. They may be bankers or factory workers—proof enough of their usefulness to society. Do we have to be 'supercrips' in order to be valid? And if we're not super, are we invalid?"[6]

The Disabled Person As a Threat: Evil and Warped

Conflict and suspense are central to most movies and television shows. Usually, this means a threatening, evil character whose very presence implies danger for the protagonist. Modern screens abound in portrayals of villains whose evil presence is exemplified by some obvious physical limitation—a limp, a hook for a hand, a black patch over the eye, a hunchback. All of these play on subtle and deeply held fears and prejudices. It would be naive to think that these attitudes, which have been nurtured through the years by Hollywood portrayals, do not carry over into attitudes toward others with similar limitations in real life.

The Disabled Person As Unable to Adjust: "Just Buck Up!"

In recent years television programs have often featured the person with a disability who ended up maladjusted, unable to handle the trauma of his or her problem. Simply put—and the shows put it very simply—these people are bitter and full of self-pity because they have not yet learned to handle their disability.

Most of these shows feature a confrontational scene in which the protagonist, usually a friend or family member, sets the pitiable character straight. "Just buck up and take control of your life" is the usual message. There is no mention made of social prejudice or the role of social programs in helping alleviate the problems. Almost always the non-disabled person is shown to understand the problem better than the one with the disability. For instance, in an episode of "Night Court" during the 1980s, the young judge, Harry, is asked on a date by a young woman who has lost her legs. When he turns her down because he is too busy, she is devastated, so he naturally sets her straight. The problem, he tells her, is all in her attitude, not in her legs. A few minutes later she walks in on artificial limbs that she had with her all the time, smiling now. All she needed, it seems, was Harry's insightful advice.

Such messages imply that persons with disabilities don't really understand their own situations. These insights are provided by others. Therefore, says this myth, those with disabilities need guidance, since they are unable to make sound judgments themselves.

The Disabled Person As One to Be Cared For: The Burden

One consistent portrayal of those with disabilities is that of the frail person who needs to be taken care of, the burden on family and society. Foremost is the view that this is a duty that needs to be faced. At the same time, the implication is that a burden is difficult to bear and must be avoided. Thus the portrayal dehumanizes those with disabilities. As a dramatic device, this depiction is often used to show the noble intent and generosity of those who furnish the care, which makes the disabled person little more than a prop rather than as a human being capable of interacting with others to the profit of both.

It is that way in Johanna Spyri's 1881 novel *Heidi*, whose title character is hired as a companion to the "rich little cripple" Clara. Through the loving attention of Heidi, Clara gets well. In reality, Clara's role is only included to show the virtues of Heidi. Tiny Tim in Dickens's *A Christmas Carol* serves the same function.

The Disabled Person As One Who Shouldn't Have Survived

One of the most sobering portrayals of those with disabilities comes under the heading of the "better off dead" syndrome. This reflects the attitude that those with a serious disability would really be better off if they hadn't survived. It echoes the belief that anyone with a serious physical impairment cannot live a fulfilling and happy life, and therefore might as well not be alive. During the 1980s several dramas reflected this attitude: the play and movie *Whose Life Is It, Anyway?*, the television movie *An Act of Love*, and the play *Nevis Mountain Dew*. In each of these, quadriplegics and paraplegics beg to be assisted in suicide because they say their lives are not worth living. A rather frightening subtext in these dramas is that in a time of spiraling medical expenses, it costs a fortune to keep people alive who would be better off dead anyway.

This portrayal also deals with the fear and loathing that some people feel in dealing with those with handicaps. For many, the sight of serious physical disability is an unpleasant reminder of their own mortality and vulnerability. Longmore (1985) suggests that in these dramas, disability alienates a person from society and deprives the individual of self-determination.[7] Death is shown as preferable, partly because it relieves society of the problem of dealing with the long-term needs and rights of those with disabilities. The chilling implication is that this attitude is a step toward justifying euthanasia for those whose lives—in someone's judgment—"are unworthy of life."

These distortions occur over and over in dramas that fill our living rooms almost every night. Only in recent years have there come changes in attitude that balance the stereotypes with more accurate and individualized depictions.

TELEVISION PORTRAYALS

One of the interesting findings of sociologists is that on television the lives of people with disabilities are obviously empty, excluded from important roles as husbands and wives, as fathers or mothers. One survey showed that two-thirds of them were single, even childlike, often victims. Thus, power and strength were denied them. Their lives centered on their disability.[8]

Another study of eighty-five half-hour prime-time television shows noted that, although what were called "handicapped characters" were sometimes seen in major roles, they seldom appeared in incidental roles. In fact, in the entire study not one handicapped character appeared in a minor role except in juxtaposition with other handicapped characters. None were visible in groups of shoppers, spectators, jurors, customer, or workers. Handicapped people were thus invisible among the thousands of people in the background.[9] Indeed, considering how often disabled people have been shunted out of sight, it is not remiss to call them "the invisible minority."

In the above study, Donaldson found that positive portrayals appeared less often than negative portrayals. When they were portrayed positively, those with a disability were shown valiantly struggling against a dominating facet of their life such as blindness or paralysis. In a sense these portrayals are positive, but at the same time they strengthen the stereotype that the disability is the central focus of a person's life. What was absent was the portrayal of a person who lived a full and rich life in which a disability was an incidental facet—a successful lawyer or professor who happened to use a wheelchair, for instance.

Just as important, J. Donaldson reported, those with disabilities were seldom shown living their lives in interaction with those who did not have disabilities:

The absence of positive portrayals that belie stereotypes and depict comfortable interaction between handicapped and non-handicapped people suggests that prime time television is not exerting a significant influence in shaping positive societal attitudes toward individuals who are handicapped, nor is it facilitating comfortable relationships by providing models of interaction.[10]

As might be expected, Donaldson found that those with disabilities were often shown in "extremely negative roles." When they were shown as evil threats to society, the negative portrayals of the handicapped showed their disabilities as only incidental to the plot. In other words, their disabilities were not shown to dominate their lives, as was the case in the positive portrayals.[11]

THE RISE OF THE MEDIA ACCESS OFFICE

One positive influence at work for the disabled is a group known as Media Access Office (MAO) that has operated since 1978 on the Hollywood scene to exert quiet pressure in favor of the disabled. Made up of approximately 250 actors and actresses with varying disabilities, the group advocates the use of actors with disabilities to portray characters with disabilities and more normal treatment of people with disabilities by writers, producers and directors of movies and television. They particularly encourage roles in which the disability is seen as incidental. For instance, former MAO Chairman Alan Toy recalls a commercial he made in which he portrayed an ordinary businessman carrying a briefcase and walking on crutches, which is how he normally gets around. "If only we could get that image of normality projected more," he says, "the more audiences would get used to seeing us as human beings, and the less aghast they'll be when they meet us in the street."[12]

MOST IMPORTANT INFLUENCES: STEREOTYPES IN THE MIND

Of all the stereotypes about the disabled that plague the public, none is so insidious as the one that dwells inside the mind as a result of being exposed to all the media stereotypes. That is, the accumulation of all the movie portrayals, the television characterizations, and the real-life experiences that all of us are exposed to during our lives result in expectations of how those around us will act, given certain signals.

The signals of disability, such as a wheelchair, an unsteady gait, or a tremor, elicit reactions that one might expect from some unenlightened people. Take the example of someone portraying a person with cerebral palsy, for instance. In preparing to star in the film *My Left Foot*, Daniel Day-Lewis strove to get inside Christy Brown's head. To accomplish this Day-Lewis used a wheelchair, was lifted in and out of cars, spoke with impaired speech and had someone feed him in some of Dublin's best restaurants.

"It's strange what happens, even though everybody knew who I was and what I was doing," he explained later. "When people see someone in a wheelchair, their attitudes change . . . . They start treating you like a child." He found that people talked around him instead of to him. He had become one of the invisible disabled.[13]

The average person walks around with these expectations—the pictures in his or her head—and only slowly are changes coming. But changes are taking place in how society treats the disabled, and how they are portrayed in the media. These improvements are partly fueled by the Americans with Disabilities Act of 1990 and by a growing awareness that those with disabilities are first of all people and only secondarily defined by any impairment they might have.

CHANGES GOING ON

The past two decades have been times of monumental social change in American society. The growing awareness of the rights of minority groups has been one of the hallmarks of this century. Granted, deeply held archetypal fears and attitudes do not shift 180 degrees in a few years. But it has become apparent in the last two decades that attitudes toward those with disabilities are undergoing some major shifts. The culmination, of course, came with the passage of the 1990 Americans with Disabilities Act, which guarantees a new deal for those with disabilities, particularly in such matters as access to public accommodations and employment. Perhaps what is most important is that passage of this act signals a change in public expectations and attitudes regarding this important group.

In the media also there are signals that the traditional stereotypical treatment is no longer acceptable. Major changes have occurred that reflect these new attitudes. Indeed, new attention is being given to the representation of the disabled in the media. For instance, in the fall of 1991, NBC's "Reasonable Doubts" broke new ground by featuring a deaf actor, Marlee Matlin, as a deaf district attorney who delivered some lines in sign language. Most important was the fact that the NBC series was not about a disabled person, but a district attorney who incidentally is deaf.

Similarly, in the early 1990s popular ABC series "Life Goes On," the central character was acted by a young man with Down's Syndrome. Perhaps most noticeable is the growing number of users of wheelchairs who showed up on television ads in the early 1990s who are shown as normal people doing the things that normal people do. In the growing catalogue industry more and more models are showing up in wheelchairs for such retailers like Eddie Bauer and Nordstrom.

Since the early 1980s, of course, ads featuring disabled people have appeared on television, but by 1992 the roles were more frequent and more varied. Many of these show workers in law offices and in such high-profile places as newsrooms carrying out routine tasks without fanfare like everyone else in these offices. In other words, the message is that those with disabilities have a place on the job like everyone else.

Similarly, in an ad for Target discount stores, a photograph of a child in a wheelchair was included in a sales circular. This occurred at the suggestion of a vice president of marketing whose daughter was born without a left hand. He approved the ad with some trepidation, but the reaction of the public was enthusiastic. The company received more than 2,000 letters of praise, he said.[14]

In the words used to describe those with disabilities, there has emerged a new spirit of self-identification and activism among the disabled community. In recent years, disabled people have recognized themselves not as victims of disease and disablement, but as members of a stigmatized cultural group, discriminated against, segregated, and denied the opportunity to participate equally in the good life of normal society.

In an effort to change perceptions inherent in traditional pejorative language, such neologisms have been fashioned as "differently abled," "physically challenged," or "handicapable." In 1991 the National Cristina Foundation announced a $50,000 prize for the best word that put a positive spin in describing those with disabilities From 50,000 entries, the winner was "people of differing abilities," which brought hoots of derision from those in the disabled community.[15] While none of these terms have won wide acceptance, the growing move among the disabled to describe themselves pridefully as an "in group" is suggested by the trend to describe others as TABs (temporarily abled bodied) or ABs (able bodied). Such emerging language is a sign of their refusal to accept the role of a stigmatized group who are only marginally recognized as human beings.

As we are poised at the turn of the century, there is promise of vast improvements for the disabled community. New public attitudes seem to be building, but there remain many of the prejudicial attitudes of the past that view the disabled as invisible or unworthy of notice.

The influence of television and movie portrayals of disability can hardly be overestimated when we consider the huge audiences they draw, first in theaters and then inside hundreds of millions of homes on television. The impact of these images in changing stereotypes in the public mind cannot be overestimated. But in a world where the information superhighway is more and more taking a central role in people's lives, there is also vast promise of what can be done to alter attitudes by these powerful institutions.

Perhaps most encouraging of all, those in the disabled community have emerged with stronger images of self-empowerment. As they view themselves differently, the world may follow along.

21

The Blind in the Media: A Vision of Stereotypes in Action

Lee Wilkins

The human animal is distinct from other mammals in many ways. One of the most profound is the neural capacity of the human cerebral cortex, the portion of the brain that processes visual information. The cerebral cortex has imbued the capacity to see with qualities of myth and mental acuity. Presidents are expected to have vision; Cassandra saw the future and was cursed. These cultural understandings provide multiple meanings to an important symbol: the seeing or blind eye. Sight is fundamental to what and who we are as people.

The media, of course, are symbol transmitters. That is the focus of this chapter. Common themes about the blind drawn from Western literature and art will be applied to a selected sample of the more than 200 films in which the blind have been major characters. News accounts from the print and broadcast media will then be examined to determine how journalists use these same culturally based symbols in reporting the news. The chapter concludes with suggestions for improving journalistic performance.

THE CULTURAL MEANING OF BLINDNESS

In the popular mind, the concept of blindness simultaneously juxtaposes two contradictory notions: that the loss of sight dooms most of its victims to lifelong dependence, but that it also rewards a few of them with super human powers. Out of these twin beliefs have grown the stereotypes of the blind beggar and the blind genius.[1]

Blindness is one of Western literary cultures most common dramatic conventions. The Egyptians were the first civilization to try to medically treat sightlessness, and the Greeks introduced the metaphor of blindness into Western literature. The blind poet Homer wrote that Odysseus was deprived of sight for his cruelties.

Oedipus tore out his eyes to atone for his patricide and incest.   References in Western religious tradition link blindness with evil or sin. Lot's wife was blinded when she looked back at Sodom.   The Talmud and other Hebrew commentaries refer to the blind as the living dead.[2] Although some Eastern cultures found an economic niche for the blind (for example, in Japan they worked as masseuses), almost all ancient Western civilizations sanctioned euthanasia for the physically deformed. The Romans borrowed from the Greeks the tradition of putting blind children by the side of the road in specially constructed baskets where they were left to die.

However, "not all of the fallacies and fables about blindness are negative. There are also positive images interwoven in its mystique." These positive stereotypes include the notion that other senses can compensate for sightlessness, that blind people possess the desirable character traits of spirituality, patience, and cheerfulness, and that they have superhuman command of the non-visual senses. Humor by a blind person is often interpreted as an example of extreme fortitude or an attempt to hide sorrow.[3]

These stereotypes are sometimes accepted by blind people themselves. One survey of blind people noted that nearly 10 percent did not believe that, if they were employed in a competitive job, their work would be as good as that of the sighted; 36 percent of those surveyed thought that away from their own house, they should have a sighted guide.[4]

Helen Keller, who is discussed more extensively later in this chapter, noted the logical inconsistency of such persistent cultural views. She found

a medieval ignorance concerning the sightless. They assured me that the blind can tell colors by touch and that the senses they have are more delicate and acute than those of other people. Nature herself, they told me, seeks to atone to the blind by giving them a singular sensitiveness and a sweet patience of spirit. It seemed not to occur to them that if this were true it would be an advantage to lose one's sight.[5]

Stereotypes of the blind are among the most evocative in contemporary culture. Because blindness deals with the act of seeing, many of these stereotypes are laden with visual messages. A brief review of the most common, and their literary origins and amplifications, follows.

- The blind are deserving of sympathy and pity. Buddha taught that mercy should be extended to the deformed, and the Koran makes some exceptions for the blind. Christ asks for pity for the blind.
- The blind are miserable. Seeing double or having to squint are common motifs in folk literature. Think of the animated cartoon character, Mr. Magoo. The Greeks considered blindness the worst of misfortunes, and the Bible and Greek literature curse people who misdirect the blind. Kipling, Conrad, and D. H. Lawrence all developed blind characters who were miserable.
- The blind live in a world of darkness. Milton linked blindness with darkness, as did Dickens. However, many medically blind people report a grayness of vision, while many legally blind people retain some useful sight.
- The blind are helpless and useless. Perhaps no better encapsulation of this stereotype can be found than in Deuteronomy 28: 28-29. "May the Lord strike you with madness, blindness, and bewilderment; so that you will grope about in broad daylight, just as a blind man gropes in darkness, and you will fail to find your way." The Bible bars the blind from the priesthood.
- The blind are fools. This stereotype has its roots in both folk and elite culture. Deception or trickiness by the blind is a concomitant stereotype that Shakespeare, in *King Lear*, and Milton, in *Samson and Delilah*, employed.

- The blind are beggars. This stereotype appears to be cross-cultural. It has been found as a literary motif in folk tales from Europe, Ireland, the Philippines, and among the Navaho.
- The blind are compensated for their lack of sight. Homer was blind, but his talent was considered a gift from the gods. That the blind have the gift of prophecy is part of the mythology of Turkey, Korea, and Russia.
- Blindness is a punishment for past sins. Traditional Christian teaching has linked a variety of physical disabilities and deformities with "original sin." Folk literature in India, Sweden, Finland, Greece, Spain, Brittany, and among some native American peoples repeats this view.
- The blind are to be feared, avoided, and rejected. Psychologist Gordon Allport notes the image of a blind man is a "label of primary potency," a linguistic symbol that "acts like [a] shrieking siren, deafening us to all finer discriminations that we might otherwise perceive."[6]
- The blind are immoral or evil. Stagg in Dickens' *Barnaby Rudge* and Pew in *Treasure Island* typify this stereotype: "These characters would be despicable under any circumstances, but being blind, they are horrible."[7] However this stereotype is an improvement over others; an evil person is neither a helpless nor a useless one.
- The blind are mysterious. In *Paradise Lost,* one may lose one's sight for the purpose of redemption, but not for some other, more social purpose. The blind are believed to have magical powers in South Vietnam, Korea, among the Nuer tribes of Africa, and by some native American peoples.

Thus, blindness represents a complicated cultural stereotype. It shares with many other forms of stereotyping the human tendency to treat all people who share one trait as identical rather than as distinct individuals. The blind are transformed into a category, making it easier to treat them as a means to enhance dramatic impact than as an end.

But, unlike many other stereotypes, stereotypes of blindness include strong positive and negative elements simultaneously. Research suggests many stereotypes are "cross-cultural in nature, indicating some commonalty in man's experiences with and reactions to blindness and blind people."[8] Their universality makes it more difficult to counteract them.

THE BLIND IN FILM

Blind people have been major characters in more than 200 films, and their dramatic qualities have enhanced and puzzled critics for as long as the medium has existed. For example, in the film trilogy of *Star Wars*, fighter pilot Hans Solo loses his sight as a result of carbon-freezing induced hibernation. He regains his sight off camera, a plot irregularity that was noted by many critics of the wildly successful series. Gene Hackman's hilarious portrayal of the blind mute in Mel Brooks' *Young Frankenstein* owes a debt to the dramatic rendition of the legend in James Whales' *Bride of Frankenstein.* In both cases, however, the visual message of the blind is remarkably similar: they appear helpless, they grope about in apparent darkness, they mistake one thing for another (Solo cannot penetrate Leah's disguise until he hears her voice, while Hackman lights the "monster's" thumb instead of a cigar), and both are in some sense innocents.

Visual messages about the blind in film provide the cultural context that helps people understand messages from different sources. That same cultural context may influence how messages themselves are framed. Scholars and critics agree that there are certain touchstone films about the blind that are worth examining. Two of the earliest films to employ blind characters, Charlie Chaplin's *City Lights* and W. C. Fields *It's a Gift* represent two opposing portraits of the blind. Two other films from the 1960s, *The Miracle Worker* and *Wait Until Dark*, demonstrate not merely an evolution in dramatic technique but in some cultural understanding of the blind. A contemporary film, *Scent of a Woman*, provides insight into current popular thinking. It is against this backdrop, a funded visual memory that extends at least to the 1930s, that other messages may be understood.

Although the era of sound motion pictures had begun when Chaplin made *City Lights*, the director and star chose to keep the film silent. This decision, which has been critically acclaimed for many years, gives even more power to the imagery Chaplin as the Little Tramp chose to capture on camera. The plot itself owes much to stereotyping and to the Enlightenment. The Little Tramp falls in love with a beautiful, blind flower girl. The young woman, with encouragement from the tramp, believes him to be wealthy, a delusion Chaplin encourages as he attempts to raise money for an operation to restore the girl's sight. He succeeds, and much of the comedy in the film centers on the trials, tribulations, and mistaken identities that Chaplin must endure in his fund-raising endeavors. In the final scene, the girl discovers the true identity of her benefactor, producing one of the most poignant moments of any Chaplin film.

Innocence is one of the major themes of many Chaplin films, and *City Lights* is no exception. The blind flower girl particularly embodies an almost ethereal quality, enhanced by her beatific expression and her total acceptance of the Little Tramp at all stages of the plot. The flower girl is better than most other people; she has qualities of patience and spirituality and seems to divine the innocence at the core of The Little Tramp himself. Yet the flower girl is helpless. She must rely on others to do things for her. Her occupation is superfluous even in 1931, when the film was made, and she is so trusting that the actors and director had a delicate line to tread between enhanced perception and foolishness. The blind flower girl in *City Lights* represents ethereal beauty coupled with helplessness and emotional insight. The visual messages that Chaplin used—her costume, her expression, her manner of moving, which is in real contrast to Chaplin's pantomime—are all stereotypes employed for a powerful dramatic effect.

If Chaplin used his films to discuss the concept of innocence, then W. C. Fields' work represents experience. Only Fields, in those early days of cinema, would have used a bumbling and irascible blind character to further the plot of *It's a Gift.*

The blind character in the film appears in only one scene, where Fields employed almost every common visual stereotype of the blind. Small-town grocer Harold Bissonette (Fields) is continually harassed by everyone, including his wife and store customers. In a memorable five-minute encounter, Fields must wait on a blind man who enters the audience's frame of vision by smashing a glass window with his cane. The character wears a bowler, dark glasses, walks fumblingly and only with assistance, and despite this help breaks glass, upsets store displays, and is generally cantankerous. In addition, he's hard of hearing, a disability that also renders him foolish. It is only as the blind customer, Mr. Merkle, is leaving the store—again smashing another glass window with his cane—that Fields tells another customer that Merkle is the house detective at a local hotel. Fields then guides the blind customer out to the street, reassuring him there is no traffic. The audience's last glimpse of the character is a long shot where he haltingly crosses the street and is dodged by fire engines, police cars, and other emergency vehicles.

Fast forward three decades to Broadway, where two successful stage plays were adapted equally successfully for the screen. *The Miracle Worker,* starring Patty Duke and Ann Bancroft, re-created the Broadway play to critical acclaim. The film, and particularly Patty Duke's portrayal of Helen Keller, provides one of the least stereotypical portraits of the blind in popular culture. In fact, one critic reacted so badly to the lack of stereotypes—he would not accept that Keller had been as stubborn and as difficult as the film portrayal suggested—that as part of his review he read both Keller and Sullivan's books about their experience. He wrote "After I had written the above, I got around to looking up the sources—Helen Keller's *The Story of My Life*, and her memoir of Ann Sullivan called *Teacher*, and Nella Braddy's *Anne Sullivan Macy*—and I find that the movie is accurate literally, that Helen was indeed a holy terror and a spoiled brat."[9]

It is difficult to estimate the impact Helen Keller, popularized in a Broadway play and a film, with her own books and her life's work, has had on popular understandings of the blind. She remains a heroine to many for whom blindness represents an obstacle overcome by enormous personal courage, tenacity, and a fine intellect. The underlying issues of Keller's struggle for self-sufficiency, her grasp of the power of an idea, and her stalwart individualism also resonate deeply with popular conceptions of Americans. Myth resonates within myth. Keller, who also overcame deafness, may embody an almost unachievable ideal, representing as she does values far outside the traditional thinking about physical disability. But, like the real life it was based on, *The Miracle Worker* also provides an antidote to stereotypical thinking.

Wait Until Dark was equally influential, but with the film-making community. In this 1967 psychological thriller, Audrey Hepburn plays a blind woman who, for reasons the plot leaves completely unclear, becomes trapped in her New York apartment with three murderous thugs and a doll filled with heroine. Hepburn levels the playing field by knocking out all the lights in the apartment, rendering her assailants as physically challenged as she. The resulting action is filled with visual messages of "blind" people tumbling over furniture, the thugs groping and stumbling through the apartment, and camera work where weapons seem to come out of nowhere, playing upon the audience's perception of blindness as blackness and as filled with unpleasant surprises. Hepburn eventually foils her attackers, primarily through trickery. Some critics wondered why such an intelligent woman would not have thought to send for help earlier in the incident (a problem with the plot of the Broadway play as well). *Wait Until Dark* plays stereotype against stereotype. Hepburn is alternately helpless and capable, quick thinking yet groping in an environment she should know well, clearly a better person than the thugs who attack her yet able to trick them.

The blind also became protagonists in several films in the early 1990s, among them *Sneakers*, Disney's *Wild Hearts Can't Be Broken*, and *Places in the Heart*. Perhaps the most successful of them was *Scent of a Woman*, starring Al Pacino, who received an Academy Award for best actor for his performance.

Pacino plays a dissolute and depressed former Marine officer who through his own bull-headedness blinds himself. Pacino's character has saved his disability checks to fund one extravagant weekend at New York's Plaza Hotel that includes wine, women, and suicide. The tension in the film is provided by the high school military cadet Pacino finagles into accompanying him into the city. The young man objects to Pacino's plans to end his life and spends the weekend convincing this unpleasant and often unfeeling character that death is not a preferable option to living sightless.

The character Pacino plays represents many of the traditional stereotypes. He is maladjusted, he is useless in terms of earning money, he needs the help of a sighted person to get around, he is unpleasant, and, depending on individual interpretation of his interactions with his family, could also be considered evil. Blindness has rendered him morose. Even the title of the film—*Scent of a Woman*—borrows from stereotype: Pacino can no longer recognize women visually but he can sniff them out.

Three visual messages dominate Pacino's performance. First the actor manages to appear "blind" without many awkward physical cues. Second, while Pacino does need a cane and an arm to walk around, his bearing is that of a former military officer. There is little stumbling and fumbling.

Third, there's the tango, perhaps the most written-about scene in the film.

Pacino, having smelled out a lovely young woman, dances a forceful tango with her, never missing a step, never letting his partner out of reach, and never letting on that he is doing all of this as a blind man. In this one scene, Pacino's character contradicts almost all the stereotypes that dominate the plot. The tango provides the film-goer with a vision of what Pacino might have been, a reason to be sympathetic with him, and a visual message of what the blind can accomplish that is startling for its similarity to what we would expect from the sighted (and coordinated).

These films, of course, do not reflect all of the portraits of the blind in film. But they represent trends. The more recent films edge toward a view of the blind that is multidimensional and capable. As important, female blind characters often assume qualities of helplessness and surreal goodness while male characters are more unpleasant or evil. In film, stereotypes of women and men dramatically infuse stereotypes of the blind. It is difficult to tell which dominates.

This analysis of the characters in film is intended to be illustrative rather than exhaustive. The cultural myths that have dominated literary portraits of the blind are definitely part of the dramatic vocabulary on the silver screen. They form a cultural matrix, a set of expectations that includes visual, behavioral, and verbal cues. Audiences cannot be expected to forget those cues when they tune into the news. Journalists, as members of a culture, may also have a difficult time framing the news without them.

THE BLIND IN THE NEWS:
GROPING FROM CLICHE TO REALITY

While no one medium can represent all news organizations, several are taken to be indicative of national trends. Study after study has examined the *New York Times* as indicative of coverage in the elite press; *USA Today* represents every person's newspaper. The three national television networks provide most Americans with most of their news as well as a collection of visual messages. Examining how the blind are portrayed by these news organizations provides a sketch of what journalists are doing today.

The Lexis/Nexis database versions of the *New York Times* and *USA Today* were examined for any story that used the words blind, blinded, or blindness. The individual story was the unit of analysis, and a single mention of any of the key words in a full text search was enough to prompt inclusion of that story in the data set. Network news coverage was examined using Barrell's database. A similar methodology using the same key words and a full text search netted the database of stories used for preliminary examination.

It is worth noting the search process itself contains a conundrum. If blind people were the subjects of news stories and blindness was not mentioned, the articles would not be included. Such stories might be the least likely to rely on stereotypes.

Yet, searching without the key word "blind," for example, substituting "physical disability," yielded an unusable database. Traditional news values suggest that blindness is likely to be mentioned in news accounts. While the search yielded many stories, it is impossible to determine whether every story that included blind people is part of this data set.

There were 1,081 articles using the key words in the *Times*, 338 in *USA Today*, and 107 in nightly network newscasts during calendar year 1993.

Traditional content analysis then takes the preliminary data catch and culls it to eliminate duplicate stories, stories that use the term in a different fashion than is being analyzed, and so on. The same procedure was employed here, but the cull itself is worth comment.

Blindness appears in the news as a cliché or a colloquialism far more often than any other usage. Of the 1,081 stories examined in the *New York Times*, only 160 stories did not use the word "blind" either colloquially or as part of a cliché. About 131 *USA Today* stories did not use the word as predicted. About 25 percent, or 27 network news stories, fulfilled the same criterion.

For example, there were color-blind or race-blind people, constitutions, and other documents. People, particularly baseball players and quarterbacks, were blind-sided, as were politicians. Public officials put their asserts in blind trusts. There was blind love and blind lust in the news, not to mention Blind Faith and Blind Melon in rock-and-roll coverage. Outdoor enthusiasts could take cover in duck blinds, while home decorators found myriad uses for the venetian blind. In short, almost every colloquialism or cultural cliché about blindness found its way into news stories.

Most stories were not illustrated, and those stories most likely to be illustrated appeared on the sports pages. These illustrations often included photos of the blind engaged in various activities, for example riding a horse or calling baseball plays, in which they were portrayed as vigorous and active. Personality profiles some-times included mug shots or photos of works of art.

While photos were not common in news accounts of the blind, the images that words evoke certainly were a part of news accounts. Further, these word images followed some predictable patterns.

- Blindness was used as a label in one particular set of stories: reports on the New York World Trade Center bombing in which the fifty-five-year-old "blind, diabetic Muslim cleric" Sheik Omar Abdel Rahman was first arrested and later charged. More than 20 percent of all network news stories using the word "blind" used it as a phrase to label the World Trade Center bomber, with accompanying video of the bombing, the arrests, or courtroom procedures. The use of the label, sometimes accompanied by a mug shot, was as pervasive in print. Thus, readers and viewers who did not encounter the word "blind" in the vernacular were next most likely to find it as a label attached to an international terrorist.
- Coverage of the blind was event-centered, as for example in blind sailor Hank Dekker's unsuccessful attempt to cross the Atlantic alone or as a tragic result of war (in Bosnia) or disease (in Africa).
- The Enlightenment preoccupation with curing blindness infused medical stories. Collec-tively, these stories emphasize the disabling aspects of blindness. However, there was a more subtle aspect to this view: that blindness can only be surmounted medically and that when it cannot be surmounted it results in despair.
- A small minority of stories—fewer than fifteen in each of the newspapers and nine stories on the television networks—provided an account of the blind in which the physical handi-cap was incidental to other accomplishments. *USA Today* coverage clustered around

sports, while the *Times* focused on the arts.

In summary, news organizations, while providing some coverage that was not stereotypical, also appeared to follow cultural patterns. When blindness was not a cliché, colloquialism, or label, it appeared most often in the news as a disease to be cured or a disability to be endured. The blind were seldom portrayed as active, contributing members of society. When they were portrayed that way, it was often in the stereotypical realm of "giftedness" compensating for lack of sight, as in the case of a television network profile of Ray Charles. This view of blindness is particularly significant because the disability itself occurs relatively infrequently in the population. Most people, including journalists, may not have much first-hand opportunity to know blind people. What people know about blindness, then, becomes a mediated reality unchallenged by first-hand experience.

SOME ETHICALLY BASED CRAFT SUGGESTIONS

Journalists can provide readers and viewers with an alternate vision. They may be expected to provide readers and viewers with an additional dimension of understanding. To that end, I suggest the following:

- Eliminate, as much as possible, clichés using the word "blind" from news copy. Not only is it bad writing, but clichéd analysis can crowd out the original.
- Stop using the word "blind" as a descriptive label unless it is essential to understanding the story. The profession has already made this change with regard to gender and ethnicity. The reasoning that supported these changes should be applied in this case as well. In more Kantian terms, treat the blind as an end in themselves rather than as a means to that end. Journalists also need to understand that descriptive labels can be visual; blind people do not have to be pictured with canes or groping.
- Continue to cover medical advances. But do not include, as part of that coverage, word pictures or visual messages of hopeless despair unless they are appropriate. Such images may (and may not) be appropriate when writing about the late stages of AIDS. They are far less appropriate when the issue is diabetes, cataracts, physical trauma, or aging.
- Cover blind people who excel at what they do. Peg those stories in something other than a stereotype—the blind musical or artistic genius. Illustrate these stories with pictures of the blind in action.
- Cover blind people as whole human beings, not as the unfortunate result of one physical trait. Report on them as individuals, not as a category in which blindness equals sameness. Incorporate them, as much as possible, into daily news coverage in the same way that women and ethnic groups are now being incorporated into the news.
- Finally, be sensitive to the richness of cultural perceptions of the blind. Understand that blindness has both positive and negative elements associated with it, and that it has allowed us to ask some profound questions about ourselves as human beings. Asking those questions is hardly inappropriate. But it is the quality of the answers that matters most.

The Deviance of Obesity: The Fat Lady Sings

Linda Coulter

Americans, who claim to have a strong belief in fairness and equality, have been subjected by the media to heavy dosages of ideology about what it takes to be beautiful and successful in business, romance, education, and life. Stereotypes are so deeply ingrained in our culture that even competent government leaders are an acceptable target of jokes, sight gags, and discrimination. It is apparently no problem for marketers to use, either visually or verbally, the cliché that "it isn't over until the fat lady sings." If the stigma stopped there, the harm done would be minimal. But our society has developed a complex cultural bias against the obese, and particularly, fat ladies.

Whether the current standards of attractiveness are a long-term phenomenon or just a fad is irrelevant for the estimated 30 percent to 40 percent of Americans who are obese.[1] Each day they are faced with physical, psychological, emotional, educational, financial, and legal consequences of their body size.[2] Many communication researchers have suggested that the current thin standard of attractiveness is a product of the media and that the standard is not one that promotes physical health or mental health.[3]

There has been considerable scholarly attention played to the concept of woman as "deviant." Whatever truth may exist in that concept, there are parts of the female population who suffer from unequal status far more than men with similar demographics and evidence that obese women have been studied far more than obese men.[4]

The label of deviancy is not lightly bestowed on any subgroup but can be based on one of several definitions, each of which is generally concerned with processes, and is the consequence of power, social distance, the "norm" of a population, and tolerance by the "normal" community.[5] And while obesity is frequently used as an example of deviance in textbooks, it is rarely even listed in indices, perhaps because it is accepted as a fact by the authors.[6]

Using W. R. Gove's four criteria for deviance, this chapter will show the way American media have assisted in the development of the stigma of obesity and the harm that occurs when one group is stereotyped so completely, not because of behaviors, but because of appearance.

POWER

One of the most enduring stereotypes of obesity is that it is a problem of the lower socioeconomic classes: "The attribute which has received the most attention in the literature is the resources and power of the individual, and it is argued that persons with few resources and little power are the ones most likely to have a deviant label imposed upon them."[7]

There has been little work done to determine exactly who the obese are demographically; numbers vary by researcher and area of concern. Feldman found in 1992 that 40 percent of women age forty and over were above ideal weight. Of women polled in 1950, 1956, and 1966, 44 percent said they wanted to weigh less.[8] A National Health and Nutritional Examination Survey found that about one-fourth of U.S. adults were overweight, but 52.1 percent of black women forty-five to fifty-four years of age were overweight.[9]

No matter the numbers, one controversial stereotype endures: Obesity is associated with lower socioeconomic status, aging, and color, three of the least powerful groups in America. Bowen et al. list a lack of restrained eating, economic pressures to buy less expensive foods, which are calorie- and fat-rich, lack of adequate nutritional knowledge, and an external locus of control as possible reasons for the prevalence of obesity in poor people, a condition they show is six times more prevalent among poor women than affluent women.[10] But Fisher claims that "there are cultures and subgroups (e.g., lower socioeconomic) in which being fat has few negative connotations."[11] Wooley, Wooley, and Dyrenforth quote research in which the authors studied groups that "presumably valued fatness," including African Americans, Jewish people, and the poor.[12]

The media are showing a shift from caricatured, stereotypical roles of women in television to a reflection of the roles of women in general, but the diversity of women being reflected in the media is still heavily influenced by attractiveness stereotypes. A cursory look at the 1993-1994 television season, for instance, shows the presence of several large women on prime-time programming. With the exception of Oprah Winfrey (whose weight has drastically altered over the years, on her talk show), virtually all are confined to what Atkin, Moorman, and Lin call the "comedy ghetto."[13]

That comedy ghetto is one way society is able to maintain our stereotypical images of women. The way we see large women portrayed is reinforced by the stereotype, making it believable, and that belief reinforces the stereotype, setting up a vicious cycle: "The standardized messages become the only digestible ones."[14] The messages are acceptable because they are presented in a way that makes them seem attractive to us. Shoemaker quotes Nisbett and Ross's approach to message attraction: "Information may be described as . . . likely to attract and hold our attention and to excite the imagination, to the extent that it is (a) emotionally interesting, (b) concrete and imagery-provoking, and (c) proximate in a sensory, temporal, or spatial way."[15] According to Shoemaker, information that meets those standards is more likely to be remembered.

The large women on such shows as "Rosanne," "Thea," "Grace Under Fire," and others are usually portrayed as blue-collar workers and often as single mothers. They have children who are often out of control or are ill-mannered, and the women struggle with poverty and hardship, all the while providing us with a few good laughs. It provides a vicarious peek into the lives of "others" who may interest us, and who may even resemble us, whether we want to identify with them or not.

SOCIAL DISTANCE

Just as we associate beauty with goodness, so do we associate obesity with characteristics generally considered negative.[16] Fisher wrote, "The chubby physique of the endomorph is universally looked upon negatively."[17] Elsewhere, he wrote: "The corpulent body is usually not acceptable to its owner and is even less acceptable to others."[18]

The current standard for most women fashion models is called "waif-like" in the media, and even though supermodels have openly discussed their problems with bulimia and anorexia, they are still the women who most represent the new ideal body image. Freedman says that body image is constantly changing, based on how much real bodies look like the ideal bodies: "If there is a great discrepancy between the ideal and the real (for instance if a cult of thinness defines most women as overweight) then the majority of women feel pressured to remodel themselves to fit the popular mold."[19]

In the absence of an objective definition of correct weight or ideal size, women are left with the uneasy realization that they don't look much like the women they see most often, the women in the media.[20] And since the women in media set the standard, one that most women don't meet, the majority of women feel they are less attractive than those in movies, on billboards, in magazines and on television.

TOLERANCE

Those constant reminders of the difference between the beautiful and the fat make it difficult not to expect social distance between "us" and "them." While there are undeniably physical consequences of being overweight, including diabetes, hypertension, arthritis, gout, and other medical problems, some researchers have found the average consumer to be more concerned with the social consequences of being overweight than the physical.[21] The list of social repercussions, because of the widespread intolerance of obesity, is long.

If one is considerably overweight, he or she is viewed as physically unattractive, is prone to experience social rejection, and is likely to be trait-typed as weak, lacking in self-control, slovenly, and so on. In short, consumer demand for easy weight reduction agents is a reflection of obesity's status as a culturally deviant adaptation.[22]

Myers and Biocca acknowledge that while most people will never look like the culturally defined ideal, there is a price to be paid by those who look different: "It is reasonable to imagine that each of these body image messages is just one strike on a chisel sculpting the ideal body inside a young woman's mind."[23] There are social consequences for not meeting that standard. "The ever present danger of being deemed physically unattractive has, in fact, been a quite explicit theme— perhaps even the single most dominant one—in much advertising aimed at women."[24]

There is evidence that the overweight are penalized for their size in terms of promotions and salaries. *Business Week* reported a University of Pittsburgh study of MBA graduate students, which found that men 20 percent over their ideal weight had salaries about $4,000 per year less than their "normal weight counterparts."[25] (Baum uses the phrase "earned salaries" rather than "had salaries," but there is nothing to indicate that the men actually worked less, therefore earning less.) There were so few women MBAs who were overweight that Baum concluded that obese women "tend not to be in management" and that "bosses interpret weight gain in a woman employee as a signal that she's abandoned any hope of rising higher" in the corporate structure.

VISIBILITY

The final characteristic, that of the visibility of the behavior, takes on ominous overtones with the obese. "All fat people are 'outed' by their appearance."[26] It is appearance, not behavior, that establishes this deviation, but it is the behaviors to which the appearance is attributed.

But bodies are more than objects that are weighed and measured; they are more than possessions that are discarded or changed at will. Merleau-Ponty said a body is not just something we have; it is something we are.[27] That fundamental difference provides both a sense of ambiguity and a sense of unity to bodies. To objectify a body is to move it away from its relationship with the world of being and toward a relationship with the world of things, thus provoking the ambiguity. Are we a collection of parts—hair, teeth, skin, thighs, fingernails—or are all of those parts us? Does a person have fat or are they fat? Does an obese person have a problem or are they a problem? Is the obesity a deviance or is the obese person a deviant?

CONCLUSION

Obese people, especially women, have been told they are unattractive by their own choice, they are shunned by those who are thin and beautiful, they are more likely to be poor, and less likely to get out of the trap of poverty.

Politically, women are now beginning to have their collective voices heard on a national basis, with more women in power than ever before. President Bill Clinton's Cabinet is a better representation of what America really looks like than others have been, with women in several of the power positions. There is an increased emphasis on the importance of women in the workplace, with women's rights assuming a stronger role in legislation. But the political elite still looks much like the people we see on television.

There is no need for Hollywood to tell women that the worst thing that can happen to them is to be fat. Academic scholarship and the popular press have both covered the tragedy of anorexia nervosa, but the tabloids scream headlines about the weight gains of Liz Taylor, Tyne Daly, Oprah Winfrey, and Kirstie Alley. Teenagers binge and purge to avoid an extra pound, and diet foods, diet plans, diet books, diet schemes, and diet programs fill hours on cable television as well as advertisements both printed and broadcast. For young girls growing up, there is no phrase as cursed as, "You have such a pretty face, if only you would lose weight." You cannot be both pretty and overweight. The cultural myth won't let you.

According to Kevin Barnhurst, "(I)f ... making and recognizing pictures depends on experience with vision, there is still room for conventions. In every detail beyond whatever is essential to recognition, the powerful effects of social attitudes and norms are felt."[28]

One means of probing the context of social attitudes and norms reinforced by our media is by understanding the cultural stereotypes and stigmas, by looking beyond the surface of visual media and examining "every detail beyond whatever is essential." That is where the danger for stereotyping lies. And unfortunately, this time, it won't be over when the fat lady sings.

PART VI

SEXUAL ORIENTATION STEREOTYPES

23

Reframing Gay and Lesbian Media Images: Fundamental Problems

Marguerite Moritz

Despite journalistic claims that they don't make the news, they just report it, news organizations have a well-documented history of being selective and biased in their choice of news topics. "The works of Epstein, Gans, Tuchman and others have made it axiomatic that what mainstream journalism offers as 'news' is a highly selective text and that what it portrays as reality is highly constructed."[1]

News organizations, print and broadcast, never have been prohibited from writing and reporting on gays and lesbians. But unwritten news codes—those generally accepted definitions of what constitutes a story—for decades provided a powerful barrier to coverage of many minority groups, including gays and lesbians. Far from being independent, news codes flow out of the larger culture and reflect the attitudes and socioeconomic hierarchies in society at large. Given that system, it is hardly surprising that gays and lesbians were not considered worthy of coverage well into the 1980s.[2] In 1987, to cite one notorious case, both *Time* and *Newsweek* ignored the gay rights march in Washington, D.C., the largest civil rights demonstration in the capitol since 1969.[3]

What coverage the incipient gay rights movement did get was presented from a heterosexual framework that implicitly (and often explicitly) constructed homosexuality as deviant. In news, both still photos in print and moving images in television have been a particular point of contention. In their early attempts to depict gays and lesbians, journalists often utilized the bizarre to illustrate the homosexual look. News editors showing gay pride parades, for example, typically selected twenty seconds of footage that featured whips, chains, and bare breasts. Gay watchdog groups in cities around the country pressured television newsrooms to change. The Gay & Lesbian Alliance Against Defamation (GLAAD) still instructs media personnel on the issue: "Do not show or describe only the most unconventional members of our community. There is nothing wrong with unconventionality—many in our community quite properly celebrate it—but it is nevertheless unfair to reinforce misperceptions that all lesbians and gay men are into, say, leather or drag."[4]

News practices did begin to change and images that reflected a more mainstream look became more common. But that technique has now led some critics to complain that the "liberal" media are sanitizing the issue in an effort to be politically correct. The 1993 march on Washington, for example, became a central focus of the criticism, the charge being that images selected to illustrate the parade did not include bare-breasted lesbians, gay men in leather, crossdressers, and other unconventional-looking participants. In essence, conservative critics were now arguing for a reframing of gay images not only to illustrate perversion but also danger. This is precisely the technique used so persuasively in a videotape produced and widely distributed by the far right, "The Gay Agenda."[5]

DUELING VIDEOS

"The Gay Agenda" is a nineteen-minute videotape constructed in traditional, formal news documentary style. It relies heavily on interviews with people presented as experts and combines their comments with news footage of gay rights demonstrations and gay pride parades. In addition, the video uses footage of ads from gay magazines and still photos of a drag queen who went straight, got married, and now talks about living a happy, heterosexual life. Its audio track includes interviewees as well as the sound added for a music track and for a "Voice of God" narrator.

The video was produced prior to the 1992 elections and was made available in Oregon and Colorado, where anti-gay initiatives were on the ballots. Its creators have claimed that they distributed 10,000 copies in those two states alone, many of them handed out free of charge. After the election, the distribution effort continued, and by early 1993 "The Gay Agenda" had started circulating in Washington, D.C. When the Commandant of the U.S. Marine Corps got a copy, he told Congresswoman Pat Schroeder in a letter that he had it sent out to the rest of the Joint Chiefs of Staff.[6]

As the tape made the rounds in Washington, reportedly going to every member of Congress, a group called the Gay and Lesbian Emergency Media Coalition prepared a video response entitled "Hate, Lies and Videotape." Initially, "The Gay Agenda" video had been ignored by the mainstream news media, perhaps seen as yet another piece of predictable anti-gay propaganda. But the release of the response video created a legitimate space for the news media to enter. "Hate, Lies and Videotape" suddenly turned a piece of propaganda into a point-counterpoint story with both sides represented.[7] The creators of the response tape were, in effect, asking the news media to take up the story, examine the evidence and bring their conclusions to their audiences. Ironically, they themselves created the license for news organizations to circulate the anti-gay material.

In the case of television news in particular, this was an ideal story—low in cost, high in controversy, heavy on both visual interest and audience appeal, and neatly fitting into the news frame that reduces complex issues to simple cases of pro and con. Since television reporters could logically tell the story through and with material from the already available videotapes, most of the expense of production work was eliminated. Television news for years has operated under an imperative that demands not just pictures, but "good" pictures, that is, images that are highly compelling. Certainly this story provided that. After the release of the response video, stories on the so-called "dueling videotapes" were featured on CNN, ABC, and in the *Washington Post* and *USA Today*.[8]

Who Won?

If this indeed was a video duel, is it possible to determine how points were scored and whether either side actually won? On the level of public relations, the answer is somewhat obvious. "The Gay Agenda" won a decisive public relations victory simply by being circulated in major news media outlets, particularly television. Instead of being seen by several thousand people, it was now seen by several million. Some of its more memorable visual images were excerpted on "Larry King Live," for example, while the response video was not shown at all.

In addition, "The Gay Agenda" won a political victory because it was a more credible and convincing videotape, even though the factual content of that video has been either refuted or, at the very least, seriously challenged. Indeed, the video succeeds by employing the very codes, techniques, and stereotypes used in television news and documentary forms. In a sense, "The Gay Agenda," through its manipulation of imagery, beats the news media at their own game.

Precisely because this is a videotape, its message is carried not just by the printed word or even by the spoken word. Instead, it employs production techniques of both Hollywood cinema and documentary film to create more complex visual and aural messages. The particular ways in which these are constructed and connected—complete with casting, framing, shooting, editing and mixing devices—constitute a cinematic language with its own set of meanings and messages. Thus an analysis of the video requires not only an examination of its language but also of its filmic codes.

Production Strategies

While a number of production strategies combine to give "The Gay Agenda" credibility, the selection and juxtaposition of visual messages may be the most crucial. The video is modeled on the formal news documentary and relies on videotape footage of actual events for most of its images. In the vocabulary of news, the still photograph and the moving image have become synonymous with reality. A reporter's words may be disputed, but pictures are considered to be unmediated representations, a true rendering that is not subject to debate or interpretation. In short, news consumers have been conditioned to believe that pictures equal reality, that they are documentation that is irrefutable, and that news simply holds up a mirror to the real world.

This view, however, fails to account for both the complexities of production and of reception. Communication research has demonstrated that news—pictures and copy—is not reality but a particular construction of reality.[9] In producing video images, the decision of what picture to take and what picture to ignore, what picture to leave on the proverbial cutting room floor become determining factors in shaping a particular reality. Additionally, the ways in which pictures are juxtaposed and the ways in which they are combined with sound tracks during the editing process will also have an impact on the messages conveyed.

"The Gay Agenda," for example, opens in black with only the sound of police whistles, chants, and ominous music to draw the viewer in. When the first images appear, they show a storefront window being shattered, a street fire burning, an angry crowd, jeering protesters confronting rows of police armed with shields and helmets—a quick succession of images that together convey the by-now familiar look of an urban riot. Added to the throbbing beat of the music is the so-called Voice of God narrator, a disembodied speaker who is never identified, the authoritative voice who is never seen but who speaks as if from on high, telling the viewer what these images are about: a protest over California Governor Pete Wilson's veto of Assembly Bill 101, legislation that "would have granted special minority rights" to gays and lesbians. And thus begins the first of several references to one of the video's subtexts—that gays and lesbians want and in some cases are getting "special rights" that should not be "equated with the truly, morally neutral condition of a particular racial or national origin or other status." At the same time, this opening montage visually recalls images of race riots and thus indirectly suggests that just as angry African Americans are to be feared, so too are angry gays and lesbians.

A second set of visuals follows shortly after this opening. In this sequence, there is no narration to distract from the visuals—only pictures and a pulsating soundtrack shows a gay pride parade as a music video. In this sequence, we see simulated sex acts, nudity, whips, chains and other forms of sadomasachism, men in drag, men in nun's habits, and signs with messages such as "God is Gay" and "Fuck." Intercut with these images are shots of small children and presumably their gay and lesbian parents who also are participants in the parade. We have said that the sequencing of images can create meaning, and this is precisely the case here. By juxtaposing children with sexually provocative paraders, the video effectively taps into the often repeated myth that gays and lesbians are pedophiles, that they recruit young people into homosexuality and that they are unfit to be parents. Public opinion polls have demonstrated that for "the majority of Americans, the belief in homosexuals recruiting the young is still strong."[10] Through its editing strategy, "The Gay Agenda" reinforces and extends that belief, especially to segments of the audience who are least familiar with pride parades and the role such events play in gay and lesbian culture.

We know from studies in audience reception that there is no single reading of a text. Instead, there are multiple readings, often linked to subcultural group membership. Interpretation clusters around age, ethnicity, race, gender, religion, or sexual identity. In his review of the literature on gays, lesbians, and the media, Fred Fejes describes the phenomenon this way: "That gays and lesbians, in order to cope with the overwhelming heterosexist and homophobic bias of media content, develop complex, interpretive strategies different from heterosexual viewers is not surprising." He cites an audience study reported in *Outweek* in which African American gays and lesbians were questioned about their responses to the comedy skit "Men on Men," which is featured on Fox Television's "In Living Color." Results showed a "very complex reading with a number of individuals expressing great pleasure in an accurate and funny depiction of Black gay camp, while at the same time voicing concern and even anger that these skits will be read by heterosexual white viewers— who do not understand the source and meaning of camp—as defaming caricatures of Black gay men."[11]

Certainly gay pride parade images will be read differently by straight, white, conservative audiences than they will be by gays and lesbians who are likely to view these events as queer performance, that is, an expression that may incorporate irony, camp, comedy, confrontation of mainstream sexual mores, exotica, erotica, and more. By showing only those gays and lesbians who most critically challenge conventional standards for public behavior and cultural expression, the video implies that they represent the entire group. As many have pointed out, this is the equivalent of showing pictures of drunks during Mardi Gras to illustrate the lifestyle of Anglo, heterosexual men.

CONCLUSION

The tactics employed in "The Gay Agenda" serve as a potent illustration of the future direction of the anti-gay movement. The message that invokes science, that relies on deeply embedded visual stereotypes, and that lets "you decide" the issues is far more difficult to combat, but its effect on the lives of gays and lesbians is no less devastating. While Amendment Two's "no special rights" passed with 54 percent of the vote in Colorado, becoming the "first statewide constitutional amendment to limit civil rights in the history of the U.S.," the more harshly worded Oregon measure was defeated, 57 percent to 43 percent. Using the Colorado model, a variety of state and national organizations of the right wing are preparing anti-gay legislation for upcoming elections in more than half of the fifty states. Videotapes such as "The Gay Agenda" are a central part of the effort to sell those laws to voters.

Of course, these ballot initiatives are only part of the debate over gay and lesbian rights that will be carried out for years to come. Gays in the military, adoption rights, parental rights, depictions of gays and lesbians in the arts are just some of the issues that are starting to be confronted by the culture. Inevitably, the mass media will play a central role in framing these topics. I would like to conclude by pointing to some of the specific ways in which the news media has been implicated in perpetuating homophobia, naturalizing heterosexism, and legitimizing the agenda of the far right. My assumption is that the more frequently these practices are exposed, the more likely they are to change.

The issue of civil rights for racial and ethnic minorities, for the aged, the disabled, and the disadvantaged is no longer a matter of debate in the media. Yet the issues of civil rights for gays and lesbians still triggers what GLAAD calls the Hitler response: "Anti-gay zealots are in no sense responsible spokespersons about lesbian and gay issues, yet their hate often gets presented whenever any lesbian or gay topic is covered. A Ku Klux Klan member or neo-Nazi is not included to discuss 'the other side' in every story about African Americans or Jews."[12]

Not only is the far right position given prominence, but its spokespersons are rarely challenged on the accuracy of their claims. One news reporter explains the process this way: "You have a lot of stuff getting into the paper and on TV from extremist bigots, and it goes unchallenged . . . . Somebody will say, '85% of homosexuals are pedophiles,' and because this is a quote it gets in unchallenged, simply because the editor in charge has no idea whether that's real or not."[13]

If the media have a role to play in terms of determining the credentials of nominated spokespersons, they are also responsible for explaining basic legal principles. The countless letters to the editor that appeared in Colorado papers after the passage of Amendment Two is a case in point. After the amendment passed, an immediate challenge to its constitutionality was launched in the courts. Letter writers by the score wrote to argue that such a challenge was wrong because the people had spoken and therefore the law must be followed.

In our system of government, however, minority groups are in fact protected from discrimination by the will of the majority. As Charlene L. Smith writes in the *Washburn Law Journal*, "If the majority of the people had the power to decide who is, and who is not, worthy of equal protection, the Equal Protection Clause would be meaningless." This principle was explicitly stated by the Supreme Court in a 1943 decision that reads in part, "One's right to life, liberty and property . . . and other fundamental rights may not be submitted to vote; they depend on the outcome of no elections."[14]

The media, however, seem far more interested in the sensational than the instructional. So as recently as 1993, we see the NBC flagship station in New York carrying a three-part series on the man-boy love association. After protests from GLAAD, the station did respond with another series, this one looking at substantive issues such as domestic partnership.[15]

Story selection is one obvious place where the media's role is critical; use of language and selection of images are two others. In the case of language, the far right has been highly successful in exerting its influence. Just as it succeeded in renaming and thus reframing its anti-abortion stand into a "pro-life" position, just as it turned anti-feminism into "pro-family," so has it successfully turned the issue of civil rights for gays and lesbians into one of "special rights."

In the case of imagery, the right has been less able to push its agenda, but here too its efforts have had some impact, as was evident in the aftermath of the 1993 march, on Washington. Unlike the 1987 march which got virtually no media coverage, the 1993 event was heavily covered by national and local newspapers and television stations. Much of the coverage emphasized the peaceful nature of the march and the everyday character of the participants. Immediately, the charge came from the far right that liberal media had sanitized the parade. Soon thereafter media critics, reporters, and editors were questioning whether they had indeed been hiding and protecting their audiences from the real gay community, the one depicted so graphically in "The Gay Agenda." Headlines such as these soon followed: "What the Gay Didn't Say About the Gay March—and Why" and "Did the Networks Sanitize the Gay Rights March?"

At this point the issue is shifted once again to the complex terrain of cultural conformity and morality. And it is in this very complexity that clarity is so sorely needed:

The fight for equal rights for gays and lesbians is a myriad of complicated issues and emotions. Like abortion, the legal issues are often subordinated and confounded by religious and moral beliefs. The rights of gays and lesbians, however, are not moral or religious issues. They are legal issues—issues that define the new frontier of civil rights.[16]

Perhaps there is much to be hoped for in the legal arena. The courts in Colorado thus far have rejected the constitutionality of Amendment Two and there is reason to believe that the Supreme Court will follow. But because legal debates and decisions take place within a culture, changes in the law do not necessarily translate into changes in practices, beliefs, and attitudes. That struggle takes place in a variety of venues, not the least of which is represented every day in the morning paper and every night on the evening news. Let us hope it will be represented fully and fairly.

24

Don't Ask, Don't Tell: Lesbian and Gay People in the Media

Larry Gross

In the summer of 1992, the daytime TV serial "One Life To Live" (OLTL) began what was to be the longest and most complex television narrative dealing with a lesbian or gay character. Billy Douglas is a high school student who moved to Llanview (the fictional small town outside Philadelphia where OLTL takes place) and became a star athlete and class president. When Billy confides, first to his best friend and then to his minister, that he is gay, he sets off a series of plot twists that differ from the usual soap opera complications in that they expose homophobia and AIDS-phobia among the residents of Llanview and thus offer the characters—and the audience—an opportunity to address topics that U.S. media have generally preferred to ignore.

The plot featuring Billy Douglas was the dominant thread of OLTL from July through early September 1992, after which Billy appeared less frequently until he left Llanview for Yale the following spring. Billy Douglas was played by a young actor named Ryan Phillipe, in his first professional role, and he found himself at the center of a great deal of media and audience attention. He received an unusually large amount of mail, even for a good-looking young soap opera actor. Even more unusual was the fact that the majority of the several hundred letters he received during the months that he appeared on OLTL came from young men, most of whom identified themselves as gay. Many of the young gay men—and several of the older men—wrote that they were particularly moved by and grateful for Ryan's sensitive portrayal of an experience much like their own, being isolated and vulnerable in a society that would prefer not to know they existed.

MINORITIES AND THE MEDIA

The familiar term "minority group" has been applied to ethnic and racially defined people as well as to women, in terms of their relative powerlessness despite their numerical majority, and it is now commonly applied to lesbian women and gay men. All of these are categories are marked by their deviation from a norm that is defined as Anglo, male, and heterosexual, and these deviations are reflected in the mirrors that the media hold up before our eyes. In brief, minorities share a common media fate of relative invisibility and demeaning stereotypes. But there are differences as well as similarities in the ways various minorities are treated by the mass media. And, given important differences in their life situations, members of such groups experience varying consequences of their mediated images.

Sexual minorities differ in important ways from the "traditional" racial and ethnic minorities; they are, in an interesting sense, akin to political minorities (so called radicals and "fringe" groups). In both cases their members typically are self-identified at some point in their lives, usually in adolescence or later, and they are not necessarily easily identifiable by others. These two groups also constitute by their very existence a presumed threat to the "natural" (sexual and/or political) order of things, and thus they are inherently problematic and controversial for the mass media. These characteristics can be seen to affect the way members of such groups are depicted in the media (when they do appear), and also suggest ways to think about the effects of such depictions on the images held by society at large and by members of these minority groups.[1]

Close to the heart of our cultural and political system is the pattern of roles associated with sexual identity, our conceptions of masculinity and femininity, of the "normal" and "natural" attributes and responsibilities of men and women. And, as with other pillars of our moral order, these definitions of what is normal and natural serve to support the existing social power hierarchy. The maintenance of the "normal" gender role system requires that children be socialized—and adults retained—within a set of images and expectations that limit and channel their conceptions of what is possible and proper for men and for women. The gender system is supported by the mass media treatment of sexual minorities. Mostly, they are ignored or denied–symbolically annihilated. When they do appear, they do so in order to play a supportive role for the natural order and are thus narrowly and negatively stereotyped. Sexual minorities are not, of course, unique in this regard. However, lesbians and gay men are unusually vulnerable to mass media power.

Of all social groups, we are probably the least permitted to speak for ourselves in public life, including in the mass media. We are also the only group (except, at present, for Arab "terrorists" and Latin "drug dealers") whose enemies are generally uninhibited by the consensus of "good taste" that protects most underrepresented cultures from the more public displays of bigotry. It is unthinkable in the 1990s that any racial or ethnic minority would be subjected to the sort of rhetorical attack that is routinely aimed at lesbian and gay people, by public figures who do not encounter widespread condemnation for their bigotry. When Roberta Achtenberg, a member of San Francisco's board of supervisors and a prominent legal activist, was nominated by President Clinton as Under Secretary of Housing and Urban Development, Senator Jesse Helms went on the attack: "She's a damn lesbian . . . working her whole career to advance the homosexual agenda. Call it gay-bashing if you want to. I call it standing up for traditional family values." One would have to go back decades to find a remotely similar example of unabashed bigotry directed against a member of a racial or ethnic minority on the floor of the U.S. Senate.

The reason for our vulnerability to political attack and media stereotyping lies in large part in our initial isolation and pervasive invisibility. The process of identity formation for lesbian and gay people requires the strength and determination to swim against the cultural stream one is immersed in at birth. A baby is born and immediately classified in two critical dimensions. One is presumed to be known before birth—when a baby is born no one asks, "What race is it?"—because we believe in a fairly rigid and deterministic set of racial identities (and, in our Anglo supremacist society, if you're not "all white," you're "not white"). The other identifying attribute is the subject of that first question: Boy or girl? The newborn infant is held up, inspected, and wrapped in an appropriately colored blanket. And, as ample research has shown, the blue blanket babies and the pink blanket babies are treated differently from that moment on, by doctors, nurses, parents, and everyone else. But another determination that is taken for granted at the same time also affects how that baby is treated: That baby is defined as heterosexual and treated as such. It is made clear throughout the process of socialization—a process in which the mass media play a major role—that baby will grow up, marry, have children, and live in nuclear familial bliss, sanctified by religion and licensed by the state. Over and over, through a multitude of messages in myriad media, that child encounters the taken-for-granted assumption that his or her future is that of a heterosexual, and a fairly "traditional" one at that.

How do those of us who are not Anglo, male, middle class, Christian, and heterosexual come to a sense of identity and self-worth in a society that privileges attributes we do not and mostly cannot possess? For one thing, we all can observe the people around us as well as those we encounter through the lens of the media. Women are surrounded by other women, people of color by other people of color, and so on, and can observe the variety of choices and fates that befall those who are like them. Mass media stereotypes selectively feature and reinforce some of the available roles and images for women, national minorities, people of color, but they operate under constraints imposed by the audiences' immediate environment. Lesbians and gay men, conversely, are a self-identifying cultural group. We are presumed (with few exceptions, and these—the "obviously" effeminate man or masculine woman—may not even be homosexual) to be straight, and are treated as such, until we begin to recognize that we are not what we have been told we are, that we are different. But how are we to understand, define, and deal with that difference? Here we generally have little to go on beyond very limited direct experience with those individuals who are sufficiently close to the accepted stereotypes that they are labeled publicly as queers, faggots, or dykes.

And we have the mass media. The mass media play a major role in the process of social definition of lesbian and gay people, and rarely a positive one. In the absence of adequate information in their immediate environment, most people, gay or straight, have little choice other than to accept the narrow and negative media stereotypes they encounter as being representative of gay people.

The mass media have rarely presented portrayals that counter or extend the prevalent images of lesbian, gay, and bisexual people. On the contrary, they take advantage of them. But there is more to it than stereotyping. For the most part, gay people have been simply invisible in the media. The few exceptions have been almost invariably either victims—of violence or ridicule—or villains.[2]

UP FROM INVISIBILITY

Until the 1960s, gay people were rarely if ever mentioned in the news media and only hinted at in movies, following the restrictions imposed by the Hollywood

Motion Picture Production Code introduced in the 1930s and abandoned only in 1968.[3] During the 1950s gay people were mentioned in the press when they were identified as part of the "commie-queer" menace targeted by such Cold War crusaders as Senator Joseph McCarthy. As the flames of the 1950s witch hunts cooled, the news media remained oblivious to the existence of lesbian and gay people, despite the first stirrings of a lesbian and gay movement that had begun to coalesce in several urban centers around the United States.[4] Through the mid-1960s lesbian and gay people began to break the silence of decades, demanding an end to laws that criminalized gay people and promoted discrimination and harassment. When the editors of the *New York Times*, then as now the nation's leading newspaper, first put gay people on the front page in 1963, they were motivated to break their silence by the realization that gay people were beginning to live their lives more openly. That this was not a development welcomed by the *New York Times* could be seen in the headline and lead paragraph of the first-ever front-page article focusing on gay people:

Growth of Overt Homosexuality
In City Provokes Wide Concern

The problem of homosexuality in New York became the focus yesterday of increased attention by the State Liquor Authority and the Police Department. The liquor authority announced the revocation of the liquor licenses of two more homosexual haunts that had been repeatedly raided by the police . . . . The City's most sensitive open secret—the presence of what is probably the greatest homosexual population in the world and its increasing openness —has become the subject of growing concern of psychiatrists, religious leaders and the police.[5]

The *New York Times* editors were not alone in noticing the increasing visibility and militancy of lesbian and gay people and their growing demand for an end to stigmatization and oppression by the institutions of law, religion, and medicine. *Life* and *Time* devoted attention to the emerging homosexual movement in the mid-1960s, but after relatively positive articles in *Life* in 1964 and 1965—the latter called on New York to follow the lead of Illinois and decriminalize homosexual behavior between consenting adults—they reverted to McCarthy-era hostility. In a January 1966 essay, "The Homosexual in America," *Time* paid brief acknowledgment to the growing belief among psychiatrists that homosexuals were not mentally ill, but then devoted most of the essay to undermining that perspective. It concluded:

It is a pathetic little second-rate substitute for reality, a pitiable flight from life. As such it deserves fairness, compassion, understanding and, when possible, treatment. But it deserves no encouragement, no glamorization, no rationalization, no fake status as minority martyrdom, no sophistry about simple differences in taste—and above all, no pretense that it is anything but a pernicious sickness.

The gay liberation movement exploded into visibility in June 1969, spurred by the examples of the black, anti-war, and feminist movements, and sparked by a routine police raid on a New York gay bar, the Stonewall, that triggered several nights of rioting by lesbian and gay people who were no longer willing to acquiesce in their own oppression. Consequently, media attention to gay people and gay issues increased in the early 1970s, much of it positive (at least in comparison with previous and continuing heterosexist depictions and discussions). By the middle 1970s, however, a backlash against the successes of the gay movement began to be felt around the country, most visibly in Anita Bryant's successful campaign to repeal a gay rights ordinance in Dade County, Florida, in 1977.

In February 1971, just a few years after Stonewall, network television's first sympathetic portrait of a gay man appeared, when the controversial sitcom "All in the Family" aired an episode, "Judging Books by Covers," in which Archie Bunker discovers that a football-player pal is gay. Possibly because "All in the Family" wasn't yet the ratings giant it soon became, the gay-theme show received comparatively little attention. But as we've recently learned, among those who did pay attention was then-President Richard Nixon, whose response was recorded by aide H. R. Haldeman on May 12, 1971:

The President wants a study done for his own knowledge. The baseball game was rained out last night. CBS . . . then put on a show to fill time. Star of show—square type—named Arch. Hippy son-in-law. This show was total glorification of homosex. Made Arch look bad— homo. look good. Is this common on TV? Destruction of civilization to build homos. Made the homos. as the most attractive type. Followed Hee-Haw.

The following year there was the more significant breakthrough of the ABC made-for-TV movie *That Certain Summer*, in which two gay men were shown touching (on the shoulder), and none of the gay characters had to die at the end of the story, although the main character, a gay father who comes out to his son, says that if he were given a choice he would choose not to be homosexual. This "breakthrough" was something of a false spring, however, as it did not herald the blooming of a hundred (or even a dozen) gay and lesbian characters. Yet gay and lesbian characters did begin to appear from time to time for one-shot appearances on network series, and in 1978 two TV movies were based on real life experiences of lesbian and gay people: *Sergeant Matlovich vs. the U.S. Air Force* told the story of the Vietnam vet who said, "They gave me a medal for killing two men and a discharge for loving one," and *A Question Of Love* recounted a lesbian mother's child custody case (the women never kiss, but one is shown tenderly drying her lover's hair).

The slight increase in gay (and less often, lesbian) visibility in the mid-1970s was quickly seized upon by the right as a sign of media capitulation to what in the 1980s came to be called "special interests." The apocalyptic tone of their jeremiads is well represented in a nationally syndicated column by Nicholas Von Hoffman, who noted that the "old-style Chinese have the Year of the Tiger and the Year of the Pig," but the "new-style Americans are having the Year of the Fag" (November 4, 1976). Von Hoffman charted the decline of the American character as beginning with a "presentable gay" in the "Doonesbury" comic strip and, "from there it was but a hop, skip and a jump to television where the flits are swarming this year." Hoffman plaintively asks, "Is a new stereotype being born? Is network television about to kill off the bitchy, old-time outrageous fruit and replace him with a new type homo?" Among the horrors he foresaw were "the Six Million Dollar Queer or The Bionic Fruit."

Since the late 1970s the gay movement and its enemies, mostly among the "religious right," have been constant antagonists (right-wing fund-raisers acknowledge that anti-homosexual material is their best bet to get money from supporters), and television has often figured in the struggle. But although the right wing has attacked the networks for what it considers overly favorable attention to gay people, in fact gay people are frequently portrayed and used in news and dramatic media in ways that serve to reinforce rather than challenge the prevailing images.

Being defined by their "problem," it is no surprise therefore that gay characters were generally confined to television's favorite problem-of-the-week genre, the made-for-TV movie, with a very occasional one-shot appearance of a gay character on a dramatic series. Continuing gay male characters began to appear in the 1980s (the first was Peter, a gay set designer in ABC's short-lived 1972 sitcom "Grant's Tomb," followed by the gay couple Gordon and George in the equally short-lived "Hot L Baltimore" of 1975) but they tended to be so subtle as to be readily misunderstood by the innocent (as in the case of Sidney in "Love, Sidney," whose homosexuality seemed to consist entirely of crying at Greta Garbo movies and having a photo of his dead lover on the mantelpiece), or confused about their sexuality and never seen in an ongoing romantic gay relationship (as in the case of the off-again-on-again Steven Carrington of "Dynasty," whose lovers had an unfortunate tendency to get killed, and Jodie on "Soap" who became involved with women). Although the lesbian character Dr. Lynne Carlson appeared for a few months in 1983 on the daytime serial "All My Children," a regular lesbian character did not appear on prime time television until Marilyn McGrath of (the also short-lived) "Heartbeat" in 1989. This small circle has recently been enlarged with the appearance of regular, if secondary, lesbian (often bisexual) and gay characters on "Roseanne," "Northern Exposure," and "Melrose Place."

The rules of the mass media game have a double impact on gay people: Not only do they mostly show us as weak and silly, or evil and corrupt, but they exclude and deny the existence of normal, unexceptional as well as exceptional lesbians and gay men. Hardly ever shown in the media are just plain gay folks, used in roles that do not center on their deviance as a threat to the moral order, which must be countered through ridicule or physical violence. (In recent years there has been a rise in the number of secondary gay characters in Hollywood films, frequently shown as sensitive gay male friends of the central, heterosexual characters.) The stereotypic depiction of lesbians and gay men as abnormal and the suppression of positive or even "unexceptional" portrayals serve to maintain and police the boundaries of the moral order. They encourage the majority to stay on their gender-defined reservation, and try to keep the minority quietly hidden out of sight. The visible presence of healthy, non-stereotypic lesbians and gay men does pose a serious threat: It undermines the unquestioned normalcy of the status quo, and it opens up the possibility of making choices to people who might never otherwise have considered or understood that such choices could be made.

AIDS VICTIMS AND VILLAINS

In the late 1970s America was confronted with the specter of the epidemic spread of a seemingly incurable disease contracted through sexual contact, genital herpes. The media were quick to point out that the causes of the epidemic were to be found in the so-called sexual revolution: "Health officials say that genital herpes became a growing problem only during the mid-1970s, after sexual codes had loosened in American society."[6] Despite all the attention it received, the panic was short-lived and the fear of herpes did not bring down the curtain on the sexual revolution. Perhaps the extent of the "epidemic" was exaggerated, or perhaps herpes, while incurable at present, wasn't a sufficient deterrent to play the role it was assigned as the chief weapon of the emerging sexual counter-revolution of the 1980s. But the stage was set for the arrival of a much more potent and deadly threat: AIDS.

AIDS provided mainstream society and the media with a double-edged opportunity and challenge. Here was the truly frightening specter of a deadly disease that could be associated with sexual permissiveness, but it was showing up among a group that the media have consistently defined as being outside the mainstream.

The first accounts of AIDS in the media emphasized its apparent link to gay men's sexuality (there were also at that time two other outsider "risk groups," IV drug users and Haitians, and the first "innocent victims," hemophiliacs). The first story on AIDS aired by NBC News began with Tom Brokaw framing the issue in a fashion that remained constant in much subsequent coverage: "Scientists at the National Centers for Disease Control in Atlanta today released the results of a study that shows that the lifestyle of some male homosexuals has triggered an epidemic of a rare form of cancer" (June 17, 1982).

Already treated as an important medical topic, AIDS moved up to the status of front-page news after Rock Hudson emerged as the most famous person with AIDS. Ronald Milavsky, then vice president of NBC, described the coverage of AIDS:

The most striking thing . . . is the low level of reporting until Rock Hudson's illness and the rather continuous high level after that. AIDS did, after all, have a focal event, like the Tylenol poisonings, the death, after thousands of others, of a famous person who most people did not think of as being homosexual. Rock Hudson's illness, death, and his admission that he was indeed dying of AIDS was a very unusual combination that was big news and stimulated the public's interest. From July to December 1985, NBC broadcast over 200 stories on AIDS— three times as many as during the entire 1980 to 1984 period. The other news media reacted similarly."[7]

Note the implication that it was the low level of *public* interest that was responsible for the lesser amount of coverage before Rock Hudson.[8]

AIDS has had the effect of finally ending the invisibility of gay people in the news media, but this is a mixed blessing. At present AIDS stories appear daily in print and broadcast news—often with little or no new or important content—and the public image of gay men has been inescapably linked with the specter of plague. Media coverage of AIDS is very likely to reinforce hostility to gays among those so predisposed—there is abundant evidence of growing anti-gay violence in many parts of the country—and to further the sense of distance from a strange and deviant "subculture."[9]

It would be misleading to focus primarily on news and documentary programming if we wish to understand television's role in helping or hindering the fight against AIDS. For most Americans, television drama is a far more potent teacher, and thus we must ask, how has television drama dealt with AIDS and gay men? Which stories have been chosen and which stories have been ignored?

AIDS reinvigorated the two primary roles the mass media offer to members of minority groups: victim and villain. Victims, as in the family-centered dramas *An Early Frost* (NBC, 1985) and *Our Sons* (ABC, 1991), are objects of pity, and when treated well by the authors they end by being tearfully reconciled with their families. Television dramatists have presented the plight of (white, middle-class) gay men with AIDS, but their particular concern is the agony of the families/friends who have to face the awful truth: Their son (brother, boyfriend, husband, etc.) is, gasp, gay! But, even with AIDS, not too gay, mind you. In the first network made-for-TV movie on AIDS, NBC's *An Early Frost*, a young, rich, white, handsome lawyer is forced out of the closet by AIDS. "We know he is gay because he tells his disbelieving parents so, but his lack of a gay sensibility, politics and sense of community make him one of those homosexuals heterosexuals love."[10]

There are some truly dramatic and important AIDS stories that we never see enacted or even reflected glancingly in TV drama, but they aren't stories of villainous AIDS carriers or abandoned victims who may finally be accepted back into the arms of their families. These are stories of how the gay *community* responded to an unparalleled health crisis with an unprecedented grassroots movement of social service and medical organizing; of sex and public health education; of research-backed militant agitation for reforms in the testing and approval of drugs; of coalition building with other marginalized groups suffering from disproportionate AIDS risk; and pushing the issue of health care and health insurance onto the national agenda.

The consistent feature of all TV dramatic programming on AIDS (and most news, public affairs and documentary programming as well) has been to focus on individual people suffering from AIDS and, if the angle of vision is widened at all, it will then include (straight) family members and possibly a lover (as long as they barely touch) and perhaps one or two friends (more likely to be straight than gay). What is wrong with this picture?

What's wrong is that it not only leaves out all of the important—and dramatic—achievements of the gay community noted above, but it falsely suggests that gay people with AIDS are alone and abandoned, unless and until they are taken back into the bosom of their family. Even the best of the TV AIDS stories fall into this pattern.

The pattern of portraying people with AIDS outside the context of the gay community and the service organizations created in response to AIDS was dramatically reinforced in Hollywood's first major film centering on the epidemic, Jonathan Demme's *Philadelphia*. Once again we meet an Anglo gay man who lives an upper-middle class life as a closeted lawyer—although he has a lover and he is known to be gay by his family—until he is stricken with AIDS, whereupon he is promptly fired from the big law firm where he had been a rising star. Shortly afterward he shows up in the office of an African American homophobic, ambulance-chasing lawyer and asks him to represent him in suing his old law firm, because he has been turned down by ten other lawyers. The ambulance chaser refuses but later reconsiders, takes the case and wins it, while at the same time undergoing a conversion to tolerance and acceptance of at least one person (we have no reason to think that the character would not be horrified were he later to learn that one of his children was gay). The film was presented and largely received as a landmark of progress in Hollywood's approach to AIDS and gay people, but in fact, it was mired in the same old stereotypes.

True, the protagonist is not rejected by his incredibly supportive family, but in most ways the film continues the familiar practice of marginalization. The homophobic lawyer is shown repeatedly in intimate scenes with his wife and children but the gay lawyer and his lover are barely allowed to touch, and their only (brief) kiss is obscured by the back of the lover's head. A scene showing the two of them talking in bed was reportedly shot but not used. The gay couple seems to have gay friends but they have few lines and are mostly confined to a costume party, presumably representing the true image of gay life.

Most dishonest, however, is the erasure of the organized response to AIDS. The biggest lie in the movie is told when the gay lawyer fired because he has AIDS says that he was turned down by ten lawyers before ending up in the office of an ambulance chasing homophobe. In Philadelphia, as in many other large cities, a person in his position would have been able to avail himself of the services of lesbian and gay legal services or even legal services especially created to deal with AIDS-related cases such as the AIDS Law Project. In other words, the dramatic premise of the film—the victimized person with AIDS ends up at the mercy of a homophobe who can then be converted to tolerance—requires the erasure of the accomplishments of the gay community, just as the fear of heterosexual audiences' sensibilities requires the denial of the realities of gay life.

KISS BUT DON'T TELL

By the early 1990s, the cultural and political battlelines were drawn across the United States. Although homosexual acts are still illegal in twenty-three states and despite the 1986 ruling by the U.S. Supreme Court that such laws are constitutional, the lesbian and gay movement has made dramatic gains. Dozens of cities and eight states have enacted legal protections against discrimination based on sexual orientation, and many cities and private employers are beginning to grant equal employment benefits to lesbian and gay domestic partners. Openly lesbian and gay people are more visible throughout society, and the movement has accomplished the goal of being taken for granted as a fact of our social life even by those who oppose us. But the degree of a movement's success can also be measured in the ferocity of the backlash it stimulates, and the gay movement is no exception. With the demise of communism as an international force, and with the abortion issue settling into a national stalemate (which is not to say that anti-choice forces have resigned themselves to defeat), the issue of lesbian and gay rights has emerged as the prime focus of the religious right in its efforts to reverse what Senator Helms has characterized as "the wayward, warped sexual revolution which has ravaged this Nation for the past quarter of a century."

The mass media have been a continuing battleground in this cultural war for the hearts and minds of America. The power of the right wing to slow down and even reverse any movement toward acknowledging and including lesbian and gay realities in the fictional worlds of the media can be illustrated by the cowardice repeatedly shown over the depiction of physical affection.

The 1993–94 television season was a landmark period for lesbian and gay visibility and the controversies it arouses. In an atmosphere shaped by President Clinton's controversial decision to end military discrimination against lesbian and gay people and the mounting crusades of the religious right in the form of initiatives to repeal and prohibit civil rights protections for gay people in states and cities across the country, the television industry inched its cautious way forward through the cultural minefields.

In the early 1990s three successful TV series made history of a sort by introducing lesbian or gay characters with continuing, if secondary, roles. Ratings queen Roseanne brought into the circle of her eponymous heroine the character of her openly gay boss (and later partner), Leon Carp (played by Martin Mull), followed by her bisexual friend Nancy (Sandra Bernhard). The story of the founding of the fictional town of Cicely, Alaska (the setting of "Northern Exposure"), by lesbian lovers Roslyn and Cicely was told in the final episode of the 1992 season. The series earlier introduced the secondary characters of Ron and Erick, a gay couple who own a bed-and-breakfast inn in Cicely. The twenty-something ensemble show "Melrose Place" features a gay man, Matt Fielding (Doug Savant) among the residents of a West Hollywood apartment complex. Matt's sexual orientation was mentioned in the pre-premiere publicity, but it is practically invisible in the show. Despite living in an area known colloquially as Boys' Town, Matt seems hard-pressed to find other gay people with whom to socialize and apparently spends most of his time hanging out with his straight friends.

On February 6, 1994, Roseanne's ex-husband Tom Arnold and former executive producer of the top-rated "Roseanne" announced that ABC had refused to air the episode scheduled for March 1 because it included a kiss between Roseanne and a lesbian character played by Mariel Hemingway. Arnold said he was told by ABC officials that "a woman cannot kiss a woman. It is bad for the kids to see," and, besides, they would lose $1 million in advertising. The announcement set off a predictable storm of publicity and debate, leading many to suspect that the whole controversy was intended to build the audience for the episode, which was slated to air at the beginning of the spring "sweeps" month (a period critical in determining ratings standings). The issue occupied a great deal of attention on the familiar forums for national conversations—newspaper columns and editorials, TV and radio talkshows, supermarket tabloids—and certainly didn't hurt Roseanne's coincidental tour promoting her newly published memoirs. Among the points made repeatedly was that there was something amiss about an industry that routinely shows us women being beaten and shot but balks at showing two women kissing.

The suspense ended when ABC agreed to air the program and began to promote it heavily (for the few hermits who might not have heard about it already) as the "lesbian kiss" episode. When the show aired it was carried by all but two ABC affiliates, attracted an audience of 32 million, and resulted in about 100 calls to the network, most of them positive.[11] What did those 32 million viewers see? Before anything else they saw and heard a parental advisory that the show "deals with mature sex themes and may not be appropriate for younger viewers." The program itself may well have been an anticlimax for those whose expectations had been built by the publicity. Roseanne, determined to show how cool she is, insists on accompanying Nancy and her new girlfriend (Hemingway) to a gay bar, and drags her sister Jackie along. The "climax" of the evening, as it were, occurs when the Mariel Hemingway character comes on to Roseanne and kisses her. The four-second kiss is obscured by the back of Hemingway's head, and we can see Roseanne's distaste as she wipes her mouth on her sleeve. The rest of the episode focuses on Roseanne's discomfort as she confronts the realization that she's not as cool as she thought she was. "But she doesn't get angry. Instead she talks out the incident with her husband, in an honest conversation that allows them to vent both their blind fears and erotic curiosity about homosexuality even as they unpiously reaffirm the strength of their heterosexual marriage."[12]

The furor over Roseanne's kiss had barely subsided when the airwaves were roiled by the threat of another assault on traditional family values. Erick and Ron, the gay inn-keepers on "Northern Exposure," decided to get married—a religious ceremony (within the peculiar definition of religion that obtains in Cicely), not a legal one—and the wedding occupies a large portion of an episode that aired May 2, 1994. The producers may have been cautious after the "Roseanne" flap, or perhaps they wished to avoid the copycat label, because the camera cut away from the two men just as they were pronounced "married" and returned only after they apparently had embraced, thus pointedly not showing the one visual message virtually every media wedding can be expected to include. The producers said they avoided filming the kiss so it wouldn't become the focus of controversy and detract from the story; in fact, the result was markedly flat and lacking in feeling. The producers' decision did not prevent the Rev. Donald Wildmon from calling for a boycott, but only two stations (in Alabama and Louisiana) refused to broadcast the episode.

ONLY ENTERTAINMENT?

The battlefield of American popular culture is likely to remain active for the foreseeable future, as the forces of conservatism continue their attempts to push us back to the mythical past of "traditional family values" and the mainstream media, in their search for large and demographically lucrative audiences, inch cautiously toward a more accurate reflection of contemporary realities. In this seesawing progress, the lesbian and gay community finds itself simultaneously sought out by adventuresome marketers and scapegoated by opportunistic preachers. And we are increasingly insisting on speaking for ourselves, both behind the scenes and even on the media stages. Gay advocates and our enemies agree on one thing: The media are more than "mere" entertainment. The mass media that tell most of the stories to most of the people most of the time are slowly shifting the terms of our public conversation toward a greater inclusiveness and acceptance of diversity, even while they shield their timid advances under the cloak of parental advisories.[13]

Rev. Wildmon and his colleagues on the religious right are right: The honest portrayal of lesbian and gay people in the media does have the potential to reach the hearts and minds of many Americans. This is reason enough to continue the struggle to transform the media.

25

Of the Avocado and the Asparagus: The Dance of the Archetypes

Julianne Hickerson Newton

And the avocado hangeth from the tree bow, ripe and swollen, holding within it the seed of life. And the asparagus riseth from the earth, firm and erect, tapering to the tender tip of sensuality. And together they honor the archetypes of human passion: the primordial feminine and masculine.

Through time and convention, we have learned to dichotomize the archetypal patterns of human sexuality and personality into yin and yang, soft and hard, female and male, pistil and stamen, and either/or. We expect one to complement the other, to fulfill a supposed vacancy of the other, to somehow complete human existence through the balance of opposites, or to validate heterosexuality as the only "natural" form of human passion.

But we have missed the proverbial boat. Rather than constructing feminine and masculine as either/or characteristics, this chapter argues for the position "both/ and." Rather than constructing sexuality and gender as oppositional, dichotomous variables, "both/and" thinking reconstructs masculine/feminine as characteristics that can manifest themselves through human personality and behavior in an infinite number of combinations, limited only by the imagination and creativity of the human body and spirit.

The limitations of "either/or" thinking as a way to interpret the archetypal human characteristics of feminine and masculine have imposed boundaries on the human capacity to feel, understand, behave, dream, and interact. "Either/or" thinking has imposed a sexuality and a sensuality and a way of understanding and constructing ourselves and our worlds that assumes feminine is attracted to masculine, masculine is attracted to feminine, and further, that one is necessary for the fulfillment of the other. "Either/or" thinking requires anyone who is not "either" or "or" to defend their very existence. It denies our capacity to love our own sex in many different ways. It denies the complex interaction of feminine and masculine within each of us. It denies the infinite variety of ways the feminine and masculine are expressed within and without human beings. While it is true that civilizations through time have constructed narrow interpretations of the masculine-feminine archetypes, it also is true that those same civilizations—at least in more ancient times—often created venues for a less simplistic understanding of the human psyche, whether expressed in internal personality characteristics or manifested through sexual behavior.

I want to propose four arguments for consideration:

1. That the instinctive nature identified as masculine-feminine archetypes has been misinterpreted, both in classical psychological literature and in popular media.
2. That the primordial basis for masculine-feminine characteristics and behavior not only has been directed into simplistic stereotypes of the masculine and feminine that impose various constructions on humankind (such as heterosexuality, dominance of one type over the other, and either/or thinking), but also has been abused as means to sell products and ideology.
3. That the dichotomous casting of human personality and sexuality into masculine/feminine has oppressed humankind, whether homosexual, bisexual or heterosexual.
4. That we must reformat society's simplistic masculine/feminine stereotypes as the infinitely variable archetypal bases for gender, sexuality, and personality within us all.

Masculine and feminine are attributes all human beings have experienced to some extent, through their biological makeup, through archetypal encoding, through socialization, and through literature, the arts, and the media. The problem with discussing masculine and feminine attributes is that they too have been confused with gender, with gender roles and with sexual orientation. A man, therefore, must have a penis, must exhibit such supposedly masculine characteristics as virile strength and aggressiveness, and must be attracted to a woman. A woman must have a vagina and breasts (preferably large), must exhibit such supposedly feminine characteristics as gentleness and sensitivity, and must be attracted to a man. These incarcerating stereotypes are made explicit in advertising, and in much of art and literature through time.

Such simplistic application of the glorious archetypes of masculine and feminine undergird public discrimination against homosexuality, providing ammunition for oppressing anyone who "doesn't fit" the mold. Abuse of the archetypal patterns imposes a false, polarized heterosexuality that abuses us all, regardless of sexual orientation. The confusion of gender, sexuality, and sexual orientation with masculine and feminine stereotypes has denied—or at the very least discouraged us all—from discovering the intricate complexity of our archetypal selves. Further, such dichotomous thinking has led to the oppression of ambiguity, the oppression of anything that "isn't the way it's supposed to be," the oppression of human beings' capacity for creative interaction, and the oppression of the lively, multifaceted spirit within us all.

One of the gifts of gayness, of lesbianism, of bisexualism, and of transsexualism is freedom:

• from stereotype
• from convention
• from the logical and the linear
• from constructed sexuality
• from constructed gender
• from being locked within a socially acceptable body

• from a life of lies and masks and constant theater
• from a life of the socially constructed self.

The abuse, misuse, and misappropriation of the archetypes of masculine and feminine into male and female biological forms means that heterosexuality has been substituted for honest communication within oneself about one's own nature. This condition has led to an oftentimes lonely and impossible archetypal search for wholeness within a rigid structure of acceptable expression of the masculine and feminine.

WHAT IF?

Archetypes versus stereotypes—what do they mean? In particular, how do the traditional archetypes of masculine and feminine alter our definitions of ourselves as male and female, and more important, perhaps, our definitions of our sexual selves? Is it possible that the Freudian and Jungian-based archetypes, also discussed in terms of mythology by Joseph Campbell, have been abused through time to deny the natural tendency all humans have to love and/or be attracted to someone, regardless of their apparent body type in terms of gender? Is it possible that a redefinition of masculine and feminine as parts of all human beings, sometimes in opposition, sometimes in harmonic wholeness, can help us see beyond our bodies? Or is it even possible that the union of masculine/masculine and/or feminine/feminine is essential for the wholeness of us all? What are we heterosexuals so afraid of? Have we not had men loving men and women loving women since the beginning of life as we know it? What if it all is metaphor? What if heterosexual hormonic and chemical compositions are constructed evolutions forced on us all by ancient prescriptions of masculine and feminine exterior characteristics? What if we were actually intended to be bisexual, or to follow our attraction instincts for sexual orientation?

If we turn to so-called nature, we find an infinite symbol system of feminine and masculine: Avocados and asparagus, apples and bananas, yoni and lingua, stamen and pistils. Do we have analogous androgynous symbols? Flowers with both stamen and pistils, watermelons (huge swollen, elongated entities with many internal seeds and a basic yoni shape), bell peppers, and trees with long, rigid trunks and rounded, flowering greenery.

Masculine or feminine, maleness or femaleness implies an either/or category. The ancients knew both were necessary—yin and yang. But the assumption was that both were necessary in terms of external union. What about different degrees of masculine and feminine uniting different degrees of masculine and feminine? This may be akin to early interpretations of left-brain, right-brain theory: that the left brain, representing traditional masculine characteristics (which also happen stereotypically to represent Western Anglo-European and so-called North American—and therefore preferred—traditions), handled such functions as linear, logical, hierarchical thinking, and that the right brain, stereotypically representing traditional feminine characteristics (which also happen to represent eastern Asian, African and Latin American—and therefore inferior—traditions), handled such functions as visual, creative, and multidimensional thinking.

WHAT KIND OF DAMAGE HAS BEEN DONE?
AND HOW HAS IT BEEN DONE?

Consider an early McLuhan work, *The Mechanical Bride*. McLuhan warned us of the media framing our very thinking processes before framing theory or social construction of reality theory or symbolic interactionism were written. Yet we continued literally to "buy" into media abuse of our bodies and sexuality and psychological composition. The media have for years played on heterosexual fears of the vital masculine-feminine components of ourselves and on homophobia in general, so that we allowed ourselves, and in fact encouraged, the continued promulgation of masculine/feminine stereotypes. In so doing, we have abused masculine/feminine archetypes almost beyond recognition. We have forced our bodies and souls into media stereotypes—non-real, post-human, mechanical selves—that categorize, homogenize, dehumanize, sexize the most precious, natural, holistic, universal, and healing parts of our natures—our basic selves, sexual, soulful, physical, and spiritual.

We have lost it, folks! Women are supposed to fit the mold defined by billboard sexuality—young, blonde, perfectly smooth legs, large breasts, perfectly small waists, and perfectly sized butts with nary a dimple of cellulite in sight. Men, of course, must be blonde or appropriately tanned/dark, with muscular legs, torso, arms, thin waist, only appropriately furry, and with that ever so carefully imaged hint of a large penis. And the greatest lesson of billboard sexuality is that all the products associated with these archetypal caricatures will, of course, bring such stereotypical and universally desired physical attributes and unlimited sexual opportunity to each of us—if only we smoke and drink and drive and buy and dress accordingly.

We have lost it, folks!

Some tell us we must fit the abused archetypal, stereotypical, media typical sex molds because the Bible tells us so. But we now know that for at least 2,000 years, even sources as traditionally relied upon as the Bible have been interpreted by patriarchal, anti-feminine voices to the exclusion of the feminine aspects of a Supreme Being Herself. To think otherwise is considered neurotic, psychotic, crazy in some way, deviant, and sad.

Isn't it fascinating that we have seen a sexual revolution to the point of anarchy in the last part of the twentieth century, right at a time when, through technology, we can be whatever gender we want—through lifestyle, surgery, chemistry, technology, or virtuality—and have sex with whomever we want? Yet we still have legislatures, ministers, doctors, and psychologists who fear such gender/sexual freedom that they tell us it is wrong. And those same people would rather see us all exposed repeatedly to billboards using sexual stereotypes to sell us death-arettes and death-ahol and sex-'em-up trucks and spend-all-your-money-on-them, cause-then-you'll-look-sexy-and-think-you've-made-it than have us exposed to honest-sensual-sexual-traditional-radical-middle-of-the-road-people who may look like what we have constructed as men or women or look like neither or both or another gender entirely. If society can construct us through every external form imaginable, how do we dare not construct our most private selves—our own identities, our own sexualities, our own physical and psychic connections with other human beings?

I hereby call on all gays, lesbians, transsexuals, and heterosexuals to scream, yell, and strip away the false media stereotypes that constrict our rights to define our own identities.

Here's to you: The avocado and the asparagus, the apple and the banana, the yoni and the lingua, because you freely exhibit the patterns of vital sexuality within us all.[1]

PART VII

MISCELLANEOUS STEREOTYPES

26

Of Fairy Godmothers and Witches: Network Television and the Teacher

John Bell

Two images drive this chapter: the fairy godmother, a dispenser of the right path, and the wicked witch, the depriver of true joy.

The first image is at the conclusion of *There Are No Children Here*, a made-for-TV movie that starred Oprah Winfrey. The movie ends in a public school auditorium with a teacher who is smiling and well-dressed. She is a fairy godmother amid a gathering of students and parents. She welcomes a lost child who has somehow found the way out of all the misery, violence, and brutality that mark his Chicago project life. She is at once a nurturing and protective teacher.

The second picture is a witch who is revealed in a commercial that was aired the same week as the movie. In a classroom of rigid rows and cowering children, the evil spinster-teacher suddenly pulls off a rubber mask to reveal a pizza delivery boy who magically displays what the children really want—a Bigfoot pizza. The children jump for joy and cheer.

From my own experience as a teacher, I can assert that education is constantly subject to public and legislative pressure. Consequently, a teacher is in part a political animal. A teacher is also a cultural-mythological animal—a set of images mapped out over time in the unconscious discourse of social roles to which we all respond. To a great extent television, I believe, constructs our views of social roles. The two sets of images launched me into some key questions:

How does network television present teachers?

What are the implications of such presentations?

What images of teachers should be cultivated for the coming century?

I will attempt to answer these questions in three ways. First, I will review the literature of teacher presentations on television. Second, I will address teacher presentations by analyzing teacher dramas. Finally, I will suggest a point of view that I hope all television viewers adopt as they watch teacher dramas.

TELEVISION AND TEACHER: THE LITERATURE

What impressed me most in surveying the research literature dealing with teacher presentations on television was how little I could find. Complete books are available about doctors, nurses, and detectives,[1] and one can easily find mention of policemen, lawyers, and cowboys in common critical sources,[2] but, for the most part, teachers have slipped through the net of critical attention.

Studies of occupational roles note only the minor presence of teachers on television, and usually teacher, per se, is not seen as a separate role. Melvin DeFleur (1964), for example, finds educators appearing eleven times out of 436 appearances in his content analysis of occupational portrayals; occupations related to the law appeared 128 times, occupations related to health and medicine thirty-nine times, and secretaries and office workers twenty-three times.[3] Teachers are not mentioned in Roberta Wroblewski and Aletha Huston's (1987) study of the effects of television's occupational stereotypes on early adolescents.[4] Leah Vande Berg and Nick Trujillo's book *Organizational Life on Television* (1989) points out that education, one of the service industries, was presented in roughly 2 percent of all industry portrayals in their fourty year portrait of prime-time television. Education portrayals also varied throughout the decades studied; they were 6 percent of the 1950s' portrayals of service industries, 5 percent of the 1960s', 13 percent of the 1970s', and 14 percent of the 1980s' portrayals. "Welcome Back Kotter" (ABC, September 1975-August 1979), "The Paper Chase" (CBS September 1978-July 1979), and "Head of the Class" (ABC September 1986-present) are cited as shows that have effected the trends.[5] But when the researchers highlight case studies of organizational cultures, no educational organization is included.[6]

Three relatively recent articles by Vicky Lytle,[7] George Kaplan,[8] and Leslie Swetnam[9] represent the main body of critical work on the presentation of teachers in television drama, along with an earlier article by George Gerbner[10] dealing with the broader issue of the teacher image in mass culture. Since the Gerbner article raises questions of the most general nature, I will postpone talking about it until later in this chapter. Lytle, Kaplan, and Swetnam note numerous shows that feature presentations of teachers: "Our Miss Brooks," "Mr. Peepers," "Mr. Novak," "Room 222," "Welcome Back Kotter," "Head of the Class," "Fame," "The White Shadow," and "The Bronx Zoo," most of which, I believe, would be called reasonably memorable by long-term television viewers, with the exception of "The Bronx Zoo."

Some programs, of course, have treated teachers and school issues realistically. "Mr. Novak," for example, is the only show in which the National Education Association (NEA) provided a script review panel. But the normal attention given to "tiny details" in the program is almost always wrong. Granted, television is preoccupied with entertaining, but why have there been so few women, so few married teachers, and so few supporting workers? Too many writers just don't seem to have done their homework.

Kaplan's concerns are larger than presentations of teachers on television dramas. He wonders why "the real drama of the learning experience somehow continues to elude" television.[11] Education is a secondary player in the television news business ("less than 1% of all reporting [is] customarily devoted to education"), and few stories have much to do with "whether or how children are learning in our schools."[12]

Swetnam's concern is the distortion of the image of teachers in the media, and the author reports on a "content analysis of eighteen teachers in popular current and rerun television programs and films."[13] Television programs mentioned include "The Bronx Zoo," "The White Shadow," "Head of the Class," and "Fame"; films mentioned include *Teachers*, *Summer School*, and *The Dead Poets Society*, but a list of the works and teachers studied is not presented.

Some of the misleading common messages are that "anybody can teach," "learning should always be easy and fun," "all teachers have an antagonistic relationship with their principal," and insulting student-teacher exchanges are presented as "witty." Common distortions are that "class sizes are minuscule," "little actual classroom instruction is depicted," and customary real activities, such as "paper grading, planning, meetings, and . . . extra duties . . . are rarely included."[14]

Damaging stereotypes observed include several negative or incompetent types: The autocrat, such as Professor Kingsfield in *The Paper Chase*; the "pied piper," such as John Keating in *The Dead Poets Society*; and the "jerk or clown," such as the science and physical education teachers in "The Wonder Years," "The Simpsons," and "Beavis and Butt-head." Another damaging type is "the superhuman teacher who easily solves all student problems and runs every class effortlessly." These are the "social worker" teachers like Ken Reeves in "The White Shadow." Such portrayals send out damaging subliminal messages that "teachers can and should solve all their students' social and family problems as well as their academic ones" and that effective teachers must be charismatic.[15]

Swetnam concludes with a call for further research to help make clear how teacher portrayals in the media affect perceptions of the teaching profession. Swetnam also asks professional educators to promote more accurate portrayals of teachers.

LOOKING AHEAD: WAVING WHAT WAND?

In a sense we have returned to our beginning: the curious mix of fairy godmothers and witches, noble human ideals versus a capitalist society. The two always seem to bump into each other.

What's most important, to me at least, in reviewing teacher presentations on television is the combination that they are unreal and infrequent. No one wants to see real schoolwork or teachers meeting about curriculum delivery in a television sitcom. No one wants to see crowded classrooms, insufficient or battered books, insufficient laboratory equipment, or out-of-date computers. No one wants to see unions in the schools, discussions of proper wages for teachers, or the complexities of good teaching. Everyone wants to see clean buildings and well-scrubbed, fashionable students, principals who serve as comic relief rather than serious educational leaders, and superhero teachers who spend most of their time being inspired psychologists and social workers.

Why can't someone write one of those "real" shows like "L.A. Law" for teachers? All we need, says the NEA, are some committed writers (meaning those who would consult the NEA) and some committed producers. Well, wasn't "Mr. Novak" really a better high art show than "L.A. Law"? I think it was, and probably the NEA does also. Why did it fail? Ratings, we are told. Viewers don't want to watch shows that begin to look real. The "real" answer, of course, is not that simple, but it is noteworthy that teacher dramas, in general, don't survive for long. Is there something intrinsic in the teacher ethos that drives this apparent truth?

One answer might be that teacher dramas are not inherently entertaining, or at least not as entertaining as doctor dramas. Teachers don't have the dramatic power of doctors, lawyers, and police workers. It is hard to write big scenes for teachers. Most of their real work is incremental and hard to see.

Another reason might be that teacher dramas are less foreign and therefore not as romantically appealing. It is much easier for an average person to imagine a lawyer or a doctor as a knight than a teacher. In some sense a teacher is more like a cost accountant who only weighs and grades. It is difficult to find a television series featuring romantic cost accountants.

Much of the trouble, I believe, lies in what might be called the dramatic possibilities of the teacher narrative. The teacher narrative may offer a chance for a quick laugh, but it rarely offers possibilities for television's other vital engines—the sensational and the melodramatic.

The trouble with the teacher narrative is that it is hopelessly embedded in the education narrative, which, like real life, is serious, subtle, and trying. For the most part, the American public want their television to radiate the magic of escape and laughter. We recoil from the grating, noisy, complexities of communal life and turn to the sorcery of the fast-food pizza.

The ultimate question for anyone concerned becomes: Is serious public discourse ever possible on television? Teacher dramas, however stereotypical, do have the salutary effect of pointing to our mixed desires. On the one hand, the programs attempt to show real communities and how we pass knowledge on to our children. On the other, in their desire to be something more—to be narratives of successful or failed romance, of discipline or of social work—television shows demonstrate a desire to turn teacher dramas into police or doctor narratives with their obvious and simple closures. The mask comes off; the pizza is eaten, and all shall be well. But the true educational narrative is mask upon mask. It is an interrogation of the qualities of the pizza. It is the continual desire to foster the self and the community within the emotions of doubt and hope. Teaching is a complex, rewarding, and frustrating narrative, without closure.

Television narratives strive to create escapist comfort zones that forever move us backward while they edge us ever so slightly forward. For example, note how often discussions of computers and interactive multimedia technologies are a part of the present discourse of education, and try to remember their presence in any recent teacher dramas.

Who knows what a teacher will do in the twenty-first century? I certainly do not, but I do grapple with the problems that computers raise in my English classes. Questions must be asked, and possible answers must be tendered, if we are to take serious measure of the future. It is hard to believe that lecturing, as we now know it, will exist in the near future. In what sense will face-to-face instruction in the classroom survive, or the school as we know it, for that matter? What will a library look like? The ProQuest system that I used to locate and retrieve a few articles for potential use in this chapter surely augurs the possibilities of a library I have never known. Did you ever see a library in a teacher drama? I can't recall one. I've seen whiz kid students enter something like the Internet on student dramas; have you ever seen a teacher do the same? Will a future teacher stereotype be a bumbling technophobe unable to make use of a computer? And what about the problems of the rich and the poor? How will we guarantee equal access to the information superhighway? Will there be legislation guaranteeing equal educational rights? Forgive me if I offer a cynical smile.

Television shapes and reflects, reflects and shapes. But because it is not a place for full public discourse, its narratives should always be resisted. We need to foster in every backyard, on every street corner, in every public room, in every school, and in every couch before every glowing screen a critical perspective begun with, "What's missing?" When the mask comes off and the pizza sits before us, we need to understand why the teacher/witch changed into a huckstering warlock who "smiles" as he gratifies our desires. As a representative of network TV, he doesn't want our discourse—he wants our money.

27

Post-Rodney King: The Reciprocal Gaze

Katherine Reed

"If Rodney King were a white man, he would have been treated the same way."
"If there had been no videotape, there would have been no outcry."
"If the assaulting cops [had] been tried by a multiracial jury anywhere in urban America . . . they would . . . have been convicted."[1]

Any one of these statements could be—and will be—debated for a long time in America's kitchens, living rooms, university classrooms, and police departments. And they should be. But one truth seems nearly unassailable in the aftermath of the Rodney King case: "Police work has been forever changed into two phases—before Rodney King and after Rodney King."[2] The reasons are complex, with roots in the 1960s civil rights and Vietnam War protests—and then much further beyond. The image of an African-American man sprawled on a city street, surrounded by police with nightsticks rising and falling, snapped an entire nation to attention. It activated a perception of police that had somehow been forgotten or mothballed by many Anglo, middle-class Americans and validated a perception long held by everyone else.

The stereotype of the ignorant, racist, brutal cop was alive and as alarming as ever, thanks to George Holliday's camcorder. Fair or unfair is beside the point. Who you are, when you were born, where you grew up and the color of your skin have everything to do with how you saw the minute and a half of amateur film that some believe changed a profession forever.

It is no exaggeration to say that to many Anglo Chicagoans, where I grew up, the police were a joke, certainly not deserving of respect. I know that many Chicagoans of my parents' generation saw them as an extension of the Daley machine, and certainly they were. And, like Mayor Richard Daley, Sr., that was a good thing and a bad thing.

But those televised images of "Chicago's Finest" savagely beating up protesters—and innocent bystanders—was another thing altogether. I was too young at the time to remember exactly what was said over dinner tables after the convention. But I do remember a certain uneasy quiet in the aftermath, the kind that spreads in a kind of ripple effect after something incomprehensible and shocking has occurred. There had to be a reason. The protesters must have provoked the police. Why else would the cops act like that?

Somehow, those widely disseminated images of brutality became part of the jarring, violent panorama of growing up in the 1960s in the United States of America. Civil rights workers were being firehosed, beaten and "disappeared" in the South; college students were resisting the war in Southeast Asia on campuses across the country; rioters—already a familiar part of the evening news before the assassination of Martin Luther King, Jr.—vented their range in southern and northern cities. The year 1968 was an extraordinarily violent year by any standard. As Jerome H. Skolnick and James J. Fyfe note in their book, *Above the Law*, "In April 1968 alone there were nearly as many disorders as there were in the entire disorderly year of 1967."[3]

Then, on the day I celebrated my birthday in 1970, four people were killed on the campus of Kent State University when National Guardsmen opened fire on war protesters. I was just ten years old. They looked like police to me.

These were the pictures I carried in my memory when I went to work as a police reporter in Columbus, Georgia., in 1982. I was not expecting Andy Griffith or Bill Gillespie, the ignorant police chief that Virgil Tibbs enlightens in the movie, *In The Heat of the Night*. I told myself that anything was possible, but I tried to keep an open mind. That is how I viewed my responsibility as a journalist, back then, before reality intervened and I realized that the best we can do in the media is to be aware of our biases, educate ourselves against them, and know when they're leading us astray.

I know what the police thought of me, because they told me: I was too forthright, not feminine enough, too aggressive, not to be trusted, in short—a journalist. And a Yankee, to make matters worse.

They were short, tall, fat, thin, stupid, smart, racist, sensitive, sexist, undereducated, well-read, dishonest, highly moral, surprising. And unsurprising. They were everything I'd ever expected a cop to be—and more. And less. The only generalities that apply to the men and women I got to know as a reporter is that they thought of themselves as members of a pariah group. They thought no one really understood what it's like to be a cop, that people looked down on them, thinking them stupid. As one of my favorite cops sarcastically put it to me one morning, "Why else would I crawl through the window of a warehouse at 2:30 in the morning with an alarm going off and only a flashlight in my hand for protection? And for 16,000 lousy dollars a year?"

They hate themselves a little bit. I often wondered if they began to believe the epithets slung at them with bottles and trash when they ventured into certain parts of town on hot summer nights (there is no other kind in Columbus) to respond to domestic disturbance calls. Tolerating a certain amount of verbal and physical abuse just seemed to be part of the job; that part they willingly talked about. Naturally, I didn't hear very much at first about how they hand it back, how they come to view the people they police.

To get familiar with my beat, I rode with a patrol sergeant as soon as the police chief said I could. The chief had done well in choosing the person with whom I would ride; he picked a good cop, a genuinely conscientious, honest man. I watched him talk to an African American boy, about nine years old, whose bike had been stolen a week earlier. He felt bad about it; he gave the kid a squeeze on the shoulder and told him he was still on the lookout for it. Then someone else approached him with another question, not strictly police-related, that reflected the sergeant's familiarity with the people on his beat. He listened carefully, offered some advice, then listened some more.

He got back into the car and began to drive again. It was a nice night. We chatted about his job, and a little about mine. I realized that I was impressed, almost awestruck at what I'd seen, which made me realize how little I'd expected. I was making a major adjustment in my attitude toward police work based on a few hours in a squad car with a man who might have been putting on a pretty good show just for me.

Then he got a call for a break-in in progress and it was as if someone had thrown a switch; radio grabbed, code exchanged, lights and siren on and we were flying about 80 mph down Victory Drive near Fort Benning. It was so sudden, I remember feeling the car seat hard against my back and the sergeant saying something like, "See what I mean? It's 95 percent monotony, 5 percent pure terror. Nothing in between."

Certainly the stack of police reports I went through every morning seemed to bear him out. There was an occasional homicide, a steady trickle of reported sexual assaults and lots of armed robberies. But many of the reports were of burglaries and thefts from cars—cases that would never be solved—with descriptions of property damaged or stolen that would never be restored or returned. Car stereos and guns were stolen from vehicles. Reports detailed fistfights outside of nightclubs. Patrol officers seemed to spend an extraordinary amount of time on paperwork, and they hated it.

Things were different upstairs, where the investigative divisions were housed. There was no shortage of paperwork, but the secretiveness that surrounds "real police work" was much more in evidence. The detectives took themselves seriously. I got used to conversations stopping in mid-sentence when I entered a room. Then word got around that I was "all right" for a journalist—they called me Lois Lane in a term of semi-affection—and I found myself actually standing unnoticed for a few minutes now and again just inside the door of the personal crimes division.

That's how I happened to catch on to what was happening to rape victims. I came in one morning about 7 a.m. and saw three detectives—one with his feet up on a desk, smoking a cigar, another eating a sausage biscuit—interviewing a rape victim. She was an African American woman in her twenties, wearing a blue bathrobe and looking extremely uncomfortable as a detective interviewed her about what exactly had happened between her and the man she said had raped her.

I had already done stories about the local rape crisis center and knew that a special room had been designated in a city building across the street from the police department especially for interviewing rape victims. It was supposed to be comfortable and private.

When I asked why this victim had not been taken to the "rape room," as it was known, I was told that it was inconvenient. It wasn't always available. I found out that it was seldom if ever used, but that was only the tip of the iceberg. Many rape victims were being talked out of their rapes. They were described to me as prostitutes or "not really a victim. After all, she took a ride home with the guy."

I began to notice subclasses of victims, from the police perspective. I would nod and scribble in my notebook as a criminal event was described to me as a non-event, a somebody was transformed into a nobody.

Perry Jones was a nobody, until he ignored police commands to come out of a barbecue restaurant he'd broken into, climbed up its chimney onto the roof and was shot dead by a police sergeant, who'd once won a marksmanship award. Within forty-eight hours, the police chief had declared Jones' killing a "justifiable homicide," long before the internal investigation was completed.

I should have known by then what a mere formality that investigation would be.

But in my naiveté, I approached the shooting of Perry Jones like a criminal event, with a suspect and a victim. I talked to people, some of them cops. Jones was believed to be armed when he climbed onto the roof of the Dynasty Barbecue. When police shone lights on him inside the restaurant, he'd had a cleaver in his hand, which he was apparently using to hack meat out of a freezer. He'd dropped the cleaver when he began his scramble up the chimney onto the roof.

But the police didn't know that when at least seven of them surrounded the small, squat Dynasty Barbecue. "He could have jumped off that building and hurt someone with the cleaver," the chief told me.

The sergeant was taken off patrol duty pending the investigation; an evidence technician who called Jones a "nigger" during the shouting that preceded the shooting was suspended for fifteen days. The coroner, who publicly asserted his right to hold an inquest into Jones' death, decided not to exercise that right. He held a press conference and said that the family of Perry Jones did not want an inquest. They just wanted the whole matter closed.

I was puzzled. Family? What family?

After the shooting, I'd attempted to talk to someone—anyone—who could tell me anything about Perry Jones, nineteen, address unknown. I hadn't been able to locate a single soul. It had been a long time since he'd even had a fixed address. After the press conference, I tried again. I finally reached the funeral home director who buried Jones in rural Alabama, and he asked me to hold the line; he would have to run down the road and get Perry's sister. She sometimes saw Perry.

About 15 minutes later, Perry's sister came on the line. She hadn't spoken to the coroner since the day they learned of Perry's death, she said. I asked her if she'd asked that there be no inquest.

"Inquest?" she said, pronouncing the word haltingly. "What's an inquest?"

The coroner had counted on Jones' nobody status to cover his misrepresentation of the truth. I should not have been so surprised by that. His sister wasn't. His grandmother, whom I finally found living in a shotgun shack, wasn't either. She seemed utterly unfazed by his death and the way he died. It was as if she'd expected it. I'd come through her door with Anglo, middle-class expectations of justice and left with some sense of hers—which is to say, no expectation whatsoever.

Dr. Peter Tarlow at Texas A&M University, who has researched the relationship between police and tourism, says that police have very little knowledge about other cultures. He made two other statements that interested me: The majority culture in a society tends to see authority as an extension of its culture; the minority culture sees authority as a threat.

Some who have given the Rodney King videotape close, repeated viewings see his physical behavior—the fact that he appears to be trying to rise—as nothing more ominous than an effort to escape what he saw as his certain fate: to be killed by the police. If Los Angeles police had a reputation for brutality that was well known among those most likely to be at the receiving end of it, one can see how his fears and his struggle might be well-justified.

The fact is, the Los Angeles police were, under Police Chief Daryl Gates, the nation's most likely to kill. The Christopher Commission, appointed to look into the conditions that created the Rodney King beating, found evidence of racism and excessive force in the department. Los Angeles police killed 3.0 people and wounded 8.1. per 1,000 officers in 1986; in second place were Detroit's police, with 1.2 and 5.0 per 1,000.

Possibly the strongest evidence of a police department gone awry (under Gates) was the LAPD's Special Investigations Section, which stalked career criminals, watched them plan and execute repeated crimes, then sometimes surrounded and killed them with heavy gunfire. Members of the squad have been sued repeatedly, and in the case of the slayings of three McDonald's restaurant robbers who were shot to death in their car, a jury held Gates and the five officers who fired the shots personally liable. An attorney for the victims' family characterized the officers as "assassins."

In a poll by the *Los Angeles Times* published on March 10, 1991 (a week after the King beating), nearly two-thirds of the L.A. residents polled—a majority of them Anglo—said they believed "incidents of brutality by Los Angeles police are common, with 28 percent saying such incidents are very common." Research conducted at the Crime Victims' Research and Treatment Center in Charleston in the fall of 1992 found that more than half of the 400 South Central residents polled (53.3 percent) said that police "often or sometimes" are disrespectful and/or use insulting language; 51.2 percent of the polled South Central residents said they had been frisked without reason, and 40.8 percent were arrested without reason.

Take an "us and them" mentality, sanction it in explicit and implicit terms within a department, characterize crime control as a "war," and it becomes entirely clear how the King incident—and the many incidents just like it that are not filmed and never come to light—could happen. Police tend to think of themselves as misunderstood and outcast; they characterize some of the people who represent their most difficult policing problems as less than human, "garbage," and "the scum of the earth." The highly controversial recordings of retired LAPD detective Mark Fuhrman made public during the O.J. Simpson murder trial supports this stereotype of the police.

George Holliday's video recording was seen by 96.9 percent of the 800 L.A. county and South Central residents in the South Carolina study. Two-thirds said they found it tremendously upsetting and 67.1 percent said they had a more negative view of police as a result of the viewing.

The videotape—and the way it was used by the media—doubtless gave law enforcement a black eye, but it also seems likely to have accelerated the movement toward a different kind of law enforcement, one that deemphasizes the gulf between the police and the policed. After all, "assuming that the public is the enemy is not compatible with serving the community."[4]

Is the public finally seeing police as they really are? As they sometimes are? Rarely are? There is surprisingly little research on public attitudes—in general—toward police. The public seems interested in police work, if the number of new television police dramas is any gauge. In the new generation of shows, "NYPD Blue" and "Homicide," police are smart, passionate, frustrated with "the system" and, above all else, intensely human. They play the cello, agonize in the locker room about how "to be helpful" to their girlfriends—and sometimes lose their cool.

Then there is the "reality" program "Cops," which shows police involved in the day-to-day routine of police work—arresting drunken drivers and prostitutes and trying to mediate domestic disputes. I watched an episode recently in which the police were trying to pull over a motorist, who was driving erratically and ignoring police efforts to stop his car. Suddenly, there were four, maybe five vehicles involved in the pursuit. When the driver finally pulled the car to the curb, the camera followed as two officers approached the car. With difficulty, the driver got out of his car and the arresting officer threw him to the ground, pulled the suspect's hands behind his back and handcuffed him. After the suspect had been placed in the back of a waiting patrol car, the arresting officer returned to speak to the ranking officer on the scene, who was being interviewed.

The camera zoomed in on the arresting officer. His jaw worked and his eyes glittered as he described the events preceding the traffic stop. His hands were clenched at his sides and he seemed to be trying to catch his breath as he stood tensely in the street. If I had been walking through the room where the television was on, I would have taken one look at the man in the uniform and known in an instant that he was terrified. Fear is a difficult emotion to mistake.

That's the 5 percent the sergeant in Columbus told me about. It is hard to know the impact that 5 percent had on the behavior of the police in the Rodney King case—the four who participated in the beating and the estimated twenty-three at the scene. How afraid could they be of an unarmed man on the ground, with that many armed police officers—and two in the air in a helicopter—on hand for protection? Does fear play a part in vengeance? Were they "getting back" at a dimly perceived group—the so-called underclass—through the beating?

It's interesting that two of the bystanding officers in the King beating who expressed disapproval of the beating were women—officer Melanie Singer of the California Highway Patrol and rookie LAPD officer Ingrid Larson, who interpreted King's physical behavior as self-defensive. Women know fear: We experience it every time we walk alone down a dark street. Efforts to recruit more multicultural members and women into police work are based on the premise that a more representative department is likely to be more sensitive and less brutal. But until those from diverse groups are in positions of power, their impact is unlikely to be felt.

Community policing may represent one of the best hopes for the future of police because it means that the police are looking at us, the people they police, and the realities of the communities we live in. George Holliday's video recording symbolizes the beginning of a reciprocal relationship: We are now returning that gaze, with a stubborn expectation of justice.

28

Dueling Stereotypes of Politicians

Keith Kenney, Lee Zukowski, and Carl Glassman

Quickly think of an image of a politician and you will either imagine an all-American, intellectual, patriot or a fast-talking, hand-shaking, mudslinging self-promoter.

The two different pictures—positive and negative—are both stereotypes that describe a specific cultural group. Now consider which type of image you are likely to see in photographs published in newspapers and news magazines, why most photographs show politicians in a positive light, and which stereotype of politicians will you encounter when reading editorial cartoons. The answers to those questions are the subject of this chapter.

Especially during political campaigns, photographers take positive pictures and editors select positive pictures of politicians. Dynamic and upbeat imagery of candidates so permeates visual campaign coverage that many assume the pictures were crafted by media handlers who used the picture press like putty to shape candidate imagery at will. Cliché pictures convey excitement, public involvement, and dynamic attractive personalities.

In an article on still photographic coverage of the 1988 presidential campaign, Carol Squiers attributes the standardization of candidate photographs to "a variety of reasons having mainly to do with editorial formality and protocol."

Most campaign photographs look uniformly similar because politicians have learned to manage press coverage of their campaigns: "Candidates and their staffs have become the ultimate journalistic gatekeepers, deciding what is and is not news by allowing access only to those events which they wish to publicize."[1] As *New York Times* political reporter Maureen Dowd put it, "Now the press are led like cattle to one perfectly controlled event after another."[2]

It's true that politicians and their staffs try to control photographers, but they don't always succeed. Arthur Grace photographed the 1988 presidential campaign.[3]

Without special access he was able to show candidates looking small and vulnerable against an expanse of sterile walls and empty stages. The usual grins and forceful gestures were absent, as were the adoring crowds. Grace provided glimpses of reality that were available to any news photographer wishing to capture them rather than stereotypes.

America is founded on a belief in the common man. This common-man ideal holds that "citizens are more or less equals in their influence on elites; and elites accept the policy consensus which the public develops."[4] Indeed, the Declaration of Independence states: "Governments are instituted among men, deriving their just powers from the consent of the governed." Having escaped the encumbrances of elitist European society—monarchy, titles of nobility, and state church—early settlers looked upon European ways as improper for Americans. They had an aversion to government and an almost holy belief in agrarian life.

Immediately following the Revolution, however, a philosophical split emerged between the majority of Americans, who were farmers, and the capitalists and bankers residing the growing commercial centers of the East. This split between "agrarian democrats" and "aristocratic capitalists" represented a fundamental disagreement about the nature of property and the nature of man.[5]

Andrew Jackson's election in 1828 symbolized the triumph of the common man.[6] In his veto of a congressional rechartering of the privately held Bank of the United States, Jackson noted that the rich and powerful "bend" acts of government to become even more rich and powerful, while "the humble members of society—the farmers, mechanics, and laborers—who have neither the time nor the means of securing favors to themselves, have a right to complain." A stand must be taken, he said, "against any prostitution of our Government to the advancement of the few at the expense of the many."[7]

The idea of populism remains in the 1990s, especially during political campaigns. Politicians like to be photographed with farmers, blue-collar workers, police, and cowboys. These are "real" people, not elites. In contrast, suburban, white-collar workers are rarely pictured with politicians because they don't fit the populist ideology. Viewers of photographs also rarely see the political players who truly influence the political process—major contributors and well-financed special interest groups. Instead, the press follows the populist ideology that "the people" have more influence and involvement in government than they actually do.

Four different stereotypes of politicians follow the populist ideology. First, there is the "glad-to-see-you" politician. We see photographs of a politician waving, shaking hands, or giving a thumbs-up sign to "common people." The politician shows his or her enthusiasm and concern for ordinary people by visiting a bakery, factory, daycare center or other facility where he or she can ostensibly learn about workers and issues that affect their lives. A variation is the classic photograph of a politician with tie loosened, hair tousled, coat off and slung over one shoulder wearing a *blue* (not white) dress shirt. This projects an image of a hard-working "man of the people." Rarely do photographs show the politician visiting the kinds of nondescript offices where most business and bureaucratic work takes place. Never do politicians appear sad, pessimistic, or distressed.

Second, stereotyped photographs show politicians as athletes or outdoorpersons. Politicians throw balls, pitch horseshoes, fish, hunt, bowl, and run in order to tap into the nation's obsession with sports and to convey energy, strength, and a competitive spirit. Some sports, however, are more suitably populist than others. During the 1992 campaign, aides discouraged President Bush from "manic rounds of his favorite elitist pastimes, golf and boating" because such pictures "reinforce the image of an aristocratic president out of touch with the common man."[8]

Third, the politician appears as a father figure. Contrary to popular belief, politicians rarely kiss babies, but they do hug them and hoist them into the air. By appearing with a child, politicians are cast in a glow of reflected innocence and they project a concern for education and the future. "Father figure" pictures are so common they create the false impression that politicians spend a disproportionate amount of their time wooing people who are too young to vote. A study of the 1992 campaign found more pictures of candidates with children and youths than with representatives of business and labor combined.[9]

Related to the "father figure" role are the many photographs showing a candidate with his/her spouse, children, or parents. The fourth stereotype, that of family figure, is used to convince voters of the politicians' respectable and virtuous character. Politicians appear as human as we are. For men, the politician's wife also must play a stereotypical role for the cameras. The press supplies photographic evidence of a warm and loving wife who wants nothing more than to support her husband. Cliché photographs of Nancy Reagan and Barbara Bush were inevitable. With Hillary Rodham Clinton, photographers and editors have a choice: they can follow the stereotype or portray Mrs. Clinton as the tough, independent lawyer she is in reality. In its year-end retrospective issue, *Life* chose a shot of the Clintons in front of a huge American flag. Mrs. Clinton is demure and slightly in back of her husband. Her eyes are raised skyward in a boys-will-be-boys look of girlish charm.[10]

POLITICAL CARTOONS

Cartoonists also exploit stereotypes. There's the donkey, the elephant, Uncle Sam, and the Statue of Liberty. Russians are drawn as Boris Yeltsin, Chinese as Deng Xiaoping, and Somalians as a starving child. Politicians succumb to the vices of arrogance, cantankerousness, hypocrisy, and greed. Surely these are oversimplified images. "The basic building block of a political cartoonist's armory is stereotype," said Martin Medhurst, a scholar who frequently studies cartoons. "Whether it's personal or cultural, they couldn't operate without stereotypes." But just as surely, cartoonists' stereotypes differ from photographers'.[11]

Unlike news photographers, who either help politicians control their own images or succumb to their manipulations, cartoonists cut through conventions and surface appearances. "One would hope that [politicians] are besmirched, that their PR and spin are not always in control, that reality comes through sometimes," said Pulitzer-Prize winning cartoonist Doug Marlette. Syndicated cartoonist Kevin Kallaugher said political cartoonists are the only news workers successfully resisting spin doctors and communicating opposing messages: "Being the only group of satirists in the journalistic community, in a country that is pretty low on satire, and having the tool of visual caricature, cartoonists are one of the only enemies, the only counter-spin doctors to all of the bull that's thrown out about politics."

With a irascible tone and some bite, cartoonists seek to keep politicians honest by pointing out their faults and encouraging reform. They also deflate politicians' egos. Cartoonists can tell the painful truth because they make us laugh. If they keep the laughter high, they can slice unusually deep. Their rapier-like cuts are most likely to force political changes when their cartoons focus on a local political issue and reach a large audience.

Politicians normally welcome attention from photographers, or at least they don't fear cameras, because they know that photojournalists have internalized a set of unwritten rules. In her article about photo opportunities in the Reagan White House, Carol Squiers writes that photographers abide by the rules and often remind one another about the permissible limits of their activities.[12]

Maybe politicians fear cartoonists because they don't follow the rules. As "point men of the First Amendment," cartoonists constantly push the boundaries of press freedom. They must work outside the normal practices of journalism to achieve the goals desired by all news workers—to frankly and honestly tell the truth. "Journalism is about fairness, objectivity, factuality," Marlette said. However, "Cartoons use unfairness, subjectivity and the distortion of facts to get at truths that are greater than the sum of the facts," he added.

Cartoonists rely upon visual metaphors and cultural allusions—for example, the robed female figure carrying a scale, which is the traditional symbol for truth and justice—to quickly communicate their messages. These symbols, along with Uncle Sam and Boris Yeltsin, are more of a visual shorthand than a stereotype that harms a group of people.

Cartoonists also rely on caricature. The Italian verb *caricare* literally means to load or overload, as with exaggerated detail: "The classic theory of caricature says that the caricaturist seizes the essence of his victim, destroys his victim's persona (the mask he wears in the drama of life) by penetrating to the reality behind the appearance, and reveals the man in his essential littleness and ugliness."[13]

Caricature is actually two concepts: exaggeration and individualization. Because of the individual nature of caricature, it is impossible to categorize cartoons as we did for photographs. There are no equivalents to glad-to-see-you or father figure photographic stereotypes of politicians. David Perkins has written: "A caricature typically exaggerates features of its subject and exaggerates so as to differentiate the subject from his fellows."[14] Present-day cartoonists exaggerate politicians' "intelligence, honesty, age, morality, charisma and leadership."[15] More specifically, cartoonists have characterized perceptions concerning "[Ronald] Reagan's age, [Jimmy] Carter's incompetence, Richard Nixon's duplicity," said former Reagan campaign manager John Sears. Through caricature, "they can make these characteristics more arresting, vivid, memorable."[16]

Caricatures differ from stereotypes not only because they concern individuals rather than groups, but also because caricatures represent the specifics rather than unfair, musty clichés. The caricature may be unpleasant, but it is based on particular actions or words of a particular politician. It is a slant on the news rather than an empty generalization.

Cartoonists who can't draw well use more stereotypes and get in more trouble, said Kallaugher. Poor cartoonists learned to draw from books that showed a few standard drawings of various cultures—Africans, Chinese, Latin Americans—and that's all they learned, so their drawings all look the same. Better cartoonists can draw more realistic images, he said.

Kallaugher, who draws cartoons for the *Economist* (London), the *International Herald-Tribune* (Paris), as well as the *Baltimore Sun*, said stereotypes of politicians are more defined in European cartoons than they are in American cartoons. "When I draw British congressmen, they're always tall and thin and wearing hats that civil servants usually wear. They also tend to be upper-class, conservative and more wrinkled, unless they're [blue-collar party] politicians; then, they'd be drawn heavier and shorter," said Kallaugher.

Robert Ariail, cartoonist for *The State* in Columbia, South Carolina, draws well but admitted that he may stereotype politicians and other groups without intention. A reader reprimanded him because all of his drawings show southerners as slightly overweight. "I never really thought about it," said Ariail, "it's just the way I do it." He also stereotypes politicians:

You make a politician look like you think they are, maybe greedy or vicious, people who will do anything to get where they want to go, or maybe you think they're stupid. Whatever it is, you can put that into a caricature of somebody. You can do general caricatures of politicians—the good ol' boy, the fat-vested, fat-cat, boss-hog politicians. I probably [create stereotypes of politicians] every day, but I don't think that I'm doing it.

Cartoonists sometimes imitate each others' caricatures of well-known politicians—who could draw Ross Perot without huge ears?—yet caricatures have been known to evolve as the politician serves his or her term. For example, many cartoonists focused on President Ronald Reagan's wrinkles during his first term in office. During his second term in office, however, cartoonists de-emphasized the wrinkles and instead constantly drew Reagan with a look of oblivion.

Political cartoons also appear to be changing due to political correctness. Kallaugher, for example, said he pays particular attention to the mix of people in his cartoon crowd scenes. "I make sure I have a good mix in there—women, men, minorities. I think that's only fair when you're trying to talk to a whole group of readers that you try to represent the whole group of readers." Because of politically correct values that have been ingrained in his mind since the equal rights movement of the 1960s, Kallaugher tries to avoid using placid stereotypes when drawing women or minorities. In recent years, cartoonists have been chastised for using stereotypes that were once considered acceptable.

Pulitzer-Prize winning cartoonist Pat Oliphant said the so-called Age of Political Correctness is having a chilling affect on all cartoonists: "It's killing us all. We are slumping back into the fearful '50s. It's a repressive time we're in; it's almost like McCarthyism."

Public criticism of cartoonists has gone too far, said Lee Salem, vice president and editorial director of Universal Press Syndicate. "I happen to believe that an artist has a right to put his or her thoughts on a page, and if someone's offended, then tough. That's what opinion's all about, to offend people," said Salem. "Now, that's not to say that we don't get more complaints and mail that fall under the rubric of political correctness, but I generally ignore it. The artists and writers I know of are aware of it, but I don't think it influences their work too much."

Sometimes the cartoonist portrays a sexist or racist attitude in order to hold it up for ridicule. Unfortunately, some people are unable to distinguish what characters say and do from what the cartoonist is condoning or advocating. Readers simply need to lighten up and see the humor in political cartoons rather than quickly take offense at an imagined slight. As Steve Platt writes, "The cartoonist doesn't have an unqualified need to be offensive . . . any more than he or she has an unqualified right to be offensive. But neither does anyone else have an unqualified right to be offended. We must all tread a thin black line."[17]

Joel Pett, a syndicated cartoonist working for the *Lexington Herald Leader*, stops himself from drawing only negative stereotypes of politicians. "I think our political system is all we have, so I don't take pot-shots at all the politicians of a party or all of Congress. They're not all ignorant or corrupt. In fact, most have good intentions. It's really a shame that the public has such little regard for political institutions."

In conclusion, both positive and negative stereotypes make up our mental image of politicians. Photographers perpetuate a limited number of generally positive stereotypes of politicians while cartoonists almost always depict politicians negatively. The truth, if such an elusive concept can ever be portrayed, is somewhere in the middle.

29

Lawyer Stereotypes

Tim Gleason

Images of lawyers as greedy, aggressive, and cold-hearted pervade mass media in the United States. But at first glance, it may appear that the portrayal of lawyers is a question of little or no importance in a discussion of images that "injure." Where, outside a bar association meeting, would we find a sympathetic audience for the argument that producers of media images should be concerned about stereotypical portrayals of lawyers? Lawyers, most would argue, are quite capable of taking care of themselves.

A negative image of lawyers is hardly a new phenomenon. There is evidence from the New Testament to the most recent American Bar Association survey that the public has always had, at best, a love/hate relationship with the legal profession. An anti-lawyer sentiment is deeply ingrained in the American psyche because lawyers are so much a part of the country.[1] In the nineteenth century Alexis de Tocqueville observed, "Scarcely any question arises in the United States which does not become, sooner or later, a subject of judicial debate." In twentieth-century popular culture, legal issues are first thirty-second sound bites and then made-for-TV movies.[2]

The argument in this chapter is that the portrayal of lawyers in American popular culture should be of concern on at least two grounds:

1. Image producers have a primary obligation to do no unnecessary harm to the subjects of media images, regardless of the subject's station in life.
2. Mass media have an obligation to present the public with a complete picture of all aspects of life.

The claim that media practitioners should do no unnecessary harm should be unremarkable and noncontroversial. The case for it can be made using every available ethical theory generally used when discussing either individual or professional ethical norms. After all, what possible argument could be made that media practitioners are justified in causing harm absent a compelling greater interest?

However, photojournalists, editorial cartoonists, film directors, and other media practitioners tend to bridle at the claim. "What do you mean," they say, "if we are going to tell the truth, people are going to be harmed." Editorial cartoonists are the extreme example. Most good editorial cartoons take direct aim at a specific individual or institution. *New York Newsday* once advertised Doug Marlette, one of its Pulitzer-Prize winning editorial cartoonists, as being a "Semi-Automatic Assault Weapon."

The principle of "do no harm" or "minimize harm," as the authors of the recently published *Doing Ethics in Journalism* define it, does not require that image makers avoid harming individuals in every instance, but it places a burden on the practitioner to justify the harm.[3]

This principle can also be viewed as an affirmative obligation. For example, Sissela Bok's model for ethical decision-making requires "empathy for the people involved"; a social responsibility ethical framework calls for ensuring equality for all members of the society; the Radio-Television News Directors Association's Code of Broadcast News Ethics urges members to "respect the dignity, privacy and well-being of people with whom they deal."[4]

Viewed as either a negative or affirmative obligation, the principle of "do no harm" requires that the image maker justify the image that may cause harm by reference to the greater good served. In other words, the image maker must hold himself or herself accountable to the larger community for the harm caused. One need not fully accept the "communitarian ethic" put forth by Clifford Christians et al. in *Good News* to argue for media accountability here.[5] There is simply no case to be made that image makers may harm individuals absent reference to a public good or a community norm.

A skewed, distorted portrayal of lawyers leads to an arguably undeserved negative public perception of lawyers and the legal system based, in part, on the public's lack of understanding of the legal system and the legal process. In a democratic society, this lack of understanding weakens the legal system's ability to deliver justice and erodes the people's ability to govern.

The injury is to lawyers as individuals in the society and to the society itself.

LAWYER BASHING

Given the principle of "do no harm," can "lawyer bashing" be justified?

Lawyers have been the targets of humor and criticism throughout history; however, the current wave of "lawyer bashing" is notable for, as one legal observer put it, "the intense hostility with which it is invested."[6] Another attorney notes that "lawyer bashing may be the only remaining socially acceptable prejudice" in our society.[7]

David Letterman and Jay Leno regularly target lawyers in their monologues. Then Vice President Dan Quayle (a lawyer himself) made bashing the legal profession a part of the Bush/Quayle campaign in the 1992 presidential election. Publishers turn out books with titles like *Lawyers and Other Reptiles* and *Lawyers from Hell Joke Book*. Audiences at *Jurassic Park*, Stephen Spielberg's dinosaur extravaganza, cheer when an attorney becomes a meal. And in Cleveland, an insurance salesperson started the "Shark Line, " a 900-number where for $1.49 a minute callers can listen to lawyer jokes.

The most vocal opponent of the genre, Harvey Saferstein, the president of the State Bar of California, called for a moratorium on lawyer bashing, which he labeled a form of hate crime. It is, he said, "as heinous as all other forms of bigotry that encourage hatred against another group of people."[8]

In response, Wiley, the cartoonist who draws the syndicated cartoon "Non Sequitur," where he frequently directs his acid pen at lawyers, said, "Because of political correctness, lawyers and white males are about the only two groups left in America that you're allowed to use as foils."[9]

Is this reaction simply a case of a few attorneys with too thin skins? Are lawyers fair game for any and all jokes, cartoons, and parodies, no matter how cruel or pointless?

One of the most controversial examples of lawyer bashing is the Miller Brewing Company's "Big Lawyer Round-Up" commercial in which roping and hog-tying terrified tax and divorce lawyers is a rodeo event. In one part of the ad the announcer says, "There's Billy Pugh going after that divorce lawyer that took away his bass boat!" as the viewer sees a cowboy lasso an overweight attorney. The ad is part of a campaign in which the beer company also takes shots at cooks, golfers, football players, hockey players, beauty queens, and sumo wrestlers.[10]

Shortly after the ad started to run, a man carrying a semi-automatic rifle walked into a San Francisco law firm office and randomly shot fourteen people, killing eight. Some lawyer advocates linked the killings to lawyer bashing and pointed to the Miller ad as an extreme example. Miller withdrew the ad for a short period of time, but then put it back on the air. Miller spokespersons defended the ad, rejected the idea that there was any relation between the ad and the shooting in San Francisco, reported that everyone but lawyers liked the ad, and, in effect, told lawyers to get a sense of humor.[11]

Efforts to link the violent behavior of any individual to a specific mass media message or even to the entire "lawyer bashing" phenomenon runs contrary to all we know about the effects of media messages, but the "do no harm" principle doesn't allow us to stop with a simple "it's not the media's fault" defense.

The "Big Lawyer Round-Up" ridicules lawyers and at the very least is embarrassing to the legal profession. The ad is funny, but is the harm justifiable?

In the current climate, where lawyers as a group are not well regarded by the public, the ad plays on a negative stereotype to sell beer; there is little else going on in the ad.

There is a long tradition of lawyer cartoons in the United States. One of the frequently cited examples of lawyer bashing is the work of Wiley, especially his collection of cartoons titled, *Dead Lawyers and Other Pleasant Thoughts*. Wiley builds on a tradition of lawyer cartoons, for example those published in *The New Yorker* magazine; however, his cartoons have a much sharper edge.[12]

For example, the cover cartoon in *Dead Lawyers* shows a rather nebbish-looking, white, male attorney about to cross a street next to a sign that says "LAWYER XING—NO SPEED LIMIT." Another shows children building sand castles on the beach. A boy wearing glasses is building the largest castle which is surrounded by a shark-infested moat. The caption reads, "How to spot a future lawyer."[13]

Wiley is reported to have said that his commentaries are justified because "it's not bashing, it's a means of getting even. The legal profession is such a monolith. People feel defenseless against it. The only weapon left is humor."[14]

Social commentary is a means to correct the ills of society and to correct imbalances of power among groups in a society. As Wiley notes, humor can be a powerful weapon in efforts to reveal the flaws in the social or legal order.

One of the checks on the use of social commentary is the need for truth in humor. Lawyer bashing is popular because the public finds some truth in much of it.

But most media portrayals of lawyers are not "lawyer bashing." Most Americans get most of their information about lawyers and the legal system from television and film. The picture we see has little in common with the practice of law or the legal process.

THE LAW AS DRAMA

News

Turn on the local news and there is the local district attorney saying a suspect has been arrested for murder, followed by the defense attorney claiming her client is innocent. Switch to the national news and watch the twenty-two-second sound bite of well-known defense lawyer William M. Kunstler telling reporters that he will introduce a "black rage" insanity defense for his client in a New York subway shooting, or Alan Dershowitz explaining why former heavy weight boxing champion Mike Tyson should be released from prison. The names change but the stories remain the same.

Crime and punishment dominate television news coverage, especially local television news coverage. One recent study found that a Miami station known for its extreme crime coverage devoted 49 percent of its newscast to crime.[15]

Law as television drama reached new heights in the early summer of 1994 as the O.J. Simpson murder saga unfolded on television in "real time" before our eyes. From the first reports of the murder of Nicole Brown Simpson and Ronald Goldman through the televised preliminary hearing (broadcast live on CNN and the three major networks, which pre-empted soap operas for the legal drama) viewers watched real lawyers play a wide range of roles from criminal defense attorney to play-by-play commentator in a plot that no script writer could ever write.

When a lawyer is seen on television news, it is usually in the context of criminal law and the focus is on the result of the legal proceeding, rather than the proceeding itself. As one legal scholar wrote, "In news programming, legal information comes out in tiny bites that convey upshots, not theories; results, not reasoning."[16]

Given the focus on criminal litigation and on results, is it any wonder that the average citizen has little understanding of the legal process and even less appreciation for the role of lawyers in that process?

The view from the print side is little better. The news values identified above are not unique to television. Print journalists also focus on crime litigation and results. Frequently, the only visual message readers have of lawyers is a photograph of an attorney standing with a client who, more often than not, looks guilty outside a court room or in court.[17]

The public is left with the impression that a large percentage of lawyers work in criminal law and that a high percentage of criminal cases result in trials. Both of these impressions are false. In fact, only 2 percent of the members of the American Bar Association identify themselves as practicing criminal law and only about 6 percent of all criminal cases ever reach trial.[18]

More important, the audience has little chance to understand the theories or the reasoning of legal decisions. Absent a richer presentation of the thinking and reasoning that leads to the decisions lawyers make, how can we expect the public to appreciate or evaluate what lawyers do?

Court TV, the cable channel that provides coverage of actual trials, expressly tries to move beyond the sound bite coverage of local and national news programming, but again the focus is on criminal law and on trial coverage. Court TV's coverage of the William Kennedy Smith rape trial or the trial of the Menendez brothers gave viewers an opportunity to see the actual trial process in all of its excruciating detail, but high-profile sensational trials of this sort are far from the norm of legal practice.

"ENTERTAINMENT"

Entertainment programming on television and in movies probably offers the media their greatest opportunity to influence the public's understanding of lawyers and the legal system.[19] In the era of "infotainment," where the made-for-TV movies about the legal dramas of people such as Tonya Harding, Amy Fisher, or mob-boss John Gotti move seamlessly from real courtrooms to television sound stages, the distinction between news and entertainment becomes less and less meaningful.

Entertainment television and film are heavily populated with lawyers. Watch the Lifetime channel and there is Arnie Becker on an "L.A. Law" rerun having yet another affair, or Michael Kusak delivering a brilliant two-minute summation. Click again and catch Raymond Burr in one of the 271 episodes of the original "Perry Mason" television series or maybe one of the newer TV movies. Click, and you're watching the latest made-for-TV movie "loosely" based on the sensational crime of the week or an episode of "Law & Order" ripped out of yesterday's headlines.

During a local commercial break, an ad for a personal injury lawyer in your community urges you to call the next time you're hit by a truck. That is followed by an ad for Reebok shoes that imagines a "perfect world" as one in which there are no lawyers.

Then you head off to the video rental store where you are confronted with a difficult choice: Do you want to watch Tom Cruise as lawyer Mitch McDeere in *The Firm* or as a Navy lawyer in *A Few Good Men*, with the added bonus of Demi Moore playing a lawyer; or *Philadelphia* in which Tom Hanks is a lawyer fired because he has AIDS, Jason Robarts plays the evil managing partner of the law firm and Denzel Washington is Hanks' lawyer; or *Jagged Edge*, where Glenn Close falls for her client; or Debra Winger in *Legal Eagles*; or Julia Roberts as the law student who uncovers a plot to kill Supreme Court justices and her law professor lover in *The Pelican Brief*; or Mary Elizabeth Mastrantonio in *Class Action*, where she defends automakers who deliberately covered up a design defect that cost lives; or, moving to the classic film section of the store, Gregory Peck as Atticus Finch in *To Kill a Mockingbird*, for a depiction of the lawyer as hero; or looking for a less reverent portrayal, Groucho Marx as Thaddeus J. Loophole in *At The Circus*. Perhaps you're in the mood for animation, so you select *Tom and Jerry: The Movie*, featuring a lawyer named Lickboot.[20]

Since the beginning of television programming in the late 1940s, the networks have given us more than 500 series about the law. Hundreds of movies have featured lawyers as leading or central characters, and lawyers have appeared daily on news and public affairs television and radio programs. Those who have looked carefully at the portrayal of lawyers in entertainment television and film find, not surprisingly, that the portrayals seem to reflect the attitudes of different periods. Prior to the 1970s lawyers were generally portrayed as heroes, but "in the post-Watergate era, the public's image of the law is more Attica than Atticus. The public has followed the change in pop-culture lawyers from crusading loners to big-firm lawyers, from solo litigators to corporate attorneys, from heroes to antiheroes."[21]

Lawyers and the law are clearly one of the major food groups of the our popular culture diet. Is this good news or bad news for the legal profession, the legal system, democracy, and society?

Some within the legal profession argue that the media portrayal of lawyers contributes to the low esteem in which the legal profession is held in the United States.

While media images may not enhance the image of lawyers, the evidence does not support any strong correlation between media portrayals of lawyers and negative images. In fact, television appears to enhance the image of lawyers!

• An ABA poll in 1993 found that those who got most of their information from television had a more favorable view of lawyers than those who got their information elsewhere.[22]
• A *National Law Journal* poll found that two of the twelve lawyers most admired by respondents were fictional television lawyers Perry Mason and Matlock.[23]
• Perhaps most disturbing to the legal profession was the finding by the ABA that the people who hate lawyers most are the ones who actually deal with them.[24]

However, television and film are not off the hook. While the negative perception of lawyers cannot be squarely placed on mass media, the public's misperceptions about the legal system and the practice of law is attributable, at least partially, to television and the movies.

There is little doubt that "L.A. Law," Judge Wapner of "The People's Court," and the televised actions of the attorneys involved with the O.J. Simpson double-murder trial have been major cultural influences on the public's perception and on lawyers' perception of "legal culture," which Lawrence Friedman defines as "the ideas, attitudes, values, and opinion about law held by people in a society."[25]

"L.A. Law," Judge Wapner, and all the other television and film portrayals of lawyers clearly do influence the legal culture. The evidence suggests that what the public sees results in a public perception of the legal system and legal practice that is far removed from reality. But it would be unreasonable and undesirable to claim that dramatic portrayals and of lawyers must or even should be constrained by an obligation to accurately portray daily life in the law.

The problem is the absence of significant opportunity for the average citizen to see an accurate portrayal of lawyers and the legal system in the mass media. Both news and entertainment media give us far less than a complete picture of lawyers and the law. How then can the public understand or judge the performance of this important aspect of our lives?

The failure to meet the obligation to provide the public with a complete and comprehensive picture of the legal system and the lawyers who work in it should be of the greatest concern. This failure injures all of us.

Stereotyping True Believers: The Clash of Reductionism and Symbolism

Craig Denton

Unlike racial, age, or sexual stereotypes, there are fewer examples of religious stereotyping in mass media. That's why this subject is somewhat unique. Religions and religious followers don't get much page space or screen time. Religion is an awkward, if not taboo, subject for media gatekeepers, and if religion is covered at all in the newspaper, it's often relegated to the back pages with listings of church events. Or if religion is a front-page story, it's usually as part of a larger news story of conflict, for instance the abortion fight, dissension during the pope's visit or the presidential candidacy of a cleric. This lack of coverage of religion, visually or verbally, should be evaluated in the context that, while a community newspaper will devote hundreds of column inches annually to high school football, it will devote much less space to covering religion's role in that community, despite the fact that attendance at religious services greatly exceeds attendance at high school sporting events over the course of a year.[1]

Mass media, especially the news media, have grown up under the philosophical umbrella of libertarianism. That philosophy suggests that individuals can attain truth by rigorously grappling with all information, falsehoods included. Because humans are inherently good, they will discover the truth, especially if they are schooled in methods of critical, scientific analysis. Science, then, is the ultimate helpmate of liberalism, and scientific truths have consummate legitimacy in public discourse.

Religious truth, on the other hand, ultimately relies on faith. It can't be proved with the scientific method. Media gatekeepers tend to feel uneasy with information tinged with emotional absolutism. They try to keep the two spheres—religion and the secular, faith and rationality—separate, with rationality reserved for news. That schism is ironic, considering that religious and press freedoms in the United States are guaranteed by the same First Amendment. Apparently, the writers of the

Constitution felt that the those liberties sprout from the same roots.

In the abortion battle photographers often capture members of Operation Rescue, the militant pro-life group involved in the illegal blockading of abortion clinics whose alleged members sometimes kill or wound doctors, with Bibles in their hands. The Bible, then, becomes the visual symbol for irrationality and inhumanity, defaming millions of people who swear allegiance to biblical teachings but who would vigorously oppose using it to justify violence.

In the current spate of stories regarding priests and ministers who have been convicted of sexual abuse of children, there is a special problem when the perpetrator is a priest. While some ministers wear street clothes as their official attire, other ministers or priests wear a collar. If the commonly dressed minister is pictured in a photograph accompanying a report on his indictment for child abuse, there is no visual symbol other than his person that is linked to the charge, unless it might be a dark or black suit. But if a Catholic cleric is wearing a collar, that collar symbolizes celibacy, among other things. Celibacy is linked to sexuality, even though it's the flip side. Ironically and unfortunately, in a photo of a priest with a collar accused of child abuse, the visual symbol and the church he represents through that symbolism become negatively linked with the charge of pedophilia.

A complex mixture of symbol reduction and deconstruction occurred in 1992 when the Irish-born, Roman Catholic-reared singer Sinead O'Connor, who shaves her head like an ascetic, appeared on the television program "Saturday Night Live." To demonstrate her support of abortion rights, she ripped apart a photograph of Pope John Paul II, a metonymic symbol of the anti-abortion forces, calling him a man of sin. In that same program she enlisted support from the reggae lyrics of Bob Marley's "War" and put them in a new context—war against the anti-abortion forces. To make the symbolism and stereotyping even more confusing, Marley was a Rastafarian, a member of a Jamaica-based religion that is admittedly anti-Catholic but that is also vehemently against abortion. Then, O'Connor used a Star of David in her visual protest, the Star of David being a symbol common to both Rastafarianism and Judaism. The Jewish Anti-Defamation League apologized to the pope the following day, thinking that O'Connor had included the Star of David as a Jewish symbol, when she had not. In that episode, there were multiple examples of injurious visual stereotyping of religion, but few operated as intended.

Political cartoonists are given a great deal of leeway in their characterizations. It's assumed that using visual stereotypes, usually negative ones, is necessary to make a political cartoon's visual point unequivocal and rapier-like. But, sometimes political cartoonists step over the line. During the 1993 Christmas season, the *St. Petersburg Times* ran a syndicated cartoon by Pat Oliphant that depicted two priests on the steps of a Catholic church. A caricature of Michael Jackson, the rock star who had been accused of child molestation, looked up from below. One priest said to the other, "Mr. Jackson, it seems, would like to join the priesthood." Oliphant's commentator penguin said in the bottom corner, "He probably heard such nice things about you." The public outrage was such that the *St. Petersburg Times* apologized to its readers on its opinion page on Christmas Day saying, "We agree that the timing and content of the cartoon were in poor taste."[2]

In entertainment media like film or television, screenwriters and directors consciously draw their visual images for specific characterizations and narrative effect. Sometimes, they rely on visual stereotypes already lodged in the public memory to effect communication. They draw from the reservoir of cultural images already in place rather than try to create new images that might not be as easily understood. For instance, Steve Martin's itinerant, big-top preacher in *Leap of Faith* relied on the negative image of an evangelist as being a conniving, lecherous, hypocritical reprobate with one hand on the billfold in your back pocket and the other hand under the robe of comely choir member. But Martin's characterization wasn't new. It had been presented some thirty years earlier by Burt Lancaster in *Elmer Gantry*, which of course relied on imagery originally developed by Sinclair Lewis in his novel of the 1920s.

In advertising, creative directors sometimes borrow religious symbols for their metaphorical and subliminal qualities. A photographer might shoot a model with a cross around her neck to suggest virtue. A casting agent might choose a Muslim woman with a veil over her face to suggest hidden sexuality. An art director might place a nun in habit in the photograph of customers at a bank, with the tag line "Everyone comes to our bank," the message subconsciously labeling the nun as an oddity and a fish out of water. While these symbols might not be used negatively, taken out of their religious context, they are exploitative and demeaning at best. At their worst they trivialize or distort what the symbols really represent, which is another form of injurious visual stereotyping.

SEEDS OF THE PROBLEM

Visual stereotypes are more virulent and penetrating than verbal stereotypes simply because they can be understood by the illiterate or alliterate, as well as the literate. However, it's difficult to analyze visual stereotypes apart from their companion verbal stereotypes. Inevitably, words become integrated with visual messages, and indeed good communication design encourages a marriage of the visual and verbal. Libel and privacy case law also makes the point that a visual message might not be defamatory on its face, but it can become so in association with the words in the accompanying caption that modify it and direct the meaning and intention of the visual message. In some instances a person might not be automatically identified in a photograph as fulfilling a primarily religious role in society, as would an image of a nun in habit, a priest in collar or a Hare Krishna in saffron robe. The symbolism isn't overt in the image. Lacking symbolic visual detail, the person is identified as fulfilling a religious role in a news story in a verbal description in a caption. Sometimes, the selected words are what forge the injury and negative stereotype, as in phrases like "Muslim terrorist," "Bible-thumping Christian," "rock-ribbed fundamentalist," "Bible-Belt believer," or "member of the righteous right."

When faced with complexity, the media aren't always as energetic as they should be in making distinctions. In the rush of deadlines, in the attempt to make a point, the media have a tendency to boil down things, to make a soup with a single, distinctive taste when the offering really should be perceived as collection of separate tastes. The media tend to make things monolithic, and they probably indulge in more of that easy categorization with religion than with any other institutions.

For instance, if an art director needs a symbol of religion, a nun in habit, priest in collar, or mullah in turban likely will be the first image chosen because the symbolism is on display and immediately understandable. The religions those symbols are drawn from, then, tend to be pictured in mass media more often, becoming the default image and majority religion when collectively their numbers might place them in a minority.

The media never have understood the difference between "evangelical," "funda-mentalist," and "religious right." They treat the terms and their visual referents as interchangeable. But an "evangelical" really isn't an itinerant gospel preacher. An "evangelical" is a Protestant believer who emphasizes the authority of the Gospel and seeks salvation through faith and grace rather than by displaying good works. Most mainline Protestants fit this description. A "fundamentalist" really is a historic term referring to a person in the late nineteenth century who opposed modernism by adhering to the doctrine that interpretation of the Bible should be literal. Evangelicals are less rigid and welcome more people into the fold. A Christian charismatic believes in the active agency of the Holy Spirit, including such spiritual gifts as healing and speaking in tongues. While a Pentecostal, a more generalized descriptor, has some things in common with a charismatic, all Pente-costals wouldn't ascribe to all evidence of spiritual gifts.

True believers, then, live in fear of being miscast, misrepresented, and misplaced in mass media. They have come to understand that the mass media are not sensitive to religious multiculturalism. For instance, I once photographed a documentary of a religious group called the Aaronic Order. Its Sabbath services were filled with music and congregates exuberantly waved their arms in time with the music in celebration of their faith. When I showed the work prints of the service to the first and second high priests of the church, they had different responses. The priest charged with the order's public relations was concerned that the images might confuse a secular audience with insufficient knowledge. He worried that the Aaronic Order would be seen as Pentecostal when he knew there were distinct differences in the theologies. The first high priest granted the second's concerns, but he was more willing to let the visual symbolism stand. "That's the way of our Sabbath service," he said, regardless of how others might interpret it.

A complementary problem occurs when a religious group's numbers are few. That religion likely will never be seen or its symbols used or misused in the mass media simply because of the media's ruthless absorption with demographics. A group either has to register on the scale through sheer weight of numbers to be noticed, or it has to be swept into the media spotlight due to its unwitting inclusion in a larger news event, usually one driven by conflict or violence. Then, the inevitable categorization and stereotyping would begin.

But all groups in society have a right to be seen.[3] In an era when being seen reifies existence and makes you a player in decisions regarding not only your own community but overall social governance, to be denied access to visibility is tantamount to slow cultural suffocation. In our visually driven society, to be heard you first need to be seen. Religions are placed in an awkward situation. Should they want to show their good works, or should they want to project themselves into public debate on a moral issue for which they feel they have a valid perspective and message, they have to accept the real risk of being visually misrepresented and miscategorized by mass media that are insensitive to religious distinctions if not somewhat alienated from religion in general.

Injurious visual stereotypes in entertainment media often are more subtle and complex. Since dramas are inherently make-believe, journalistic objectives of balance and fairness aren't preeminent in story-telling. The positioning of religion in the entertainment context becomes as important as the overt display. While most of the information about religious groups in television fictions is made available to the viewer through visual, non-verbal symbols, there is a layering effect. Religion provides textural detail. Usually, however, it is sketched as background detail.

Seldom do screenwriters give it foreground treatment. While organized religion is treated in the content of prime-time television frequently, only rarely do the writers allow that fictional religion to have a direct influence on the behavior of the characters or drive the narrative.[4] By placing it in the background, religion is pictured as inconsequential.

SEMIOTIC ABUSE

The essential problem of injurious visualization of religion and religious follow-ers in mass media is one of semiotic interpretation. Religions are steeped in symbolism, and religious iconography is a physical manifestation of that symbol-ism. Icons are signs that are sacred to a religion's understanding of itself and its relationship with God. The visual symbol and its spiritual or metaphysical referent are linked inextricably. The symbol is charged and fused with the spirit, whether it's a Communion wafer, a Torah or the Koran. Religions use colors, clothing, and insignia as symbols connoting specific meanings. While they don't expect a lay public to necessarily understand those idiosyncratic meanings, religions do want those visual symbols to be their earthly calling cards. When a religion is messianic, those symbols become super-charged, the embodiment of will and a God-fearing singularity.

As skilled practitioners in the use of visual symbols too, mass media are amenable to using those signs of religion. Symbols are a visual shortcut to identification, a handy stereotype. But a problem arises because the mass media lack an understand-ing of the symbolic meaning of religious signs as well as divergent religious interpretations of signs. Because mass media use symbols for communication to a secular world, religions and true believers lose control over their symbols in mass communication. Instead of being inclusive, their symbols become exclusive. Religions and their symbols wind up looking odd and foreign.

The problem is complicated by the similar, parabolic functions of religion and mass media. Both institutions are wedded to the allegorical. Both are inveterate story-tellers. Both usually end their parables of life with a lesson. Religions use symbols in their allegories, and they ask us to look for meaning in the narrative as well as in the symbols. The mass media like to define people and groups as archetypes and have them tell their stories so that the speaker, the story, and the lesson become one. They do that in the name of "balance," "fairness" and "equal time." Both religion and mass communication are story-makers and story-tellers. And, as visual signs in either medium reduce complexity by becoming allegorical symbols, they also become stereotypes.

Just as visual and verbal stereotyping are entangled, so too are religion and ethnicity.[5] The injurious stereotyping of ethnic groups often gets transferred to the religions practiced by those ethnic groups, and vice versa, especially when public perception equates a single religion with that ethnic group. The symbols of ethnicity become intermixed with religious symbolism. As a mass medium injures one, it can malign the other by association.

Ethnic and religious stereotyping is prevalent in media treatments of black religions like Santeria and *vodun*, or voodoo, as it's more commonly labeled. Researchers who immerse themselves in black religions find them complex systems of social, psychological, and spiritual communication.[6] But when filmmakers with little direct experience with the religions take hold of the imagery, black religions become "black magic." They are pictured as uninhibited and violent expressions of human malevolence and degradation. In each of the three movies *Angel Heart, The Serpent and the Rainbow*, and *The Believers*, the hero is tempted into personal destruction by the seductive lure of a voodoo ceremony while he views it in hiding. It is also important to note that in all three movies the hero is white and his security and personal value systems are threatened by a black culture cast as base and corrupting.

In 1992 Jean H. Webb and Israel K. Malupo of the World Peace Movement (WPM) sued the Mormon Church-owned *Deseret News*. Their civil rights suit stemmed from a 1990 incident in which the *News* published the text of a paid advertisement for the WPM but refused to include a head-and-shoulders drawing in the ad. The drawing was a bearded figure that seemed to be meant as a representation of Jesus Christ. The *News* argued that the picture looked too much like Malupo, who is a Polynesian from Tonga and an excommunicated Mormon, and that the picture was in bad taste and could be offensive to the newspaper's readers, even though the morning newspaper in Salt Lake City, *The Salt Lake Tribune*, ran the complete advertisement. The attorney for Webb and Malupo said the *News*'s refusal was a "combination of racial and religious" prejudice, citing the dark skin of the person in the ad.[7] The court eventually ruled for the *Deseret News*.

Native American religions also are often tinged with ethnic stereotyping. What B-grade cowboys and Indians movie was complete without the ceremonial war dance at midnight before the murderous ambush on the morrow with the pounding drums and the agitated prancing depicted as heathenism? Filmmakers never provided the Saturday matinee audience with the religious symbolism of the dance in its proper context, assuming that such dances ever were held for such events; neither did they sponsor roundtable discussions after the movies and the popcorn were consumed.

Today, Native American religious symbolism is challenged by another kind of visual defamation. When media producers accurately display but incompletely document a ceremony with the participants wearing full regalia, they force the audience to make sense of the symbolic artifacts. While the eagle feathers in the headdress honoring the spirit of the animal could have been legally obtained or passed down from generation to generation, producers leave the audience wondering whether another symbol, the bald eagle, was put to an untimely death to satisfy the demands of an atavistic ritual.

Visual symbols are tenacious. Their half-lives are the only phenomenon in mass media that approaches the longevity of radioactive decay. Consider the effects of political cartooning in the late 1800s. As America was struggling with its pluralism and its idealistic platform of equal rights for all, cartoonists often lumped together "troublesome" groups, those outside the mainstream, with the overall negative image a sum larger than the individual negative images of the various parts. When *Wasp* magazine in 1879 wished to make an editorial comment on the problems of minorities in the United States, it pictured a political cartoon of Uncle Sam beginning to kick Mormons, Chinese, Africans, Native Americans, and the Irish out of the national bed and encouraging the government to do so.[8]

Before the Mormon Church renounced polygamy in order to win statehood for Utah in 1896, the national press vilified the church for its "peculiar institution." Political cartoonists of the middle and late 1800s typically pictured a Mormon as either a satyr-like figure with horns and cloven hoofs, like the oversexed Greek mythological figure, or as a rooster with grand tail strutting around his harem of hens. Polygamy isn't grist for the editorial page anymore. Nevertheless, every year or so some official at the Utah State Travel Council will report an episode where a tourist comes into the office demanding to know where all the Mormons are. The puzzled official will ask for more detail. Then the disappointed tourist will say that, in spite of coming to Utah to see the Mormons, he hasn't yet spied anyone with either horns or a tail. Whether pulling the leg of the tourist official or not, the visual image is tenacious.

IMPROVING THE VISUAL ENVIRONMENT
FOR RELIGION AND RELIGIOUS FOLLOWERS

Devout religious followers say that mass media are inherently hostile to religion and seek to place religion in a negative light. As proof, religionists typically will note a survey by S. Robert Lichter of George Washington University and Stanley Rothman of Smith College in 1980 that polled 240 journalists at seven news organizations based in New York or Washington. When questioned about religious affiliation, 86 percent said they seldom or never attended religious services. But research doesn't show any kind of direct link of negative visual stereotyping with ingrained hatred of religion by the media.   In fact, a 1993 study by the Freedom Forum's First Amendment Center at Vanderbilt University found that 72 percent of 266 managing editors and three-fourths of the ninty-nine reporters specializing in religion who responded to the survey declared that faith is "very important" in their lives, while only 9 percent of editors and 4 percent of religion writers said "none" for religious preference. It is important to note that the Freedom Forum survey also reported that many of the journalists indicated that the issue of their personal beliefs was not relevant to how they did their jobs. Only 17 percent or the writers and editors surveyed agreed that "reporters who cover religion regularly should be active in a religion." The authors of the study concluded that there are serious problems with much media coverage of religion, but they attributed those problems largely to ignorance rather than antipathy.[9]

The current media interest in multiculturalism needs to be extended to media representations of religion and religious followers. As we strive to make sure that all elements of society, especially minorities, are honestly covered on our news pages and programs and in our entertainment media, we need to extend that same right to true believers, probably the largest demographic group in our pluralistic American culture.

What is needed in mass media visual depictions of religion and true believers is more symbolism. Right now, the cultural reservoir of visual messages is stagnant and depleted. The visual symbols are overtaxed and often misrepresent because they fail to reveal the rich pattern of religious diversity in American life. Mass communicators need to learn what religious symbols mean in the contexts in which they are used, rather than overlaying their own interpretations on those meanings. While it's unlikely that we can rid the mass media of stereotypes, due to their facilitation of mass communication, it is possible to offer more and more varied stereotypes and to present those new stereotypes in contexts that are not value-laden. Even constantly positive stereotypes are harmful because they preclude diversity, humanism, and depth of understanding. Society needs to be able to see religious stereotypes and simply not react either positively or negatively.

For their part, religionists need to stop looking at the mass media as the devil incarnate. They need to engage the media in dialogue that could lead to a fuller understanding of both institutions. If religions do not like the way their symbols are being used, they need to intervene by sympathetically presenting correct interpretations or wholly new offerings, not by crying blasphemy.

One religious order is doing just that. To reverse a dramatic fall in their numbers, in 1993 the Ursuline order of nuns hired an advertising agency to help them sign up people for a lifetime of poverty, chastity, and obedience, an admittedly tough sell. But, rather than using the old visual stereotypes of black habit, big white collar, and a hand gripped tightly around a ruler, the order decided to present their more contemporary face. The print ads show them as contemporary women in street clothes doing social projects. One nun pounds away with hammer and nails on a housing renovation project. In another ad a speech pathologist works with a developmentally impaired boy.

The news media need to be conscious of the context in which they use religious symbols. Often, events become newsworthy due to conflict embedded within them. Sometimes, religion and true believers will become part of those larger social morality plays, especially when the news event is about abortion, women's rights, and child abuse. If possible, the news media need to separate the person from the institution. Symbols represent institutions, not persons, and the news media need to separate the religious symbolism from the reportage. Even if newsmakers thrust themselves into the vortex of public debate and carry the symbols of their religion as their almighty sword and shield, they do so as individuals, not necessarily as representatives of the religion. Journalistic balance and fairness should mean treating religious symbols with the same kind of careful scrutiny as is offered to innocent bystanders or people who find themselves swept up in a news story through no fault of their own.

The news media also need to pay closer attention to the temporal context of reporting. Photo and graphics editors should realize that a visual message might not be injurious at one time, but given a news event and the negative implications of that event, there could be an association that unearths a stubborn negative stereotype. Often, religious symbols have meaning grounded in the millennia of human experience, and news gatekeepers treat them shabbily when they disregard that history and tag religious symbols in the moment.

For their part, mass media entertainment producers need to resist the temptation to treat religion and true believers as tokens or to sensationalize by casting religion in the chorus of things occult and generally strange. Religion should be depicted in the foreground of human experience. If nothing else, gross numbers of weekly worshippers should suggest that placement. People representing religion should be treated as full bodies on the continua of all possibilities of general attractiveness and unattractiveness, intelligence and stupidity, emotional and apathetic, and so on. Then, we no longer would be talking about stereotypes, positive or negative. We would use a better phrase—full characterization.

31

Stereotyping of Media Personnel

Walter B. Jaehnig

Political commentator and author Richard Reeves tells this story about one of Walter Mondale's ill-fated campaigns for the U.S. presidency.

Members of the press covering the early primaries appeared to be favorably disposed toward the young U.S. senator from Minnesota. A product of that state's Democratic-farmer-labor tradition, Mondale had made a number of populist speeches, calling for welfare reform to address the enduring needs of the American poor. For weeks, his aides had promised release of a radical plan to recast the nation's welfare system, providing details of this major element of Mondale's campaign.

On the appointed day, the nation's news media flocked to a Minneapolis hall for the unveiling. In advance of the candidate's appearance, reporters were given elaborate press packets containing detailed descriptions of the welfare plan, complete with tax tables illustrating the depth of the federal income tax increases needed to finance it. Almost in unison, Reeves recalls, reporters turned to a table that figured tax increases by personal income. And almost as a person, they realized that experienced reporters in the 1970s earned incomes sufficient to number them among the targets in the Mondale plan. While newsroom mythology might place them on the side of the poor, elderly, downtrodden, and other social underdogs, the new affluence of modern journalists linked them with other elements of middle class, established groups in American society. Mondale's support among the working press drained from the Minneapolis hall that day and never returned.

An apocryphal story? Perhaps. Mondale had a creditable political life even without this press support, serving a term as vice president of the United States, losing a bid for re-election with Jimmy Carter, and losing again to Ronald Reagan in 1984 in his last hurrah. The story also is based upon an unlikely premise: that a crowd of political reporters, representing a variety of newspapers, magazines, wire services, broadcast networks, radio and television stations, as well as an untold number of special interest publications, could simultaneously reach the same conclusion on any matter and respond in a uniform manner. And would all these reporters in Minneapolis, or even the great majority of them, put selfish interests ahead of their professional training and experience, sacrificing all for a few dollars of unassessed taxes?

But if the story is not literally true, maybe it should be. It illustrates how easily anecdotal materials can be turned into stereotypes characterizing any group or segment of a population. The best stereotypes always contain an element of truth, instead of the whole truth. (The worst contain no truth, or no attempt to find the truth at all.) And while they too often unfairly and inaccurately label a group or individual, serving as a substitute for original thought on the part of the beholder, they also can help us find order in chaos, see patterns in a life that often seems totally random.

STEREOTYPING THE STEREOTYPERS

Journalists, possibly more than any other occupational group, provide the images upon which most social stereotypes are based. But they are trained and rewarded for describing the world around them; this means they do not often provide insights into their own professional world, even when it might benefit the public to know more about who they are and how they work, or even when their most disreputable competitors err or otherwise misbehave.

This oversight means we have to look elsewhere for stereotypical material on media personnel. Fortunately, it is available: hundreds of novels, dozens of films, and countless broadcast and dramatic productions burn repetitive images about journalists into the public mind. Many books and reports, some academic and most of a critical nature, have been published about the journalistic world and the people who populate it. And a few journalistic insiders, such as Richard Reeves, produced perceptive descriptions of professional colleagues, though more often this material is found in autobiographies, written long after the fact, that seem more quaint than enlightening.

But there are problems in using this material. The first has to do with that troublesome word, "media," and what we are talking about when we use it. "Media" is conventionally used in its plural, collective form, referring to a range of print and broadcast communications organizations (and, accordingly, in the Associated Press stylebook, requiring a plural verb). This is consistent with a pluralistic political philosophy that assigns a limited, informational role to a press institution composed of a diverse range of news organizations, under different ownerships, representing a full range of views in the "marketplace of ideas." In a system of checks and balances, the media have no more power and influence than other institutions.

But increasingly in recent years, popular usage of the word has given it singular connotations (a trend evident to United Press International editors in producing the UPI version of the style manual) that represent more powerful conceptions of informational institutions. Sometimes, "media" seems to refer to television alone, as when the small-market television station reporter shows up at a fish fry, struggling under the weight of camera, light, battery packs, and someone says, "The media is here!" More often, it is used to refer to a singular, monolithic (and distinctly non-pluralistic) institution with a mind and values of its own in which all news employees are grouped together, no matter who they work for or what they do. Usually this singular usage is antagonistic in character, expressing disapproval of whatever news organizations have done and their perceived power to do it, as if the values displayed by "the media" differ distinctly from those held by ordinary (non-media) people. Note the singular verb form, for example, used in a recent statement by the governor of a Midwestern state who was criticizing news coverage of a Ku Klux Klan rally on the capitol steps marking Martin Luther King, Jr.'s birthday: "I don't think they'd get much notice unless the media covers it."[1]

If "media" is problematic, "media personnel" is even more so. Clearly, the term refers to much more than newspaper editors, reporters, photographers, and graphic designers and their occupational equivalents in broadcast organizations. Within the communications industry, we might make significant distinctions among newspaper reporters, soap opera actors, book authors, talk show hosts, television camerapersons, trade magazine publishers, advertising promoters, network commentators, sportswriters, or disc jockeys—to name only a few visible, media-related occupational positions—but it is not at all clear that members of the general public make the same distinctions.

Not only is the term "media" inclusive, but it is complicated by the increasing blurring of lines between traditional media forms and functions. Talk show hosts became reporters and newsmakers in their own right in the last presidential election. Infomercials borrow television talk show formats and purvey product attributes as if they were newsworthy. And with the heavy celebrity orientation of the new media, disc jockeys and sportswriters are as likely to relay newsy bits of information to their audiences as persons conventionally considered to be news reporters.

Finally, even within traditional news media, crucial distinctions might be made between those connected with what has been termed the "elite media"—usually referring to the Washington/New York/Los Angeles news and entertainment axis— and the rest of the country. The same stereotypes hardly seem to apply to a newspaper photographer in Carbondale, Illinois, and a Washington political commentator on a Sunday morning television panel discussion, but to members of the media audience, they both are "media personnel."

Simply put, it is difficult to identify nearly a million people working in a variety of "media" occupations under the same stereotypes.[2] This chapter emphasizes the common strands contributing to stereotypical views of persons producing news in the print and broadcast industries.

JOURNALISTS AS STEREOTYPES

Most descriptions of journalists make them colorful people. As M. Parenti pointed out, there have been consistent elements in the Hollywood image of the reporter over the years.

The fedora and typewriter are gone now, and bad coffee comes in Styrofoam instead of cardboard, but the basic stereotypical image remains in recent movies, novels, plays, and television dramatic productions. But the general picture has been updated in others ways—women are as likely to be journalists as men. Megan Carter, Sally Field's character in *Absence of Malice*, is a "relentless investigative reporter" and symbolic of changing gender roles in the 1980s. News employees from under-represented groups are visible in these accounts but usually do not play central or significant roles. Their ages seem to have been reduced, in the sense that stereotyped journalists in these accounts are invariably young, though directed by grayer figures of authority. This observation might reflect demographic changes in the journalistic population, or represent an appeal to the age groups of the movie-going or paperback novel-reading populations.[3]

Journalists traditionally have been stereotyped as seedy and cynical. The seediness is an occupational hazard, a product of chasing tough stories through city streets, knocking cigarrete ashes into the lap during hurried telephone conversations, and writing interview notes on shirt cuffs. This portrait has changed in recent years, especially with the release of movies such as *Broadcast News* about ambitious journalists in the television industry who must, so we should understand, shop in decidedly upscale stores. Exceptions are films about journalists as foreign correspondents, covering events in the world's seamiest trouble spots. Style is definitely out in films such as *Salvador*, *Under Fire*, or *The Year of Living Dangerously*, and James Woods, Nick Nolte, and Mel Gibson must struggle along in sweaty dungarees or military fatigues.

A negative view of the press has been a familiar platform for politicians in recent years, especially those trying to deflect attention from their own records. It is also found in novels. One example is *The Spike*, by de Borchgrave and Moss, which purports to show how the American news media concept of objectivity is used by Soviet disinformation specialists to the disadvantage of Western nations and to blind their citizens to Soviet imperialist ambitions.[4]

Photojournalist Russell Price (Nick Nolte) knowingly fakes a photograph in the film *Under Fire* in Nicaragua, thereby contravening both American interests and journalism ethics, when he violates professional standards and gets personally involved with the war. Playwright Tom Stoppard, a former journalist himself, cataloged the failings of journalism in *Night and Day*, a play about a rebellion in the fictitious African state of Kambawe. Though supporting the concept of free expression in the play, Stoppard's two main journalistic characters are hardened professionals with warped senses of public responsibility. His third journalist, the idealistic young Jacob Milne, is killed chasing a story while his scoop fails to be published because of a journalists' strike.

This stereotype about journalistic values has been reinforced by the publication of many nonfiction works critical of the field. Most notably, Lichter, Rothman, and Lichter studied 238 "elite journalists" working for the *New York Times*, *Washington Post*, *Wall Street Journal*, *Newsweek*, *Time*, *U.S. News and World Report*, ABC, CBS, NBC, and PBS and subtitled their book *America's New Powerbrokers*.[5] In their case, it was not so much that journalists had no values, but that they were the wrong values. The Lichter study found that elite journalists were white (95 percent), male (79 percent), college graduates (93 percent), had incomes above $30,000 (78 percent), were politically liberal (54 percent), and had no listed religious affiliation (50 percent).

Not surprisingly, the Lichter study's profile of elite journalists was amplified by a variety of conservative and Christian authors in reinforcing the stereotype that journalists generally possess liberal values and promote them in their news coverage.

University of Texas journalism Professor Marvin Olasky argued further that we should look beyond the liberal/conservative debate to see how the news media have rejected nineteenth-century spiritual values. He wrote that some conservative reporters are as materialistic as their liberal colleagues: "Non-Christians of both sides tend to give only half the facts."[6]

But others concluded that journalists' relatively low standing in the public's eyes is due to their behavior, rather than their politics, religious beliefs, and lack of values. Tom Goldstein, dean of the School of Journalism at the University of California at Berkeley, argued that "journalists have brought much on this on themselves. They are almost inarticulate on the subject of what they do and why they do it. They often are careless or incompetent, and they acknowledge mistakes reluctantly."[7] And P. Stoler noted that the "war against the press" is not new; it has existed in American politics at least since the time of Jefferson.

PERCEPTIONS AND EXPECTATIONS

It is one of the paradoxes of our time that as public estimation of the news media seemingly drops lower and lower, people apparently spend more and more time and money with media products, watching television, going to movies, buying books, searching electronic information services, and reading newspapers. This use of the media is paralleled by another paradox: that as people and political parties complain more and more loudly about taxation and the size of government, they continue to demand services, re-elect candidates and support decisions that lead to larger public expenditures.

It has become a truism that we live in an era of public distrust of major institutions, not only that of the news media. Until the Clinton/Bush/Perot race, voter turnout had been declining with each continuing election. Criticism of public education has become a major growth industry. Public authorities seem to have lost the capacity to control violence in the nation's cities and towns. Attendance in established churches and membership in traditional religious denominations continue to slide.

In this context, it might be surprising—and even worrying—if the news media, like other public institutions, had not generated stereotypes basically negative in character. Journalist? Politician? Lawyer? As Goldstein pointed out, "as individuals, journalists are probably no more or less ethical than doctors, lawyers, politicians or business executives,"[8] and these fields have encountered similar problems with public trust. What sort of journalism would produce stereotypes totally positive in nature? As seen by the O.J. Simpson murder case, American society in the 1990s seems to be quite capable of creating events that lead to media feeding frenzies with regularity, providing abundant opportunities for public criticism of news obsessions, invasions of privacy, creation of false values—while the nation's viewers remain glued to the television sets.

But stereotypes contain at least an element of truth, and this is one reason that we should pay close attention to them. In the case of the news media, we should examine the size of the discrepancy between the news media's stereotype and their performance. It is one thing to claim that journalists are political liberals or anti-Christian, but quite another to demonstrate that liberal or anti-Christian values determine the content of informational messages journalists produce. What sort of information do we receive from journalists and how ethical are the methods they use to produce it? These are the sorts of questions we should ask of the news media.

Equally, we need to remember the value of a pluralistic media system with a diversity of viewpoints, of a gigantic mixture of media organizations with countless programs, editions, and messages produced. Simple stereotypes can apply to a fraction of the people involved in the media industries, so long as pluralism and diversity can withstand alarming economic drives toward concentration and elimination of competition.

Finally, if it is important to question who watches the watchdog, it also seems important to examine the stereotype of culture's main stereotypers and the often self-serving interests of those constructing it. J. Tebbel argued that it is inevitable that journalists will be considered "liberal" because of the nature of their occupation. "Reporters know what people in public life are really like," writes Tebbel. "They see events in their raw, unvarnished state.[9] The ordinary citizen believes what he wants to believe about public events; the reporter believes what he sees and is able to evaluate what he hears."[10] Ultimately, the news media "ought to pay less attention to their critics, few of whom are worth listening to, and more to improving their product in terms of thoroughness, readability, and accuracy."[11]

32

Media Victims

James W. Brown

> To see life; to see the world; to eye witness great events; to watch the faces of
> the poor and the gestures of the proud; to see strange things—machines,
> multitudes, shadows in the jungle and on the moon . . . to see and take pleasure
> in seeing; to see and be amazed; to see and be instructed.
>
> *The Manifesto of* Life *Magazine, 1936*

> Of Many Hues
> And Many Faces,
> Many Tongues
>   And
>   Many Races;
> All our peoples
>   Truly one:
> We have
>   One Earth,
> Under One Sun!
>   *E. Paul Sechrist, jr., 1994*

Pictures help us understand the world and the people in it. They can take us to the
heights of elation and the depths of despair.

The often-reproduced Dorothea Lange photograph of Florence Thompson, a
migrant mother with despair lined on her face, symbolized the struggle to survive
with little or no resources; Joe Rosenthal's photograph of the flag-raising at Iwo
Jima captured the struggle and the spirit of U.S. soldiers in World War II; W. Eugene
Smith helped define the picture essay form with stories in *Life* magazine on Albert
Schweitzer's work in Africa, the country doctor, and life in a Spanish village.
Gordon Parks, the first African American *Life* photographer, picked the camera as
his weapon to fight discrimination.

Wilson Hicks, the late executive editor of *Life* magazine, wrote about the power
of words and pictures together in journalism.[1] He described the basic unit of

photojournalism as one picture with words. The *Life* magazine that I grew up with was the foundation of the picture story. Photographers and writers worked together on stories; they worked as a team with their editors. Their words and pictures, together, were stronger than either alone.

Just as pictures may educate and inspire us, they may also harm the sensibilities of subjects and viewers. Almost all news pictures have human beings as subjects. Often subjects are shown in difficult circumstances—a daughter grieving for her father who has just perished in a hotel fire, the mother who has just discovered her child, drowned in the backyard swimming pool, a crumpled bicycle that was minutes earlier carrying a happy child down the street, the government official who called a press conference and committed suicide by shooting himself in the head before startled reporters, the man leaping to his death from a bridge. We have seen all of these, and more, as part of the regular press coverage of life and death in America. It's all part of what we have come to expect as news.

We naturally empathize with the victims shown in pictures; we hope that neither we nor our loved ones are ever in similar situations. But readers and viewers often rebel against graphic coverage of gruesome tragedies. Death tends to make events more newsworthy, but people don't want to see too much of the detail of death in their morning paper.

When photographers lack professionalism, their subjects become victims. No professional is born knowing what to do in difficult and fast-moving situations. Under deadline pressure, professionals often don't have the luxury of time to refer to ethics books when working through a decision process. Professionals are human; they make mistakes. But being professionals, they learn from their mistakes.

One of the best places to learn how to be a journalist is as a member of a college newspaper or broadcast station. It is a place to learn about the First Amendment in practice. It is a place to learn from mistakes, and it is a place to learn responsibility. It is a place to practice ethics and to learn news judgment.

A CASE STUDY

A picture published in *The Sagamore*, the student newspaper weekly at Indiana University-Purdue University at Indianapolis (IUPUI), precipitated a period of campus unrest.[2] The facts in the case and the reaction to those facts provide a rich context to think about media victims.

The picture ran six by eight inches on the upper fold of the Monday, October 11, 1993, issue. *The Sagamore* frequently runs a feature picture without a story in that location. The photograph showed a campus police officer frisking a student for possible possession of a handgun. The picture was made on university grounds (public property) outside one of the main classroom buildings on campus.

As pictures go, this one was a simple record of a frisk for a weapon made from about fifteen feet away (too far away for good visual impact). The photographer, Matt Bingham, asked the student being frisked for permission to photograph him for *The Sagamore*. The student, Kay Kay Williams, gave his verbal permission.[3]

A line at the top of the picture read, "Spread 'em." The cutline stated, "Kay Kay Williams was searched for suspicion of possessing a firearm by Alfred C. Paul, IUPD officer."

There are three other pertinent facts surrounding the publication of the picture. A gun was not found. The police officer was Anglo and Williams was African American. In addition, the picture was published six days before a highly publicized

Ku Klux Klan (KKK) rally at the Indiana State House, about six blocks from campus.

What were the issues in this matter? Should the picture have been published? What was the newspaper's obligation to Williams? Was Williams a media victim? Did the picture discredit African Americans as a class?

THE REACTION TO THE PICTURE

By late Monday morning, the day the paper was distributed, the editor in chief of *The Sagamore* and some staff members knew there was a problem. Several students, one representing the Black Student Union, and some faculty voiced anger with the publication of the picture. The campus affirmative action officer, Lillian Charleston, called Patrick McKeand, the faculty publisher of the paper, and alleged the publication of the picture was planned in sympathy with the upcoming KKK rally.[4] Charleston had not interviewed any of the staff but immediately assumed the publication of the picture to be a racist act. Williams, the subject of the picture, spoke with the assistant news editor, Brian Mohr. He admitted granting permission for the photograph, but was displeased with the way in which it was presented. Trent McNeeley, the editor in chief, joined the conversation and asked Williams if he wanted to discuss the matter further. According to McNeeley, Williams had to leave to go to work but gave him a telephone number and asked to be called on the following Thursday.[5]

On Tuesday, McNeeley made the first of three calls to the Black Student Union to discuss the matter. The calls were not returned. In the meantime, newspapers were stolen from distribution sites.

On Wednesday, Williams and members of the Black Student Union were distributing fliers about a rally scheduled for the next day to protest *The Sagamore's* publication of the picture.

On Thursday, McNeeley was called from his office to address a rally of approximately 150 people, in which members of the Black Student Union had been joined by the Black Panther Militia, led by Mmoja Ajabu.[6] Several speakers at the rally called for the resignation of McNeeley.[7] Timothy Langston, dean of students, read a statement at the rally. He said:

It is unfortunate, however, that *The Sagamore* newspaper felt compelled to run the photograph involving police action without any comment on the events or circumstances which were depicted in a photograph. The image does not portray the overall view of student and academic life at this campus that we witness daily. IUPUI is a place where all people meet and work free from intimidation or intrusion. IUPUI is a safe, fair and civil place.

Langston added, "But *The Sagamore* is a newspaper with its own independence and rights that are protected by our commitment to a free press and the U.S. Constitution. We do not agree with their decision to run the photograph, and they have been told of our concern."[8]

Many people attending the rally marched on Chancellor Gerald Bepko's office.[9] When faced with questions about the matter, Bepko replied:

I began this meeting today saying I thought it was despicable and inexplicable and the views of the university administration have been made known to *The Sagamore*. I have not talked to them myself, but others have.[10] We have to look into all of the circumstances and, when we have understood everything that went on, we will make some concluding report and may take some other actions. But I can't prejudge what those would be at this point because we don't know everything.[11]

The protesting group wanted no less than the firing of the photographer, the news editor and the editor.

The Sagamore's advisory board met to discuss the matter. At no time did any member of the board suggest firing or punishing anyone on *The Sagamore* staff. The board reviewed published reports and letters from political groups in Indianapolis, from student organizations and from IUPUI administrators and faculty members stating that the staff's performance was despicable and racist and demanding the dismissal of the editor in chief, the reporter, and the photographer involved. A letter written by Trevor Brown, dean of the system-wide School of Journalism, was sent as a response from the board and the school to Chancellor Bepko. Brown wrote:

We understand how publication of the photograph without context has wounded some and outraged many.
We are also aware that during the past year on college campuses nationally the journalist's impulse to find out and report what's going on has provided a counter-impulse to fire or punish student journalists, to suppress or destroy campus newspapers. The notion that punishment and censorship are cures for even the most egregious error and misjudgment or for unpleasant truths and unpopular opinions is deeply disturbing in a democratic society. It's especially distressing in institutions dedicated to the pursuit of knowledge and truth and to education and learning.
We are educators, not employers. *The Sagamore* is an integral part of students' learning experience, and our responsibility is to ensure that students learn from experience, from error, misjudgment and insensitivity. Their constitutional freedom of speech and press carries with it the responsibility to strive to make sound judgments. It also includes the freedom to make mistakes and the responsibility to learn from them.[12]

The next issue of *The Sagamore* ran a front-page, two column by four inch, boxed clarification that read in part:

The cutline information accompanying the photograph was incomplete. It should have read as follows: 'Kevin (Kay Kay) Williams was searched last week in front of Cavanaugh Hall for suspicion of possessing a firearm by Alfred C. Paul, IUPD officer. No weapon was found and Williams was neither charged nor arrested.'
However, in retrospect, *The Sagamore* editorial staff realizes that the photograph should not even have appeared as a newsfeature photograph, due to the lack of a complete story about the incident.
The photograph was not intended to impugn the reputation of either Williams or Paul, or to portray the African American community in a bad light.[13]

The front-page lead article of the same issue featured a news article with the headline, "Black Student Union protests campus paper." The article was complete in coverage of the issue, the protest, and editor-in-chief McNeeley's public statement at the rally indicating that he had "learned from this experience to be more culturally sensitive." Calls for McNeeley's resignation were fueled by Ajabu who said, "The policy where there is nobody of African heritage as an editor, position of power . . . until that happens there should be some way that the paper should not be able to print."[14]

The editorial for that issue was written by McNeeley. He acknowledged that the cutline should have been more complete and that "Spread 'em" was far too light-hearted for such a photograph.[15] Next to the editorial was an illustration calling for racial harmony with a text line, "Many faces, many races. A time for a change, working together without range."[16] The first of many letters to the editor on the issue was on the same page. While some letters were supportive of the way the paper handled the correction, other letters from several faculty were particularly vitriolic.

A check of the faculty in the School of Journalism indicated that the issue was used as a point of ethical discussion in every class. Additionally, the faculty agreed to develop a case study of the issue that will likely become a classic in the "Race, Gender and the Media" class taught on both the Bloomington and IUPUI campuses of Indiana University. We invited African American journalists from Indianapolis news organizations to meet with the staff of *The Sagamore* and with students in other journalism classes to help them more fully understand the reaction to this situation. We recommended the situation as a session for a planned program on race relations organized by the Indianapolis chapter of the Society for Professional Journalists, which was attended by many of our students.

Monroe Little, director of African American Studies at IUPUI, made accusations about *The Sagamore* and the School of Journalism to the Indianapolis Association of Black Journalists (IABJ), which produced a letter from that organization containing factual errors. Neither Professor Little nor any journalist from the IABJ called any administrator or faculty member from the school to discuss the issue before the letter was written. The letter stated, "Indeed, it almost seems as if *The Sagamore* staff is engaged in a battle of wills—determined not to do the right thing, which would be to admit their error and make steps to correct it."[17] *The Sagamore's* published statements and stories regarding the publication of the picture suggest just the opposite. But it depends on how one defines "error."

Was it an error to publish the picture? No. If there were errors in the publication of the picture of Williams, they were in the context of publication. The line "Spread 'em" was in poor taste. The caption was incomplete. As published, the picture had the potential to harm Williams' reputation. The staff of *The Sagamore* immediately recognized the problem of the incomplete caption and corrected it in the next issue. Should the picture have been published at all given there was no accompanying story and no gun was found? This is a judgment call. I think that the news value of the picture was significantly lowered when no gun was found. But other journalists, whose opinions I respect, saw nothing wrong with the picture except for the incomplete caption. Ultimately, it doesn't matter what I or the publisher or other journalists think about what to publish. *The Sagamore* operates under articles of operation that allow the student editors to make their own judgments about what to publish on the editorial side of the paper. The School of Journalism furnishes a publisher who supervises the business side of the paper. We believe that students should make their own judgments and be responsible for them.

Reporters for *The Sagamore* could have used their resources to report on the issue of gun violence as a social problem and not as a simple police procedure. A possible story angle could have connected the gun search to other acts of campus violence or discrimination at other campuses and our own.[18] All *Sagamore* staff had access to an online information service. Another angle would have been to explore the gun climate in the Indianapolis area. Many high school administrators use metal detectors, on a random basis, at their schools' entrances. Such efforts usually yield a collection of folding razors, switchblades, and hand guns in the shrubbery near the school entrances. Over the school year, a number of teenagers are charged with possession of firearms at school.

The Sagamore staff ran into a phenomenon that is dangerous and antithetical to the First Amendment–they published a picture that was not "politically correct."[19] Never mind that the picture was true; it depicted a member of an under-represented group in a bad light. If news organizations do that—especially campus media—they are labeled at best insensitive, or at worst racist. There seems to be an automatic implication that a picture or story applies to all members of the subject's cultural group. Consequently, colleges and universities have been reacting to special-interest group demands in an effort to be more understanding of diverse groups. But some of these efforts have backfired.

Many colleges and universities have developed restrictive codes intended to prevent critical words and deeds directed toward under-represented groups, including gays, lesbians, various ethnic groups, and women. But the goal of not offending anyone is impossible to achieve. Moreover, codes affecting conduct and speech conflict directly with First Amendment protection of free speech. The University of Michigan's "hate speech" code was struck down by a federal court as being overly broad and in conflict with the First Amendment.[20]

The freedom of speech and expression was not always available. Molefi Kete Asante reminds us that the First Amendment, ratified in 1791, extended freedom of speech to Anglo men only.[21] African slaves were not free men until after the Civil War (1865), and women were not granted the privilege of voting until the Nineteenth Amendment was passed in 1920. The Fourteenth Amendment concerning equal protection under the law has since been extended to all people but was originally ratified in 1868 to prevent holdover abuses of and indignities to Africans after the Civil War. According to Asante, the issue of political correctness causes conflict because it straddles both the First and Fourteenth Amendments. He wrote, "The problem cannot be dealt with adequately except in the context of civility, responsibility, and decency in language." Asante wants the inclusion offer by the Fourteenth Amendment but does not abandon the rights offered by the First Amendment. The real problem is: Who decides what is civil, responsible, and decent? It is a problem that also concerns textbook publishers.

Political correctness was carried to a new level of absurdity when Melvin Mencher's journalism textbook, *News Reporting and Writing*, had pictures censored by the publisher, Brown & Benchmark Publishers.[22] The pictures, which were to appear in a chapter on defining standards of taste, were of a topless woman feeding a man spaghetti in bed and a bulldog sitting on an American flag. Mencher's chapter was sent to five journalism professors for review. Four of the five feared the woman feeding the man spaghetti might prompt sexual harassment charges. One reviewer suggested simply describing the pictures. Not to have pictures that aid in the discussion of standards of taste in a textbook chapter meant to teach future journalists about such standards is ludicrous. That professors would feel threatened by sexual harassment charges from classroom discussion of journalistic standards indicates that political correctness has eroded academic freedom and chilled discussion of important issues in journalism education.

Bad ideas should be driven away with more speech, not less. Sheila Suess Kennedy, director of the Indiana Civil Liberties Union, describes the idea of more speech driving out bad speech as her "refrigerator" theory of free speech:

When you put a leftover in the back corner of the refrigerator, it gets green and moldy and it stinks. But when you put the same leftover out in the strong sunlight, it bleaches out and doesn't smell so bad. That is what our founders decided was best. When you try to suppress ideas that you don't like, they fester and mold and stink up the whole works.[23]

If we try to second-guess every word we write and every image we make as to whether we have offended some person or group, we practice pabulum journalism. Journalism becomes banal and inane. Indeed, editorial cartoonists could not exist; neither could editorial writers. Investigative journalists would have nothing to investigate and photojournalists would shoot nothing but head shots.

HAS POLITICAL CORRECTNESS AFFECTED THE NEWSROOM?

Efforts to diversify the newsroom have increased the diversity of the reporting ranks. Journalists are also splitting themselves into special interests that bear strong resemblance to the special interests found on college campuses. There are organizations for African Americans, Latino, Asian Americans, and Native American journalists. There are several organizations for women journalists and there is the National Lesbian and Gay Journalists' Association.[24] Each organization exists because it feels its particular membership cannot be adequately served by an umbrella organization concerned only with issues of journalism.

Another case study

When O.J. Simpson appeared in a preliminary hearing to determine if he should stand trial for the murder of his former wife, Nicole Brown Simpson, and her friend, Ronald Goldman, images of his case flooded the media as never before. A total of 95 million people watched, on live television, the police chase (some have call it a motorcade) of Simpson on a Los Angeles freeway. A *New York Times* graphic compared the preemptive coverage of the chase by ABC, CBS, and NBC to other important events.[25] ABC coverage of the chase was two hours and seventeen minutes; CBS interrupted regular programs for two hours and twenty-five minutes; NBC gave only five minutes to its coverage.[26] The Nixon funeral warranted only thirty-five minutes or less preemptive coverage by the networks. The January 17 Los Angeles earthquake, the worst natural disaster in the history of the United States, ranged from zero to thirty minutes. The Clinton press conference on Somalia of June 17, 1993, received zero coverage on two networks and five minutes on the other. Why did NBC show restraint by covering the police chase for a shorter time than the other networks? NBC was televising Game 5 of the NBA championship series that night. To switch to the Simpson chase would have angered millions of viewers and would have lost premium advertising revenue.

Another image of Simpson will be fodder for journalism ethics classes of the future. Both *Newsweek*[27] and *Time*[28] ran the same picture as a cover—a police mugshot of a tired O.J. Simpson. But the two covers conveyed vastly different visual messages. *Time* sent the image to an artist to convert it to an illustration. The artist darkened his cheeks and generally made the picture much more low key by using darker tones. The effect produced a more sinister and destitute look from the blank stare of the police mug shot. Although *Time* labeled the picture an "illustration," the magazine received a lot of much-deserved criticism.

Has the video image of the police chase and the *Time* cover harmed Simpson's chance for a fair trial? We may never know the answer to that question. But his celebrity as football legend, movie actor, sports commentator, and spokesman for Hertz rental cars has propelled this case into a level of unparalleled coverage.

California allows cameras in the courtroom so the public can get all the coverage it can stand. All the networks have hired their own legal experts to comment on every aspect of the hearing. "Entertainment Tonight" (ET) sent a reporter to cover the trial. The local Fox affiliate showed up to tape the ET reporter performing his job. CNN arrived to shoot the Fox affiliate shooting the ET reporter. By holding a mirror to a mirror to a mirror, one wonders if the causes of truth, justice, and fairness are being served. But this is show biz, featuring a better plot than any of the daytime soap operas the hearing interrupts.

CONCLUSION

The qualities of pictures that may cause harm—immediacy, impact, and emotion—are also their greatest assets. Pictures have the power to inform and persuade. Working together with words, they make a strong unit of communication. But they may also harm and insult people. The harm may be intentional or unintentional. The goal of the journalist is to inform the mass audience, responsibly. Journalists are given a First Amendment right to do so. But who defines that standard by which they try to act responsibly? A professional listens to her head and heart and not the rhetoric of politically correct speech. A journalist knows and evaluates the political agendas of various cultural groups and learns who will be friendly when a report is in their favor and who will be angry when it isn't.

Censorship is not the answer. The First Amendment gives journalists the right to make a statement with words and images about what they believe—even when that statement is disliked by others. Journalists should not be bound by artificial boundaries of what some people believe to be politically correct. Journalists ought to be able to write about what they think and photograph what they see. It's the only style of communication that is honest. It's the only communication that makes sense.

PART VIII

CONCLUSION

33

Images That Heal

J. B. Colson

What do media images that heal, that serve the opposite function to pictorial stereotypes that injure, look like? There is a logical question for a text that discusses media stereotypes so thoroughly, from so many points of view, but a difficult question with less certain answers than the business of deciding what imagery injures.

Stereotypes are, by definition, easy to identify. Complaints by those who feel injured or who see potential injury for others are easy to gather. But where are we to find the responses from those who say "that media image made me feel good?"

A national call was put requesting submission of "photographs that portray traditionally stereotyped members of cultural groups in positive, non-stereotypical ways."[1] The goal was to identify and discuss photography that has a positive potential.

There was almost no response. Is there really so little interest in this issue? Or should we accept that there were only a handful of submissions because of the obvious practical problems including, but not limited to: the message didn't reach enough people, everyone was busy with more promising and important enterprises, most photographers want (and deserve) more than a by-line in payment for their efforts.

Without discounting these probabilities, I want to suggest that inherent difficulty in the concept of "positive images of traditionally stereotyped people" may also have deterred potential contributors, and deserves discussion. While this phrasing is a good deal more modest in its request than "Images that Heal," it, too, calls for some significant assumptions about uncertain issues in photographic communication.

CLARITY ABOUT STEREOTYPES

Although some imagery is obviously injurious, it would be surprising if anyone who has read through this diverse and thoughtful set of writings did not at some points think to herself, "I never thought of that," and elsewhere, perhaps, "I don't agree with that." With both a lack of awareness and a lack of agreement at stake, we are less than clear in many cases about what constitutes injury and what serves to heal.

The Difficulty of Interpreting Photographic Connotation

Vicki Goldberg puts it well in her book, *The Power of Photography*: "Photographs are mute artifacts. They do not speak but can only be interpreted, and interpretation is a notoriously tricky game."[2] She explains that one reason we are so easily fooled into believing we understand photography is that we carry over the ease with which we can read its denotation into the much less certain business of connotation. Does a photograph of a disabled person performing an everyday task with effort honor that person or victimize his condition? Details in the image itself (such as camera angles and facial expressions) can certainly influence our interpretations, but usually not as much as our attitudes and expectations will influence them.

Presentation Context Directs Interpretation

Few photographs are presented without words of explanation. Titles, cutlines, headlines, and text regularly come with photography. Because the connotation of photographs is so uncertain, these words exert a great deal of force on interpretation. Change the words and you change the apparent meaning of the image and thereby also help determine its social effect.

Other important aspects of presentation context include the expectations for the specific media used (the *New York Times* versus supermarket tabloids), and image size and placement (front page versus buried inside).

We See Our Own Projections in Photographs

One of the most thoughtful and interesting books about how photographs communicate is Roland Barthes' *Camera Lucida*.[3] Central to this work of philosophical musing is a photograph of Barthes' mother, about which he says in a point of irony as well as honesty: "I cannot reproduce the Winter Garden Photograph. It exists only for me. For you, it would be nothing but an indifferent picture, one of the thousand manifestations of the 'ordinary'" (p. 73). A matter of indifference to us, but a keystone to the nature of photography for Barthes. The difference is what he brings to the image.

That uncertainty of connotation inherent in photography, to the extent that it is not directed by presentation context, is open to influence by our personal knowledge and attitudes. Regarding reactions to stereotyping, it is assumed that members of a stereotyped group will have a common negative reaction, based on their common experience as members of that group. If the corollary of that were true, only members of that group would effectively appreciate imagery showing them well, what we could hope were images that heal. This is probably true at least some of the time, but need not deny a larger appreciation of showing human diversity realistically.

Just run down the list of titles in the table of contents for this book; how many of these types do you *not* identify with? If it is difficult for us to consider stereotyping from the point of view of so many groups, it is even less likely that we can imagine the diverse personal psychology involved in responses to images.

Separation of Photographers from Viewers

Several writers in this book have noted the need for more diversity among media practitioners. The low percentages of African Americans, Latinos, and women in key media positions do not contribute to an understanding of their needs and attitudes. As this book demonstrates, we have many other identifiable and significant subcultures to know about and honor. In addition to typical differences in subcultures for producers and consumers of media, by the nature of mass media there is little chance for them to interact. To produce messages for media is to be distanced from the viewers of those messages. In closer social contexts, discussion with skill and good motivation can convert injury into healing, a process not available to most involved with mass media.

To produce media is also to be part of media subgroups, each with its own values, attitudes, and operating sociology. Newspaper photojournalists, for example, have quite different values and working methods than news writers, but both groups tend to respect deadlines, bylines, and peer group approval, so do writers and photographers for magazines, who, as a group, are defined by some important working differences from newspaper people. The issue of struggle for success in peer group terms often results in media professionals working to quite different standards than the public uses to judge their images. The dramatic angles and stunning moments of prize winners may be difficult to read or offensive to an everyday viewing public.

SOME IMAGES CONSIDERED

[Note: The photographs are printed at the end of this chapter.]

1. "Kelly Rose, left wing for Northeastern University Women's Ice Hockey Team, during 1989-90 season." Laura Gaccione, graduate student, Northeastern University.
Here is a straightforward example of a woman in a non-stereotypical situation. As with most photographs, we are left to trust the caption for information, but the name on the jacket helps authenticate the picture. Would we be more convinced of her atypical role by a play action shot? Is a female university team member playing ice hockey less stereotypical than one playing volleyball?
As a result of Title IX, which called for equity between men's and women's sports, there were many changes in campus athletics and increased opportunities for women athletes. The photographer notes that the Northeastern team, whose players largely came from the Boston area, won a silver medal in the first women's World Ice Hockey Championship (held in 1990), but received no coverage in Boston newspapers.
2. "Roanoke City police officer helps a lady from her over turned car after an auto accident. The lady was not hurt, but she didn't like being on her side, and there was fear of fire." Wayne Deel, *Roanoke Times & World-News*.
Police officers apprehending African Americansuspects constitute one of the most noted and complained-about stereotypes of news media. Here is a group of police helping a African-American woman. Does this positive gesture help counteract negative stereotypes? If the subject were an African American male, might we think a fugitive was being apprehended?

3. "Believing themselves descendants of the Levites, the musicians of the Bible, members
   of the Aaronic Order in Utah place equal weight on Old and New Testament teachings.
   They connote that theological union by using both a Cross and Menorah in their Sabbath
   services." Craig Denton, University of Utah.
   Craig Denton writes earlier in Chapter 30 about the complexities and misuse of religious
   symbolism. Here he provides an example of treating religious experience and symbolism
   with respect.
   Mass media, he notes, are reluctant to deal with religion as a general topic (outside of special religious sections), unless something or someone connected with religion has been
   propelled into news, usually in a negative way. To what extent are we and other viewers
   interested in the quiet kind of respectful image of someone else's religion that he shows us?
   By choosing a relatively little-known religious group, is he categorizing it as an oddity or
   honoring it?
4. through 7. Selection of four portraits from the exhibition "Portraits of People." Simon Fulford, free-lance photographer, Brooklyn, New York.
   With the stated goal of facilitating "the integration of people with developmental disabilities into our communities," Fulford chose the format of simple portraiture rather than activity shots that more directly show disability. His exhibition was sponsored by the New
   Jersey Developmental Disabilities Council. In the full group of the exhibition there are
   some faces quite distorted by disability and some in which the idea of disability is not suggested visually.
   His photograph of the tattooed man is especially interesting because some of its connotation, at least, seems as direct as its denotation. This is a tough and physically fit man with
   an assertive attitude. What we cannot imagine here, as in most still photography, is the
   story that explains what we see and makes it special. Fulford writes that this man is a Vietnam veteran who spent "two bed-ridden years before rehabilitating himself through martial
   arts."
   Exhibition is a significant and under-appreciated media. Some exhibitions are seen by
   far more people than most local newspapers. With the exception of books, there are few
   other opportunities for photographers to present as much work at one time or to be as personal in their work as in an exhibition.
   Because the realm of exhibition has traditionally presented fine art, it is especially useful
   to point to it here, where the discussion of media concentrates on the genres of journalism,
   entertainment, and advertising. In fact, there is a good deal of descriptive and social documentary work presented in museums and galleries, and there is a good deal of exhibition
   in more democratically public places. It is an often missed opportunity for presentation of
   images that heal.
   However, in the realm of art, and by extension, exhibition, even when the work presented
   is not intended as fine art, uncertainty and multiplicity of interpretation are encouraged.
   For journalism and advertising there is an assumption that directness, clarity, and ease of
   interpretation are virtues. Does this expectation of certainty in media photography contribute to its presenting stereotypes? Is the exhibition context of Fulford's portraits enough
   to ensure a response appropriate to his intentions?
8. "Cahuila Bird Singers, the song cycle recapitulates the creation of the world and symbolically restores its original harmony." John Bishop, independent documentary film producer, Los Angeles.
   From the book *California Artists: At the Crossroads*, published by the California Arts
   Council Traditional Folk Arts Program, this photograph honors an effort to keep alive the
   language, songs, and rituals of California Indians.
   Does it violate a caution by Lucy Ganje in her Chapter 7 on Native American stereotypes
   to avoid "imaging that places Native people only in the past?" Although the dancers are
   not in traditional regalia, they are performing traditional ceremony. This may be a fair
   question only if the presentation is considered as a single image in mass media, rather than
   part of a group in a project devoted to ethnographic art. Context often determines the likelihood that an image will injure.
9. "Dallas, 1976." Paul Martin Lester, California State University, Fullerton.
   As Lester notes in his introduction to this text, possible categories for discussion as media
   stereotypes are far more than one book can cover. A group without its own chapter that
   has currency today is the homeless. Among common stereotypes of the homeless are un-
   kempt appearance, drunkenness, begging, and visual treatment in which the subjects are
   obviously at the mercy of the photographer (as in stolen candids, looking down, photo-

graphs obviously against the will of the subject, and so on).

While there is no surety without more specific cutline information of the social situation we are seeing here, there are interesting contrasts in Lester's picture of an African-American man seated on the street in front of the legs of standing men. His position and the wrinkled paper sack next to him indicate that he may be a street person. But he appears neat, dressed in a good shirt and sports jacket. He is wearing a kind of turban with a decorative pin, and he holds close to his chest, as if to emphasize for the camera, a braided cross that he is wearing around his neck. The camera has been lowered to his level, and looks directly into an enigmatic expression, perhaps sad, perhaps challenging, that at least is not deranged. What can we reasonably assume about the subject of this picture? Has Lester treated him with respect?

10. "The Power of Absolutes: a group of friends at World Youth Day, Denver, 1993." Glenn McGaha Miller, Fort Collins, Colorado.

Jack Nelson writes in Chapter 20 that "a major problem with a disability is the lack of understanding of others." If mainstreaming disabled youth in school can succeed in creating understanding and acceptance by peers, we will have begun to mitigate that problem. Does this photograph indicate that process is underway? Will photographs like this help the process?

11.–12. "Alex held by his mother in his hospital room. Alex with mask and IV at the hospital." Bruce Jordan, graduate student, University of Texas at Austin, from a documentary on Alex's experience with cancer and its impact on his family.

In Chapter 18 Kathy Brittain McKee writes about contemporary children who are depicted as adults. She also writes about children who are stereotyped as victims. The victims are usually starving children from underdeveloped and far away places, while the little adults are usually upper middle-class Anglo Americans. A child like Alex, suffering from long-term cancer and its treatment, is another kind of victim. Pictured in his mother's arms, his suffering and his need for adult help is apparent. (Her suffering is indicated elsewhere in Jordan's documentary.) However, in a happier moment, "Alex with mask and IV" shows him behaving somewhat playfully, in spite of his attachment to chemotherapy and his location in a hospital. Does showing his trauma present him as victim and overplay a call for sympathy? Does showing his playfulness unrealistically make him a little hero? Are the two pictures together an adequate challenge to a simplistic representation of Alex's difficult and complex life as a child with cancer?

13. "Eileen and Kim spend most of the evening with Caitlin and their dogs. Their backyard is a two-year-old's paradise. Kim remarked that she wouldn't ever want to be a single parent because it would be too much work. They alternate tasks like making lunch, doing dishes, and putting Caitlin to bed." Kristine Wolff, graduate student, University of Texas at Austin, from a personal documentary on a lesbian couple raising a child together, part of a series on nontraditional families.

In her discussion in Chapter 13 of how unrealistic childbirth and parenting magazines are in their representations of families, Dona Schwartz notes: "The images of mothers illustrating both editorial and advertising copy evoke a world of blissful, predominantly Anglo, dual-parent childrearing." In Wolff's twist on this convention, a biological mother and her female partner do the dual-parent childrearing. Stereotypes of what constitutes family, of mothering, and of lesbianism are all challenged in this image. How successful can social documentation be in familiarizing us with the real lives of others we may not understand? Can non-stereotypical imagery play a useful role in lessening prejudices and our use of stereotypes?

14. "Patricia and Mike Rose with their granddaughter Samantha, 1991. In 1994 the Roses won the custody case which made Samantha theirs." Kristine Wolff, graduate student, University of Texas at Austin, from a personal documentary on grandparents raising a child, part of a series on non-traditional families.

Having raised five children, the Roses had hoped to relax some in their later years, but felt compelled to provide a home for Samantha when both the child's mother and their own son proved too irresponsible for the task. There are a variety of ways in which our society is pressing people who are older than usual into parenting roles. Will the realistic documentation of families that don't fit the ideals of advertising and illustration make us more open and accepting of alternative social arrangements? Will our respect for the capacity of older people be enhanced by images of them fulfilling what are normally more youthful roles?

15.–16. "SHOPPING. Kristi grew up in a middle class suburban household and graduated from college with a degree in East Asian studies. Her life took a detour when she became pregnant with Joslyn, her first child. At 27 she is a single mother of two struggling to subsist on welfare. Viewed as a natural appendage of middle-class mothers, a car is beyond Kristi's financial reach. She goes to the grocery store via city bus juggling goods and children. A chore that seems a bother to many women demands extraordinary effort from mothers like Kristi." "EATING. Kristi's life is defined by the needs of her children. A calendar posted on the refrigerator reminds her of the daily schedule, though she rarely consults it. Included on the list is an admonition to devote some time to herself. 'Sometimes when I go for a few days without talking to another adult human being I kinda go bonkers . . . . I'm OK not having people around us all the time, but on the other hand I do occasionally need people. I do feel kind of isolated sometimes.'" From a documentary series by Dona Schwartz, University of Minnesota.

Welfare mothers are a target of scorn and the center of angry discussions about what is wrong with welfare, government, and society.

Families are often pointed to as the basic unit of society. Many of us in adulthood realize how much we are the product of the families that raised us, and how hard it is to really understand what that means. References to family are often loaded with strong feelings. Long before the political currency of "family values" as we have it now, family was a major theme in media.

Here as with the lesbian couple, we are confounding several stereotypes at once. We are far from the make-believe images that advertising and so much media illustration give us. Schwartz makes her camera a participant in this woman's struggle to fulfill the responsibilities of motherhood on meager resources. But how interested is the general public in the beauty and the hardship of real lives? How interested are any of us in using media to confront honest human experience and to enhance our understanding of social issues rather than to confirm our expectations and prejudices? To what extent would we rather be entertained than informed by our media?

RIGHTS AND RESPONSIBILITIES OF MEDIA PARTICIPANTS

In its innocent form, imagery that injures is the result of ignorance. As malicious enterprise, it is about the abuse of power. If not ignorance and not malice, it is the result of placing values such as visual impact or the public's right to know over the feelings of people as individuals and members of groups and it will cause injury. These value judgments may or may not be ethically appropriate (and therefore justifiable, as discussed by Deni Elliott), but in all cases of social injury due to the depiction of people, ethics are at stake.

Informed communicators with positive ethical motivations are needed if we are to replace stereotypes in significant numbers with images that heal. The victims of stereotypes need to do what they can in their part of the process by calling stereotypes to task and supporting efforts in their behalf. But, because most of the power is in the hands of the image makers and those who finance them, *they* have the responsibility of producing media that recognizes the diversity and complexity of human experience.

Kelly Rose, left wing for Northeastern University Women's Ice Hockey Team, during 1989–90 season. Photo by Laura Gaccione, graduate student, Northwestern University

Roanoke city police officer helps a lady from her overturned car after an auto accident. The lady was not hurt, but she didn't like being on her side, and there was fear of fire. Photo by Wayne Deel, *Roanoke Times & World-News*

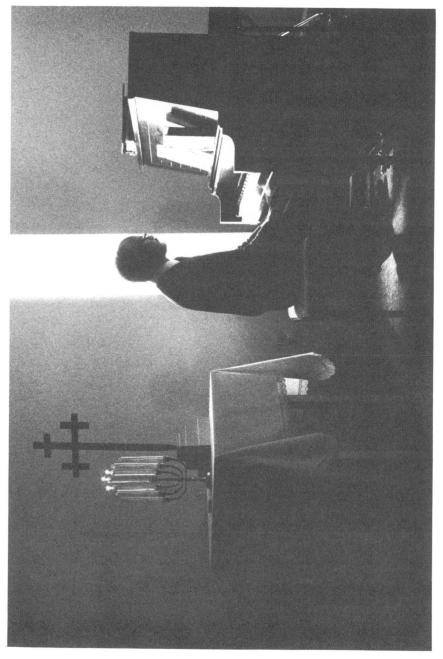

Believing themselves descendants of the Levites, the musicians of the Bible, members of the Aaronic Order in Utah place equal weight on Old and New Testament teachings. They convey that theological union by using both a Cross and Menorah in their Sabbath services.
Photo by Craig Denton, University of Utah

Selection from the exhibition "Portraits of People." Photo by Simon Fulford, Brooklyn, New York

Selection from the exhibition "Portraits of People." Photo by Simon Fulford, Brooklyn, New York

Selection from the exhibition "Portraits of People." Photo by Simon Fulford, Brooklyn, New York

Selection from the exhibition "Portraits of People." Photo by Simon Fulford, Brooklyn, New York

Cahuila Bird Singers. The song cycle recapitulates the creation of the world and symbolically restores its original harmony. Photo by John Bishop, independent documentary film producer, Los Angeles

Dallas, 1976. Photo by Paul Martin Lester, California State University, Fullerton

The Power of Absolutes: A group of friends at World Youth Day, Denver, 1993. Photo by Glenn McGaha Miller, Fort Collins, Colorado

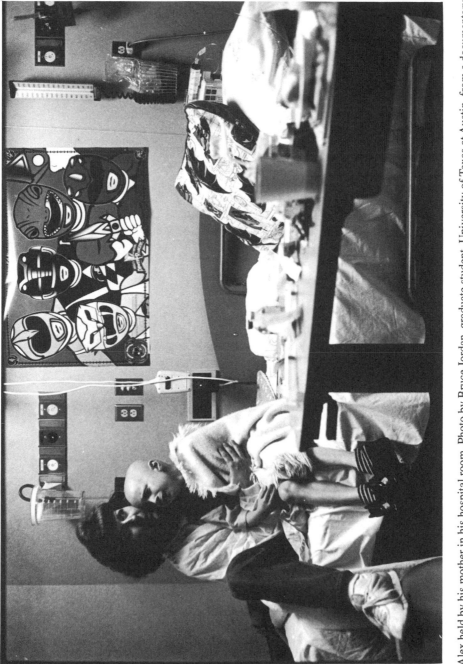

Alex held by his mother in his hospital room. Photo by Bruce Jordan, graduate student, University of Texas at Austin, from a documentary on Alex's experience with cancer and its impact on his family

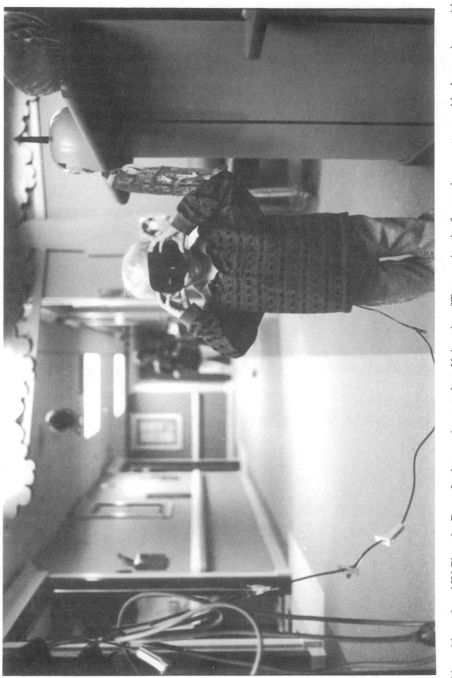

Alex with mask and IV. Photo by Bruce Jordan, graduate student, University of Texas at Austin, from a documentary on Alex's experience with cancer and its impact on his family

Eileen and Kim spend most of the evening with Caitlin and their dogs. Their backyard is a two-year-old's paradise. Kim remarked that she wouldn't ever want to be a single parent because it would be too much work. They alternate tasks like making lunch, doing dishes, and putting Caitlin to bed. Photo by Kristine Wolff, graduate student, University of Texas at Austin, from a personal documentary on a lesbian couple raising a child together, part of a series on nontraditional families

Patricia and Mike Rose with their granddaughter Samantha, 1991. In 1994 the Roses won the custody case that made them Samantha's guardian. Photo by Kristine Wolff, graduate student, University of Texas at Austin, from a personal documentary on grandparents raising a child, part of a series on nontraditional families

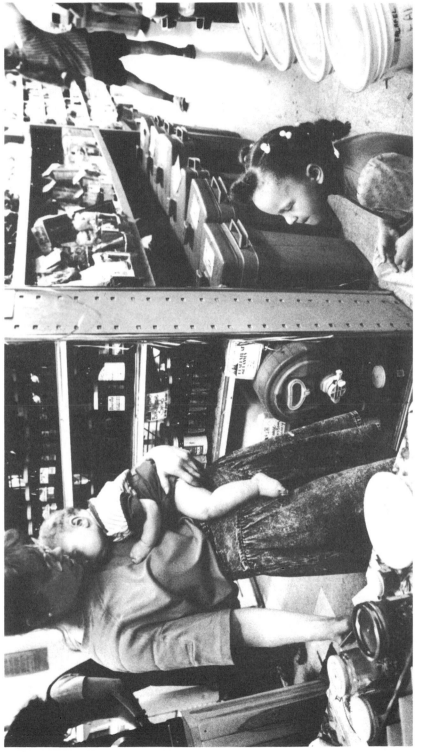

Shopping. Kristi grew up in a middle-class suburban household and graduated from college with a degree in East Asian studies. Her life took a detour when she became pregnant with Joslyn, her first child. At 27 she is a single mother of two, struggling to subsist on welfare. Although considered a natural appendage of middle-class mothers, a car is beyond Kristi's financial reach. She goes to the grocery store via city bus, juggling goods and children. A chore that is merely bothersome to many women demands extraordinary effort from mothers like Kristi. From a documentary series by Dona Schwartz, University of Minnesota

235

Eating. Kristi's life is defined by the needs of her children. A calendar posted on the refrigerator reminds her of the daily schedule, although she rarely consults it. Included on the list is an admonition to devote some time to herself. "Sometimes when I go for a few days without talking to another adult human being I kinda go bonkers. . . . I'm OK not having people around us all the time, but on the other hand I do occasionally need people. I do feel kind of isolated sometimes." From a documentary series by Dona Schwartz, University of Minnesota

34

Common Ground and
Future Hopes

Clifford G. Christians

> Sticks and stones may break my bones, but words will never hurt me.

This old saw could not be more wrong and destructive. Telling kids to ignore taunting peers is good advice in one sense, of course. But as these chapters document across the board, cruel names and distorted pictures attack our very being. They go for the jugular emotionally. Stereotypes shrivel our humanity. This book's high-level worrying about images that injure is not marginal to media studies, but central to them.

In their own way, the authors presume and exemplify a philosophy of symbolic communication. They stake a powerful claim for symbol theory, though their intentions may be elsewhere. Representational forms matter in a symbolic view; these chapters demonstrate how and why. The contributors share a commitment to social justice, but on a deeper level their common ground is epistemological. They each drive a nail in the coffin of mainstream empiricism. Communication ethicists are served with an encyclopedia of material, but the field as a whole benefits also. Stereotypes are a laboratory for examining how symbols function.

MAINSTREAM EMPIRICISM

In the received view, knowledge is built up and communicated brick by brick. The aim is clarity and efficiency in the message. Democratic societies protect it by a sacred First Amendment. We call it the stimulus-response model and go after the in-between, calibrating it empirically, insisting on a feedback loop, and quantifying the noise in the channel. It presumes the Enlightenment's fact-value dichotomy. The statistically sophisticated are assigned the heavy lifting, putting message systems into mathematical form in order to advance scientific prediction and control. In this perspective, ethical questions are left along the fringes for those with divine wisdom or hot-tempered moralists and quasi-academics.

Out of inertia or lethargy, the majority of communication scholars have assumed a priestly role as guardians of the empiricist view; they are busy, in Thomas Kuhn's terms, doing normal science.[1] Most research money still supports studies that measure observable behavior, finding in such results the precision they desire. Meanwhile, some scholars seek more elaborate and finely tuned procedures, more complex multivariate scales, faster computer banks, and longer-range experiments. It is hoped that improved methods will eliminate the remaining weaknesses.

The accomplishments of the mainstream paradigm are worth noting. We understand more clearly now the significance of audience demographics. Some differences among the media—their varying purposes and potential—have been stipulated. Media messages can be delivered today with greater impact. We speak more informatively about stimulus variables, perception, and attitude change. Sociometric scales have forced explicitness—about the way children read the television text, for instance.

But a paradigm shift is occurring in media studies these days, as in the social sciences generally. A growing number among us sense deeply that the field of communications needs a fresh theoretical foundation and a more solid set of intellectual questions. A watershed change to interpretativeness is under way. Consequently, many theorists recognize that an outdated model happily marrying political and commercial concerns, although revered by the engineering mentality found in the prestigious sciences, has just about accomplished its potential. A noted insider, Joseph Klapper himself regretted that after years at the "inexhaustible fount of variables," a systematic description of effects and their predictive applications "becomes the more distant as it is the more vigorously pursued."[2] The received view is breaking up beneath our feet and the protest grows.

In spite of good intentions and Herculean effort, communication scholars witness an ever-lengthening agenda of unresolved issues. The received view has produced an elegant handling of details, but today's issues demand a different statement of problems and theoretical inventiveness. The technically rigid left-to-right transportation model appears congenitally inadequate for the broader problems that trouble us now. Equipped with a method, we are producing mountains of information, but we lack a conceptual framework that provides connections and perspective.

The common view is a friendly companion and has a blue-ribbon pedigree reaching deep into Enlightenment maestros. But it doesn't pound on academic doors with much authority any more. There are bigger fish to fry. The mechanistic definition of communication is unhelpful when the overarching issues of this volume are at stake—multiculturalism, visual thinking, and dehumanization, for example. Cramped into Enlightenment parameters, the transportation model is little more than the crumbs left over by sociology, psychology, economics, and linguistics.

We now recognize that mathematical theories of communication are a human invention and not a body of objective truths, as the Enlightenment mistakenly assumed. Though the scientific method made stupendous gains in the natural world, generating empirically testable causal explanations, territorialists correctly insist that the quantitative motif ought not overwhelm the study of society as well. Paul Feyerabend has documented that scientific study is itself conditioned by belief systems and ideological commitments. Indeed, the repudiation of Scientism has been carried forward by a broad range of scholarship, from the Frankfurt School to Karl Popper. The epistemological foundation of social science is being re-established wholesale—over against Auguste Comte (1798-1859), who founded the new discipline "sociology" on the natural-scientific model.

SYMBOLIC THEORY

Interpretive research in the Counter-Enlightenment mode seeks insightful pictures rather than lawlike abstractions through fixed procedures. Parsimonious generalizations are still important, as they have been since William of Ockham, but only if arising from a fully developed introspective capacity—as Herbert Blumer calls it, from a poetic resonance with the data.[3] The interpretive turn recovers the fact of human agency, that is, intentions, purposes, and values. Interpretive research, in Clifford Geertz's words, "enlarges the universe of human discourse" and expands the horizons of human existence by making publicly available the manner in which "others have guarded their sheep."[4] Interpretive studies catch hold of the ambulation of history, self-consciously avoiding the assumption that social phenomena are autonomous creations arising by spontaneous combustion.

In communication theory, the Counter-Enlightenment option was established by the Italian philologist Giambattista Vico, who refused to be hoist on the Cartesian petard. His philosophy of expressivism was a brilliant achievement, contradicting the dominant doctrine of rational mind. This professor of rhetoric at the University of Naples (1699-1741) placed image over concept, language over mathematics, the mythopoetic over facts and fantasia over logic. His highly original theory of imaginative universals was a fundamental assault on the raging tide of his age.

The symbolic motif is nurtured in the ninteenth century by Wilhelm Dilthey's *Erlebnis*, Frederick Schleiermacher's *Hermeneutik*, August Schleicher's *Comparative Grammer*, Jacob Burckhart's *Civilization of the Renaissance in Italy* (1860), and George Simmel's *Problems of Philosophy of History* (1892). And it establishes definitive form in an intellectual trajectory from Ferdinand De Saussure's *Course in General Linguistics* (1916) to Ernst Cassirer's mighty three-volume *Philosophy of Symbolic Forms* (1925). For Cassirer, symbolization is not merely the hallmark of human cognition; our representational capacity defines us anthropologically. Cassirer titles his summary monograph *An Essay on Man*. He identifies our unique capacity to generate symbolic structures as a radical alternative to animal rationale that has been established since classical Greece and to the biological being of evolutionary naturalism. Arguing that the issues are fundamentally anthropological rather than epistemological per se, Cassirer's creative being is carved out against a reductionism to intellectus on the one hand, and a naturalistic neurophysiology on the other.

Cassirer collapses the hoary differences among human symbolic systems. Music, art, philosophical essays, mathematics, religious language, and Bacon's scientific method are placed on a level playing field as all symbolic constructs. James Carey calls it the ritual view—rituals as ceremonies or sacraments in which we define meaning and purpose, events of celebration (graduation, weddings, birthdays) and not merely exchanges of information.[5] In this book's effort to grapple with ethics while shifting from print to the visual, we finally feel at home theoretically.

Symbol is the critical concept. What atom is to physical science and cell to biology, symbol is for communication. Cultures are interconnections of symbolic forms, those fundamental units of meaning expressed in words (mention "power" and notice the range of affective responses), gestures (a clenched fist, for example), and graphics (swastikas or a cross burned on the lawn). Realities called "cultures" are inherited and built from symbols that shape our action, identity, thoughts, and sentiment. Communication, therefore, is the creative process of building and reaffirming through symbols. Culture signifies the constructions that result.

Human behavior, in this vision, is symbolic action—action signifying something, as does phonation in speech, pigment in paintings, sonance in music. Our world is an intricate series of piled-up inference and implication. A twitch of the eye is more than a contracting eyelid and may actually be a mischievous wink or indicate a conspiracy. News reading thus becomes a dramatic act. Readers face, not pure information, but a drama; contending forces are portrayed, nudging one another into patriotism, class antagonisms, resentments, or crusading support. Speak the verbal symbol "death" and listeners will provide their own range of understanding: cessation of brain waves or heart beat, a disembodied soul meeting God, or separation from a human community.

Our differing definitions reflect diverse values and social purposes. Humans stitch together views of the world to orient themselves and provide social cohesion. We take pieces of cloth and demand that they be respected as our national emblem. Bread signifies Jesus' body, water purifies from wickedness, and "dogs" become despicable persons. Although not identical to that which they symbolize, symbols participate in their meaning and power; they share the significance of that to which they point. In addition, they illuminate their referents so as to make them transparent; they permit us to express levels of reality that otherwise remain hidden. Symbols open up the human spirit where our world views are inscribed.

A symbolic theory of communication recognizes human creativity as this species' distinctive feature. Creative beings do not merely exist in a vast museum, but are their own curators. Their environments are not coded genetically (as with animal instinct), but organized symbolically without end. Homo sapiens is the only species that cooks its food; no balanced diets are built into the genes. Instincts produce perennially identical beaver dams and ant hills; cultures are developed and imagined, always transcending biological necessity. Humankind organizes and enlarges its environment; the porpoise cannot. Humans readily displace both time and space; animals act only when stimuli are in fact present. We possess the creative imagination to describe experience, evaluate action, and transmit ideas for public discussion. Animals demonstrate none of these traits.

Consistent with the perspective of this book, I appropriate here a semiotic definition. In contrast to anthropology, where culture refers to entire civilizations as complex wholes, and in contrast to common parlance, where culture is identified as refined manners, symbolic theories of culture concentrate on representational forms. Most definitions of culture (certainly those fostered by anthropology) are expansive, encompassing under the term virtually all social activity. Culture is thus said to involve technologies, customs, arts, sciences, products, habits, and political and social organizations that characterize a people. I find the broad definition inchoate and distinguish culture from political and social structures, from direct efforts to understand nature (such as chemistry, physics, astronomy), and from religious institutions. Culture thus becomes essentially our communicative activities and refers primarily to the products of the arts and language. Images that injure can thus be examined fruitfully, without including all types of harm to the innocent within the research frame. The semiotic focus of this volume follows in the legacy of Jacob Burckhart.

Language is the marrow of community, the public agent through which our identity is realized. H. Richard Niebuhr recognized that persons are displayed, made accessible, nurtured, and integrated into social units through symbol, myth, and metaphor. Words for him are concrete forms of life. Their meaning derives from an interpretive, historical context humans themselves supply. Symbolic forms are social, not "isolated, separate and therefore meaningless sounds."[6] Our constitutive relations as human beings are linguistic.

Language, from Niebuhr's perspective, is the matrix of humanity; it is not privately nurtured and problematic in the public sphere, as John Locke had argued in the seventeenth century. Niebuhr holds form and content together; concepts are not isolated from their representations. He weaves the social and individual dimensions of language into a unified whole. The symbolic approach to communication ransoms us from Locke's unproductive question, "How can private and isolated minds engage one another?" Through the social nature of language we integrate the message with communal formation. Consistent with this perspective, we document through these chapters that the manner in which race, age, gender, class, physical disabilities, and ethnicity is mediated provides the possibility for a just socioeconomic order. Human bonds are nurtured through language. Our first existential order, in other words, is a symbolic theater.

Symbol theory has been fertile territory—hermeneutics, the semiotics of Roland Barthes, Umberto Eco, and Paul Tillich's extensive work on symbolic language. Narrative discourse gets special treatment in Quentin Schultze's argument that popular culture serves a religious role in constituting our belief systems. Derrida's sliding signifiers, Stuart Hall's ideology, Heidegger's house of language, Baudrillard's simulacrum, and Bahktin's dialogical imagination live out of symbolic theory as well.

However, for all the vast range and depth of this book's symbolic thrust, it reminds me of a persistent problem within symbolism as a whole: Its anthropological assumptions need clarification and development. Symbol theory entails a strong claim about homo sapiens that demands further intellectual scrutiny. This first generation of scholarship has invented the wheel, but we are still riding in an oxcart. In the various debates over symbolic theory, I would argue for one that puts the radically human at its epicenter. All symbolic theories are anti-positivistic, but they accent the problem of communication in different ways: meaning, political economy, interpretation-text-hermeneutics, historically, ideology, power, and so forth. In effect, I believe we should place dialogic theory at the center of a series of increasingly narrow concentric circles—the Counter-Enlightenment, interpretive theory, and human symbolic capacity.

The ancient Greeks first identified—within Western society, at least—the interpretive impulse as a pervasive condition of human existence. They brought the hermeneutical consciousness into focus. The contemporary mind readily recognizes it. Interpretativeness is presumed among symbolic theorists today; however, it took Aristotle's genius to locate this human *ars interpretandi* explicitly within philosophical anthropology, as a property of human being. Aristotle found *hermeneia* (interpretation) worthy of a major treatise by that title, and he outlined a formal theory of communication in his *Rhetoric*. But, as Gadamer reminds us, in *Nicomachean Ethics*, interpretation is given its richest meaning. Intellection and interpretation are presumed to differ in this Aristotelian classic on ethics. *Hermeneia* belongs to the higher and purer operations of the mind, but it is not just theoretical knowledge (*episteme*). Neither is it practical skill (*techne*), since it concerns more than utility. Making a moral decision, Aristotle argues, entails doing the right thing in a particular circumstance, and to accomplish that successfully demands that we interpret the concrete situation. The moment of discernment requires that we deliberate within ourselves; yet it cannot be confused with logical analysis. In this manner, Aristotle confirmed an orienting process beyond the senses, yet differing from intellection. Discursive penetration (Anthony Giddens' phrase) is born of conscience.

What Aristotle locates in the classical period is primordial, inherent, and fundamental. While he speaks with a Greek cadence, *hermeneia* concerns a universal modality, a constituent feature of our anthropology. The most typical labels are body, mind, and spirit. Others have called it psyche, the moral imagination, and fantasia. One humanly integrated whole of three distinct dimensions is harmonized into a unique species without exception.

Through the hermeneutical modality, we experience epiphanal moments suspended outside our person. These normative manifestations of compelling force are not grounded a priori. We can appropriate everyday reality cognitively, but *hermeneia* enables us simultaneously to engage a world independent of ourselves. As Thomas Nagel contends in his *View from Nowhere*, through the interpretive impulse, we form an overriding conception of the world with us in it. We are contained within history and do not create ourselves from scratch. Thus humans consider it worthwhile to bring their values and beliefs "under the influence of an impersonal standpoint," even without proof that this more permanent vista is not illusory. An independent reality, experienced phenomenologically, is from nowhere in particular, but we think it "natural to regard life and the world in this way."[7] Thus in describing our concrete situation, we appeal to the impersonal with such phrases as, "the truth is," "my dignity has been violated," "justice demands," "innocent victims," and so forth.

Martin Buber's theory of communication makes the dialogic relation primal in his famous aphorism, "In the beginning is the relation."[8] He intends that ontology is a category of being. This irreducible anthropological phenomenon cannot be decomposed into simpler elements without destroying it. There are not three components, sender-message-receiver, to be dismembered for scientific analysis. The reciprocal bond is an organic whole forming an interpretive unit centered in human *hermeneia*. All the variables are conjugate relationships, and isolating them is academia's version of *Humpty Dumpty*. Communications rests in the spirit, in our interpretive capacity—not in the mind, cogito, or intellectus. The commonplace phrase, "We're with you in spirit," is actually a powerful truth; the oneness of our species is born along the stream of consciousness. I resonate through my spirit to the moral imagination of others. Our common humanity is not inscribed, first of all, in politics, economics, transportation, or data. Our human bond is actually an ethical commitment rooted in value-saturated symbols.

Buber categorically rejects all dualism between self and culture. And Paulo Freire maintains the same dialectical unity with this symmetrical summary: "I cannot exist without a not-I; in turn the not-I depends on that existence." "There is no longer an 'I think' but 'we think,'" he writes:

It is the "we think" which establishes the "I think" and not the contrary. This co-participation of Subjects in the act of thinking is communication . . . . Communication implies a reciprocity which cannot be broken. Hence it is not possible to comprehend thought without its double function, as something which learns and something which communicates . . . . Communication is characterized by the fact that it is dialogue. It is not the transference of knowledge, but the encounter of subjects in dialogue in search of the significance of the object of knowing and thinking.[9]

In Freire's terms, it is our ontological vocation as creative subjects to live meaningfully within the world while transforming it to suit our purposes. Freire presumes an explicit anthropology, conceiving of humans as existing not only in everyday reality but through symbols separating from it in their consciousness.[10] Humans are able to adopt postures ranging from nearly undifferentiated spontaneous response to a critical attitude that entails a conscious process of intervention. As with the dialogic tradition generally, Freire sweeps epistemology into his anthropology. He declares that we have understood reality when we have gotten inside the self-in-relation. He presumes a symbolic paradigm with the radically human as the center for meaning.

When symbolic theory revolves around a dialogic axis, the application to stereotyping in mediated images is obvious. Though the world of technological images is our linguistic home and not something alien or frivolous, we can simultaneously nurture personal arenas in dialogic terms. While critiquing mediated structures and transforming them vigorously, human beings can create oppositional symbolic worlds interpersonally within subcultures and neighborhoods. Creating and nurturing symbolic worlds that heal are never automatic anywhere; but in the free spaces, grass-roots symbol-making is likely to be participatory. Examples of local responsibility for the symbols produced exist all over the globe. Expanding their number is our primary mission for the future.

CONCLUSION

In applying and energizing a symbolic approach, this book helps accomplish for communications what Albion Small earlier attempted for sociology. Albion Small, the president of Colby College in Maine, taught a moral philosophy course to every senior, orienting them to civic responsibility before graduation. Called to the University of Chicago to start what we now know as the Sociology Department, he saw it, in effect, as moral philosophy conscious of its task: "Science is sterile unless it contributes knowledge of what is worth doing."[11]

He wanted to make sociology the organizing center of the social sciences as a whole, but without a discrete subject matter of its own. Small believed, sociology could meet its ultimate test as an index and a measure of what ought to be done.

Extraordinarily influential, he founded the American Sociological Association and served as the first editor of the *American Sociological Review*. But subsequent history ruptured his vision. In 1932, William Ogburn assumed the presidency of ASA as Small's successor. And in his presidential address, Ogburn declared: "Sociology as a science is no longer interested in making the world a better place in which to live. In encouraging beliefs. In setting forth impressions of life. In leading the multitudes or guiding the ship of state. Science is interested directly in one thing only, to wit, discovering new knowledge."[12]

Integrating facts and values has been a monumental challenge in academic life since the eighteenth century. Deep inside we agree with Thoreau that there is no sense going to Zanzibar just to count the cats, but objective science is addictive nonetheless. For communications, symbolic theory lays a new foundation on which to work in a visual age, and this book is a prototype of what to build.

Notes

INTRODUCTION

1. Walter Lippmann (1961). *Public Opinion*. New York: Macmillan.
2. Mary Catherine Bateson (1994). *Peripheral Visions Learning Along the Way*. New York: HarperCollins Publishers, p. 21.

CHAPTER 1. MORAL REQUIREMENTS AND PICTURE CHOICE

1. As is traditional in classical philosophy, the terms "moral" and "ethical" are used synonymously. Both refer to custom or conventional behavior; the difference is in their etiological roots. "Moral" comes from the Latin *mores* and "ethical" from the Greek *ethika*.
2. There are other types of harms, such as death, that will not be discussed here and other types of activities that are likely to lead to the suffering of harms, such as deception, cheating, promise-breaking, and disobeying the law, that will not be discussed here. For a complete explication of the moral scope and for full arguments of the philosophical concepts discussed here, see B. Gert (1988) *Morality, A New Justification for the Moral Rules*, New York: Oxford University Press.
3. It is, of course, possible that someone can be harmed without their knowledge. Children and other vulnerable people, for example, may suffer harms without awareness. Someone can be deceived, and thus suffer the harms associated with making a decision based on inaccurate information, and not be aware that he has been deceived. Even without perception of harm, one can suffer harms. Perception of one's own harm or likelihood to suffer a harm is a sufficient condition but not a necessary condition for an action to be morally questionable.
4. While groups of people depicted in pictorial stereotypes may be harmed, the purest form of moral analysis occurs through consideration of individuals. Communities, of course, are composed of individuals.
5. Steven Starker (1989). *Evil Influences, Crusades Against the Mass Media*. New Brunswick, N.J.: Transaction Media, p. 4.

6. See Starker, for instance.

7. Kathleen Hall Jamieson and Karlyn Kohrs Campbell (1983). *The Interplay of Influence, Mass Media and Their Publics in News, Advertising, Politics.* Belmont, California: Wadsworth, p. 3.

CHAPTER 3. MEDIA METHODS THAT LEAD TO STEREOTYPING

1. T. J. Walsh. "The Male Daze: Men Lost in the Vast Wasteland." Paper presented at the twenty-ninth Annual Convention of the Broadcast Education Association, Las Vegas, March 20, 1994.

CHAPTER 4. NEWSPAPER STEREOTYPES OF AFRICAN AMERICANS

1. Joseph Boskin (1980). "Denials: The Media View of Dark Skins and the City." In Bernard Rubin, ed., *Small Voices and Great Trumpets: Minorities and the Media.* New York: Praeger, pp. 141-42.

2. Carolyn Martindale. "Changes in Newspaper Images of Black Americans," *Newspaper Research Journal* 11: 1 (Winter 1990), 46-48.

3. Frank Stanley, Jr. "Race, Poverty and the Press," *ASNE Bulletin* (September 1967), 2.

4. Carolyn Martindale. "Significant Silences: Selected Newspaper Coverage of Problems Facing Black Americans." Winning paper in the "Significant Silences, Invisible Faces" competition, presented at the Association for Education in Journalism and MassCommunication convention, Montreal, August 4, 1992, p. 19.

5. Martindale, "Changes in Newspaper Images," p. 47.

6. "A 'Rising Star': The Political Career of Rep. William Gray," Joan Shorenstein Barone Center of John F. Kennedy School of Government, Harvard University, working paper for seminar on "Race, Politics and the Press" at Harvard, May, 3-6, 1990, pp. 1-2.

7. Ibid.

8. Ibid., pp. 19, 25.

9. Carolyn Martindale. "Coverage of Black Americans by the *New York Times.*" Paper presented at the Association for Education in Journalism and Mass Communication convention in Minneapolis, August 12, 1990, p. 13.

10. Paul Martin Lester. "African-American Photo Coverage in Four U.S. Newspapers, 1937-1990," *Journalism Quarterly* 71:2 (Summer 1994), 380-394.

11. Reported by Erna Smith in "The Color of News," *Muckraker* (Summer 1992), 3.

12. Robert Entman. "Blacks in the News: Television, Modern Racism and Cultural Change," *Journalism Quarterly* 69: 2 (Summer 1992), 350.

13. Kirk Johnson. "Black and White in Boston," *Columbia Journalism Review* 26: 1 (May/June 1987), 50-51.

14. Ibid.

15. George Curry. Panel on "News Media Performance in Covering Politics and Race," Association for Education in Journalism and Mass Communication convention, Washington D.C., August 13, 1989.

CHAPTER 5. THE MEXICAN AMERICANS

1. Rafael Perex-Torres. "Chicanos in film; a new portrayal," *Estos Tiempos* 4: 2 (Fall 1988), 28.

2. Robert Brischetto. "Marking a Milestone," *Hispanic Business* (October 1993), 6-10.

3. Decennial Report. (1990) Bureau of the Census, United States Department of Commerce;"Hispanic Households Income," (Nov. 8, 1991), Bureau of the Census, U.S. Department of Commerce; "Hispanic Median Household Income Down in 1990," (Sept. 26, 1991), Bureau of the Census, U.S. Department of Commerce; and "Where Hispanics Spend Their Money." (1991) *Hispanic Agenda: Leadership Strategies for the 90's,* 5.

4. Rick Mendosa. "A Love Affair With Movies." *Hispanic Business* (July 1993), 12-24.

5. "Numbers to be Felt in the 90's Despite Undercount." *Hispanic Agenda: Leadership Strategies for the 90's* (1991), 4.

6. Roberto Rodriguez. "Daily Papers Misread Latinos, Say Leaders," *Hispanic Link Weekly Report,* (April 9, 1990), 1-2.

7. "Newsroom Employment Survey." National Association of Hispanic Journalists. Press release, April 11, 1990.

8. Felix Gutierrez. "Through Anglo Eyes: Chicanos as Portrayed in the News Media." Paper presented at the Association for Education in Journalism sixty-first annual conference, Seattle, August 13-16, 1978.

9. Ibid.

10. "A Melding of Cultures: Latins, the Largest New Group, Are Making Their Presence Felt. *Time,* (July 8, 1985), 36-41.

11. Ibid., *Decennial Report.*

12. Ibid., *Decennial Report.*

13. Ibid., *Decennial Report.*

14. El Paso (Texas) Association of Hispanic Journalists, Colorado (Denver) Hispanic Media Association. (1993). Policy statements on media use of the term "illegal alien."

15. Frank Del Olmo. (1985). "Newspaper Innovations: Attempts to Serve the Changing Latino Community," *Telecommunications and Latinos,* 41-45.

CHAPTER 6. EXOTICS, EROTICS, AND COCO-NUTS: STEREOTYPES OF PACIFIC ISLANDERS

1. Asian American Journalists Association. *Asian American Handbook.* Chicago: National Conference of Christians and Jews, 1991.

CHAPTER 7. NATIVE AMERICAN STEREOTYPES

1. David Copeland. "'The Skulking Indian Enemy,' Colonial Newspapers' Portrayal of Native Americans." Paper presented at the Association for Education in Journalism and Mass Communication annual convention, Kansas City, August 1993.

2. *Rethinking Schools. Special Edition, Rethinking Columbus.* Published by Rethinking Schools, Ltd. in collaboration with Network Educators of Central America. Milwaukee, Wisconsin, 1991.

3. *Washington Post,* 1992.

4. *Washington Post,* 1992.

5. *Rethinking Schools.*

6. Suzan Shown Harjo (1992). "Racism in the News." Video produced by Spectra Communications, Inc., Distributed by Media Action Research Center, Inc., Nashville, Tennessee.

CHAPTER 8. JEWISH IMAGES THAT INJURE

1. Andy Goldfinger, personal communication, April 20, 1994.

2. Naomi Rivkis, personal communication, February 25, 1994.

3. Bernard Glassman. *Anti-Semitic Stereotypes Without Jews.* Detroit: Wayne State University Press, 1975, p. 152.

4. Joerg von Kirschbaum, personal communication, February 19, 1994.

5. Seth Adelson, personal communication, February 24, 1994.

6. Multicultural Management Program. *Dictionary of Cautionary Words and Phrases,* 1989.

7. David B. Davis. "The Other Zion," *The New Republic* (April 12, 1993), 29-36.

8. Bonnie Jean Chakravorty, personal communication, April 19, 1994.

9. Avner Ziv and Anat Zajdman. *Semites and Stereotypes, Characteristics of Jewish Humor.* Westport, Conn.: Greenwood Press, 1993, p. 82.

10. Claire Ellen Weinstein, personal communication, April 5, 1994.

11. Karen Ford, personal communication, April 21, 1994.

12. Bonnie Jean Chakravorty, personal communication, April 19, 1994.

13. Jessica Bernhardt, personal communication, April 19, 1994.

14. Dan Wasserman. "Visually Challenging or Visually Challenged?/A P.C. Debate by Cartoonists," *The Boston Globe*, (February 19, 1994), Op-Ed, p. 15.

15. Ibid.

16. Bonnie Jean Chakravorty, personal communication, April 19, 1994.

17. S. A. Richardson et al. "Cultural Uniformity in Reaction to Physical Disabilities, "*American Sociological Review*, 26 (1961), 244-247.

18. Laura Shapiro. "When Is a Joke Not a Joke?" *Newsweek* (May 23, 1988), 79.

19. "Definite Place at Penn State," *Time* (May 7, 1990), 104.

20. Stephen M. Eisenberg, personal communication, May 19, 1994.

21. Bonnie Jean Chakravorty, personal communication, April 19, 1994.

22. David R. Brill, personal communication, February 24, 1994.

23. Ziv and Zajdman, *Semites and Stereotypes*, p. 82.

24. Sherree Curry, personal communication, April 15, 1994.

25. Michael A. Leeds, personal communication, April 15, 1994.

26. Jessica Bernhardt, personal communication, April 19, 1994.

27. Ziv and Zajdman, *Semites and Stereotypes*, p. 82.

28. Bonnie Jean Chakravorty, personal communication, April 19, 1994.

29. Alan Asper, personal communication, April 14, 1994.

30. Ray Richmond. "Jewish Characters Stop Checking Their Ethnic Baggage," *Chicago Tribune* (November 27, 1992), *Tempo*, 3.

31. "Critics Leave Schindler Off Best Directors' List." *The Daily Telegraph* (December 17, 1993).

CHAPTER 9. THE EMOTIONAL, IRASCIBLE IRISH

1. David Rothman (1971). *The Discovery of the Asylum.* Boston: Little, Brown, p. 254.

2. George Potter (1960). *To the Golden Door.* Boston: Little, Brown, p. 168.

3. Barbara Solomon (1956). *Ancestors and Immigrants.* Cambridge: Harvard University Press, p. 153.

4. Richard Ned Lebow, (1976). *White Britain and Black Ireland. The Influence of Stereotypes on Colonial Policy.* Philadelphia: Institute for the Study of Human Issues, p. 105.

5. Ibid., p. 112.

6. Solomon, Ancestors, p. 154.

7. Andrew M. Greeley (1972). *That Most Distressful Nation.* Chicago: Quadrangle Books, p. 119.

8. William V. Shannon (1963). *The American Irish.* New York: Macmillan, p. 145.

9. Carl Wittke (1956). *The Irish in America.* Baton Rouge: Louisiana State University Press, p. 245.

10. Greeley, *Distressful Nation*, p. 5.

11. Ibid., p. 5.

12. Marjorie R. Fallows (1979). *Irish Americans, Identity and Assimilation.* Englewood Cliffs, N.J.: Prentice-Hall, p. 4.

13. See Lawrence McCaffrey (1976). *Irish Diaspora in America.* Bloomington, Ind.: Indiana University Press; William V. Shannon (1963). *The American Irish.* New York: Macmillan; Nathan Glazer and Daniel Patrick Moynihan (1963). *Beyond the Melting Pot.* Cambridge, Mass.: Massachusetts Institute of Technology Press.

14. Richard Stivers (1976). *A Hair of the Dog.* University Park, Pa.: Pennsylvania State University Press, p. 75.

15. See Margaret E. Fitzgerald and Joseph A. King (1990). *The Uncounted Irish.* Toronto: P.D. Meany Publishers, p. 313; and Greeley, *That Most Distressful Nation*, p. 143.

16. Fitzgerald and King, *Uncounted Irish*, p. 313.

17. Glazer and Moynihan, *Beyond the Melting Pot*, pp. 217-87.

18. See Robert F. Bales, "The 'Fixation Factor' in Alcohol Addiction: An Hypothesis Derived from a Comparative Study of Irish and Jewish Social Hypothesis Derived from a Comparative Study of Irish and Jewish Social Norms" (Ph.D. dissertation, Harvard University, 1944); and Donald Davison Glad, "Attitudes and Experience of American-Jewish and American-Irish Male Youth as Related to Differences in Adult Rates of Inebriety," *Quarterly Journal of Studies on Alcohol* 8 (December 1947): 406-72.

19. Louise Feroze. "St. Patrick's Day: Calgary's Irish Remember Home," *Calgary Herald* (March 17, 1994), A5.

20. Elaine Louie. "The Pub: A Center of Ireland in Exile," *New York Times* (March 16, 1994), C1.

21. Ibid.

22. Ibid.

23. Bill Reel. "When the Pot Calls Another Pot Irish," *Newsday* (July 7, 1993), 81.

24. Ibid.

25. Ibid.

26. Anna Quindlen, "Erin Go Brawl," *New York Times* (March 14, 1991), A25.

27. Pete Hamill, as quoted in Peter Steinfeld, "Cardinal Says Press Reports Reflect Catholic Bashing,'" *New York Times* (March 23, 1991), p. 27.

28. Jimmy Breslin, "The Cardinal Sins of Irish Catholics," *Newsday* (March 19, 1991), p. 27.

CHAPTER 10. ANGLO AMERICAN STEREOTYPES

1. For a sample of scholarly research on under-represented stereotypes, see Bernard Berelson and Patricia Salter, "Majority and Minority Americans: An Analysis of Magazine Fiction," *Public Opinion Quarterly* 10 (1946): 168-197, Royal Colle, "Negro Image in the Mass Media: A Case Study in Social Change," *Journalism Quarterly* 45 (1968): 55-60.

2. David Kunzle (1973). *The Early Comic Strip: Narrative Strips and Picture Stories in the European Broadsheet from c. 1450 to 1825.* Berkeley: University of California Press.

3. Edwin Emery and Michael Emery (1985). *The Press and America.* Englewood Cliffs, N.J.: Prentice Hall.

4. Arthur M. Schlesinger (1958). *Prelude to Independence: The Newspaper War on Britain, 1764-1776.* New York: Knopf.

5. Emery and Emery, *The Press,* p. 26.

6. Philip Davidson (1977). *Propaganda and the American Revolution.* Chapel Hill, N.C.: University of North Carolina Press.

7. Emery and Emery, *The Press,* p. 65.

8. Charlene Brown, Trevor Brown, and William Rivers (1978). *The Media and the People.* New York: Holt, Rinehart and Winston.

9. United States Bureau of the Census (1957). *Statistical Abstract of the United States: 1957.* Washington, D.C.

10. Christopher Lasch. "Archie Bunker and the Liberal Mind." *Channels of Communication* (October/November 1981).

11. Arthur Asa Berger (1977). *TV-Guided American.* New York: Prentice-Hall.

12. Richard M. Gardner. "Stereotypes and Media." *The Midwest Quarterly* 34 (1992-1993), 121-35.

13. Ibid., p. 124.

CHAPTER 11. ARAB AMERICANS: MIDDLE EAST CONFLICTS HIT HOME

1. Richard Behar. "The Secret Life of Mahmud the Red," *Time* (Oct. 4, 1993), 55.

2. George J. Church. "The Terror Within," *Time* (July 5, 1993), 22.

3. Behar, "The Secret Life," p. 55.

4. Ibid., p. 56.

5. David Lamb (1987). *The Arabs.* New York: Vintage Books, p. x.

6. Edward W. Said (1981). *Covering Islam*. New York:Pantheon Books, p. 26.

7. Clare Hollingworth. *International Herald Tribune* (Sept.9, 1993), 8.

8. Said interview with author, Cairo, May 18, 1994.

CHAPTER 12. WOMEN IN THE WORK FORCE IN NON-TRADITIONAL JOBS

1. Wendy Griswold (1994). *Cultures and Societies in a Changing World*. Thousand Oaks, Calif.: Pine Forge Press Series, Sage Publications, p. 51.

2. Ibid., pp. 51-52.

3. Ibid.

4. Ibid., pp. 52-53.

5. Stuart Ewen (1988). *All Consuming Images: The Politics of Style in Contemporary Culture*. New York: Basic Books, p. 112.

6. Ibid., pp. 183, 188.

7. Ibid., p. 194.

8. Michael L. Klassen, Cynthia R. Jasper, and Anne M. Schwartz. "Men and Women: Images of Their Relationships in Magazine Advertisements," *Journal of Advertising Research* 33: 22 (March/April 1993), 30-39.

9. Erving Goffman (1976). *Gender Advertisements*. New York: Harper & Row, p. 21.

10. Ewen, *All Consuming Images*, p. 194.

11. "Employment in Perspective: Women in the Labor Force." Report 860. Washington, D.C.: U.S. Department of Labor, Bureau of Labor Statistics, December 1993. The same trend shows up in a plotting of labor force participation by age groups for 1990. See pages 6 and 39 in "Working Women: A Chartbook," U.S. Department of Labor Bulletin 2385, August 1991.

12. "We the American . . . Women." Washington, D.C.: U.S. Department of Commerce, Economics and Statistics Administration, Bureau of the Census, September 1993, p. 7.

13. Ibid., pp. 7-8.

CHAPTER 13. WOMEN AS MOTHERS

1. See Katherine Arnup, Andree Levesque, and Ruth Roach Pierson, eds. (1990). *Delivering Motherhood: Maternal Ideologies and Practices in the 19th and 20th Centuries*. London: Routledge; Donna Bassin, Margaret Honey, and Meryle Mahrer Kaplan, eds. (1994) *Representations of Motherhood*. New Haven: Yale University Press; Evelyn Nakano Glenn, Grace Chang, and Linda Rennie Forcey, eds. (1994). *Mothering: Ideology, Experience, and Agency*. London: Routledge; E. Ann Kaplan (1992). *Motherhood and Representation: The Mother in Popular Culture and Melodrama*. London: Routledge; Meryle Mahrer Kaplan(1992). *Mothers' Images of Motherhood: Case Studies of Twelve Mothers*. London: Routledge; Seth Koven and Sonya Michel, eds. (1993). *Mothers of a New World: Maternalist Politics and the Origins of Welfare States*. London: Routledge; Jean F. O'Barr, Deborah Pope, and Mary Wyer, eds. (1990). *Ties that Bind: Essays on Mothering and Patriarchy*. Chicago: University of Chicago Press; Ann Phoenix, Anne Woollett, and Eva Lloyd, eds. (1991). *Motherhood: Meanings, Practices and Ideologies*. London: Sage; Kathryn Allen Rabuzzi (1994). *Mother with Child: Transformations through Childbirth*. Bloomington: Indiana University Press; Adrienne Cecile Rich (1986) *Of Woman Born: Motherhood as Experience and Institution*. New York: Norton; and Rothman, Barbara Katz (1989). *Recreating Motherhood: Ideology and Technology in a Patriarchal Society*. New York: Norton.

2. It may be worth noting that of the two versions, in 1993 only *Baby on the Way: Basics* included an article on methods of birth control. This disparity suggests the point of view that such information is more urgently needed by economically or educationally disadvantaged women than by their middle-class counterparts in order to slow the reproduction rate within under-represented communities.

3. Ewen, Stuart (1976). *Captains of Consciousness: Advertising and the Social Roots of*

the Consumer Culture. New York: McGraw-Hill.

4. Ibid.

5. Ibid., p. 169.

6. Berger, John (1972). *Ways of Seeing*. New York: Viking Press.

7. Ibid., p. 139.

8. Ibid., p. 142.

9. Ibid., p. 149.

10. These data were compiled from the following sources: John W. Wright, ed., (1994). *The Universal Almanac*. Kansas City, Mo.: Andrews and McMeel.and Children's Defense Fund Staff (1994). *The State of America's Children*. Washington, D.C.: Children's Defense.

11. Barbara Ehrenreich (1983). *The Hearts of Men: American Dreams and the Flight from Commitment*. New York: Anchor.

CHAPTER 14. WOMEN AS SEX PARTNERS

1. Louis Harris and Associates, Inc. (1986). *American Teens Speak: Sex, Myths, TV, and Birth Control*. New York: Planned Parenthood Federation of America.

2. Ibid.

3. R.J. Freedman. "Reflections on Beauty as It Relates to Health in Adolescent Females," *Women and Health* 9 (1984), 29-45.

4. L. Kaufman, "Prime-Time Nutrition," *Journal of Communication* 30 (1980), 37-46.

5. B. Silverstein et al. "The Role of the Mass Media in Promoting a Thin Standard of Bodily Attractiveness for Women," *Sex Roles* 14 (1986), 519-532.

6. D.T. Kenrick and S.E. Gutierres, "Contrast Effects and Judgments of Physica Attractiveness: When Beauty Becomes a Social Problem," *Journal of Personality and Social Psychology* 38: 1 (1980), 131-40.

7. S. Jhally (Writer and producer). (1991). *Dreamworlds* (videotape). Amherst, Mass. Center for Media Education.

8. N. Malamuth and J. Briere. "Sexual Violence in the Media: Indirect Effects on Aggression Against Women," *Journal of Social Issues* 42: 3 (1986), 75-92; and D. Zillman and J. Bryant "Pornography, Sexual Callousness and the Trivialization of Rape," *Journal of Communication* 32: 4 (1982), 10-21.

9. B.S. Greenberg (1993). "Summary and Research Agenda." In B. S. Greenberg, J. D. Brown, and N.L. Buerkel-Rothfuss, eds. *Media, Sex and the Adolescent*. Cresskill, N.J.: Hampton Press, Inc., pp. 293-306.

CHAPTER 15. SUPER BOWL COMMERCIALS:
THE BEST A MAN CAN GET (OR IS IT?)

1. Ellen Neuborne, Van Jones and Julie Schmit. "Super Bowl; By the Numbers," *USA Today*, (January 31, 1994), 5B.

2. "Super Bowl XVI Fact Book," *Marketing Week* (January 13, 1992), 19.

3. Joe Mandese. "Super Duper Deals for Super Bowl Price," *Advertising Age* (January 31, 1994), 26.

4. Julie Liesse. "Super Bowl Runneth Over With Munchies," *Advertising Age* (January 24, 1994), 3.

5. Fara Warner. "Advertisers Score High Recall on Super Bowl," *Brandweek* (February 8, 1993), 10.

6. J. Tierney. "The Aging Body," *Annual Editions: Aging* (1987), 42-47.

7. Bernice Kanner. "Quarterback Sneak," *New York* (February 5, 1990), 22.

CHAPTER 16. RAMBOS AND HIMBOS:
STEREOTYPICAL IMAGES OF MEN IN ADVERTISING

1. B. Svetkey. "Here's the Beef," *Entertainment* (March 18, 1994), 26-27.

2. Ibid., p. 26.

3. J. Leo. "Madison Avenue's Gender War," *U.S. News and World Report* (October 25, 1993).

4. Svetkey, "Here's the Beef," p. 26.

5. O. A. S. I. S. *Stale Roles and Tight Buns: Images of Men in Advertising*. Film available from O. A. S. I. S., 15 Willoughby St., Brighton, Mass., 02135.

6. J. Nickolson. "The Advertiser's Man," *Adbusters* (Summer 1992), 20-6.

CHAPTER 17. THE DISPOSABLE SEX: MEN IN THE NEWS

1. Robin Morgan (1977). *Going Too Far*. New York: Random House.

2. Lee Jolliffe. "Comparing Gender Differentiation in the New York Times, 1885 and 1985," *Journalism Quarterly* 66: 3 (Autumn 1989), 683-91; Lee Jolliffe. "What's in a Name? On Sex-Role Stereotyping and the Naming of Men," *ETC: The Journal of General Semantics* (Winter 1992/93), 490-94; and Lee Jolliffe and Turner Bond. "Sex-Role Stereotyping in Two Newspapers in 1885: The Influence of the Pioneer Effort." Paper presented at the AEJMC annual convention, Memphis, Tennessee, August 1985.

3. Sam Keen (1981). *Fire in the Belly: On Being a Man*. New York: Bantam.

4. Alison Laurie (1983). *The Language of Clothes*. New York: Vintage Books, p. 20.

5. Patricia Madoo Lengermann and Ruth A. Wallace (1985). *Gender in America: Social Control and Social Change*. Englewood Cliffs, N.J.: Prentice Hall, p. 228.

CHAPTER 18. THE CHILD AS IMAGE:
PHOTOGRAPHIC STEREOTYPES OF CHILDREN

1. F.E. Barcus (1983). *Images of Life on Children's Television*. New York: Praeger.

CHAPTER 19. GROWING OLD IN COMMERCIALS: A JOKE NOT SHARED

1. Kevin Goldman. "Seniors Get Little Respect on Madison Ave.," *Wall Street Journal* (Sept. 20, 1993), B4.

2. Mary Nemeth. "Amazing Greys," *Maclean's* (Jan. 10, 1994).

3. Goldman, "Seniors."

4. Joseph M.Winski. "Marketers Mature in Depicting Seniors," *Advertising Age* (Nov. 16, 1992), S-1.

5. Ibid.

6. Alan L. Otten. "The Old Grow Older, But Mostly They Grow," in his "People Patterns" column. *Wall Street Journal* (Dec. 10, 1993), B1.

7. Christy Fisher. "Boomers Bringing Buying Power," *Advertising Age* (Nov. 16, 1992), "Special Report on The Mature Market," S-2. An excellent summary of the statistics on the elderly can be found in Arnold A. Goldstein, "The Elderly Population," *Population Profile of the United States, 1993*, Current Population Reports, Special Studies Series P23-185, U.S. Department of Commerce (May 1993), 42-43.

8. Mary M. Walker and M. Carole Macklin. *Journal of Advertising Research* (July-August 1992), abstract in Business Index.

9. Fisher, "Boomers," S-2.

10. Quoted in Laura Muha. "Shattering Stereotypes of Old Age. Study Shows Seniors Often Happy With Life," *Newsday* (Dec. 30, 1993), 1C.

11. "Sonya Live," CNN transcripts (Sept. 15, 1993).

12. Cyndee Miller. "Image of Seniors Improves in Ads," *Marketing News* (December 6, 1993).

13. "Parting Gifts" in *American Spending*, American Demographics Desk Reference Series No. 5.

14. Elsie Martinez. "You're as Young as You Think," *Times-Picayune* (Oct. 24, 1993), E7.

15. Rebecca A. Clay. "AIDS Among the Elderly. Stereotypes of Aging May Hinder Diag-

nosis," *Washington Post* (Nov. 15, 1993), Z10.

16. Kent Shafer et al. "Vocational Rehabilitation of Older Displaced Workers," *The Journal of Rehabilitation* (July 1993).

17. Anne Dempsey, "Friedan and the Challenge of Old Age," *The Irish Times* (Oct. 27, 1993), p. 13.

18. Miller, "Image of Seniors."

19. Ibid.

CHAPTER 20. THE INVISIBLE CULTURE GROUP: IMAGES OF DISABILITY IN THE MEDIA

1. J. Donaldon. "The Visibility and Image of Handicapped People on Television," *Exceptional Children* 47:6 (March 1981), 413-16.

2. F. Mankiewicz and J. Swerdlow (1978). *Remote Control: Television and the Manipulation of American Life*. New York: Ballantine Books.

3. Paul K. Longmore. "A Note on Language and Social Identity of Disabled People," *American Behavioral Scientist* 28:3 (January/February 1985), 419-23.

4. *Salt Lake Tribune* (Sept. 8, 1992).

5. "Editor Wins Grant to Improve Image of the Disabled," *Louisville Courier Journal* (Oct. 23, 1988), 1B, 12B.

6. Joanmarie Kalter. "Good News: The Disabled Get More Play on TV, Bad News: There is Still Too Much Stereotyping," *TV Guide* (May 31, 1986), 41-42.

7. Paul K. Longmore. "Screening Stereotypes: Images of Disabled People," *Social Policy* 32 (Summer 1985).

8. K.I. Zola. "Depictions of Disability - Metaphor, Message and Medium in the Media: A Research and Political Agenda," *The Social Science Journal* 22(4) (1985), 5-17.

9. Donalson, "Visibility and Image."

10. Ibid., p. 415.

11. Ibid.

12. Daniel B. Wood. "Redrawing US Portrait of the Disabled." *Christian Science Monitor* (March 2, 1989), 14.

13. Paul K. Longmore. "The glorious rage of Christy Brown," *Disability Studies Quarterly* 10:4 (Fall 1990), 23-25.

14. "People Gain Roles in Ads and on TV," *New York Times* (Sept. 23, 1991), 14.

15. M. Johnson. "Where Do You Get Your Information About Disability Issues?" *The Disability Rag* (September/October 1987), 24-27.

CHAPTER 21. THE BLIND IN THE MEDIA: A VISION OF STEREOTYPES IN ACTION

1. Francis A. Koestler (1976). *The Unseen Minority: A Social History of Blindness in America*. New York: David McKay Co., p. 7.

2. Ibid.

3. Michale E. Monbeck (1973). *The Meaning of Blindness: Attitudes Toward Blindness and Blind People*. Bloomington: Indiana University Press.

4. Ibid., p. 10.

5. Ibid., p. 4.

6. Ibid., p. 83.

7. Ibid., p. 58.

8. Ibid, p. 63.

9. *Esquire* (January 1963), 112.

CHAPTER 22. THE DEVIANCE OF OBESITY: THE FAT LADY SINGS

1. C.R. Jasper and M.L. Klassen. "Stereotypical Beliefs about Appearance: Implications

for Retailing and Consumer Issues," *Perceptual and Motor Skills* 71 (1990), 519-28; S. Haarsagar."Fables, Fame, Fat and Female Foibles: An Analysis of Tabloid Newspaper Style and Content." Paper presented at the annual meeting of the Northwest Communication Association, Coeur d'Alene, Idaho, April 1993; H. Schwartz (1986). *Never Satisfied: A Cultural History of Diets, Fantasies, and Fat.* New York: Free Press; E.D. Rothblum. "Women and Weight: Fad and Fiction," *Journal of Psychology* 124 (1990), 5-24; A. Epstein. "Fat may be the Final Frontier in Acceptable Bias," *Wichita* Eagle (January 6, 1994), 1A; and B. Silverstein, L. Perdue, B. Peterson, and E. Kelly. "The Role of the Mass Media in Promoting a Thin Standard of Bodily Attractiveness for Women," *Sex Roles* 14 (1986), 519-32.

2. Rothblum, E. D., D. J. Bowen, N. Tomoyasu, and A.M. Cauce. "The Triple Threat: A Discussion of Gender, Class, and Race Differences in Weight," *Women & Health* 17 (1991), 123-43.

3. B. Silverstein et al. "The Role of the Mass media"; A.C. Downs and S.K. Harrison. "Physical Attractiveness Stereotyping on American Television Programs: A Content Analysis" (Report No. IR 010 917). Paper presented at the annual meeting of the Western Psychological Association, San Francisco, April 6-10, 1983 (ERIC Doc. No. ED 238 396); P.N. Myers and F.A. Biocca. "The Elastic Body Image: The Effect of Television Advertising and Programming on Body Image Distortions in Young Women," *Journal of Communication* 42:3 (1992), 108-33; L. McBride. "The Slender Imbalance: An Overview of Body Image Related Problems and Solutions (Report No. CG 018 423). Paper presented at the annual conference of the National Association of Women Deans, Administrators, and Counselors, Milwaukee, April 10-13, 1985 (ERIC Document No. ED 260 330); and R. Stein. "Comparison of Self Concept of Nonobese and Obese University Junior Female Nursing Students," *Adolescence* 22 (1987), 77-90.

4. A. Radley (1991). *The Body and Social Psychology.* New York: Springer-Verlag. Bowen, Rothblum and Fisher, in a chapter on "The Obese Condition." In S. Fisher (1986). *Development and Structure of the Body Image.* Hillsdale, N.J.: Lawrence Erlbaum lists fifteen studies in which subjects are identified by gender. Ten of the studies used women only.

5. W.R. Gove (1974). *The Labelling of Deviance: Evaluating a Perspective.* New York: Sage.

6. For example, see S. Fisher (1986). *Development and Structure of the Body Image,* Vol.1. Hillsdale, N.J.: Lawrence Erlbaum, p. 196; W.R. Gove (1974). *The Labeling of Deviance: Evaluating a Perspective.* New York: Sage; E. M. Schur (1983). *Labeling Women Deviant: Gender, Stigma, and Social Control.* Philadelphia: Temple University Press.

7. Gove, *Labelling*, p. 10.

8. E. D. Rothblum. "Women and Weight: Fad and Fiction," *Journal of Psychology,* 124:5 (1990), 5-24.

9. Bowen, "The Triple Threat."

10. Ibid., p. 130.

11. S. Fisher (1986). *Development and Structure of the Body Image,* Vol.1. Hillsdale, N.J.: Lawrence Erlbaum, p. 196.

12. O. W. Wooley, S.C. Wooley, and S.R. Dyrenforth. "Obesity and Women - II. A Neglected Feminist Topic," *Womens Studies International Quarterly* 2 (1979), 81-92.

13. D.J. Atkin, J. Moorman, and A.C. Lin. "Ready for Prime Time: Network Series Devoted to Working Women in the 1980's," *Sex Roles* 25 (1991), 677-85.

14. M. Parenti (1992). *Make Believe Media: The Politics of Entertainment.* New York: St. Martin's Press, p. 207.

15. P. Shoemaker (1991). *Communication Concepts 3: Gatekeeping.* Newbury Park, Calif.: Sage, p. 22.

16. M.J. Baker and G.A. Churchill, G.A. "The Impact of Physically Attractive Models on Advertising Evaluations," *Journal of Marketing Research* 14 (1977), 538-55.

17. Fisher, *Development*, p. 123.

18. Ibid., p. 150.

19. R. Freedman (1985). *Beauty Bound.* Lexington, Ky.: Heath/Lexington Books, p. 27.

20. Rothblum, "Women and Weight."

21. D. J. Bowen, E.Z. Woody, and P.R. Costanzo. "The Socialization of Obesity-Prone Behavior." In S.S. Brehm, S.M. Kassin, and F.X. Gibbons, eds., (1981). *Developmental Social Psychology: Theory and Research.* New York: Oxford Press.

22. Woody and Costanzo, "Socialization of Obesity," p. 211.

23. Myers and Biocca, "Elastic Body Image," p. 111.

24. Schur, *Labeling Women Deviant*t, p. 68.

25. L. Baum. "Extra Pounds Can Weigh Down Your Career." *Business Week* (August 3, 1987), 86.

26. J. A. Coleman. "My Turn: Discrimination at Large," *Newsweek* (August 2, 1993), 9.

27. Quoted in A. Radley (1991). *The Body and Social Psychology.* New York: Springer-Verlag.

28. K. Barnhurst (1994). *Seeing the Newspaper.* New York: St. Martin's Press, p. 31.

CHAPTER 23. RE-FRAMING GAY AND LESBIAN IMAGES: FUNDAMENTAL PROBLEMS

1. Marguerite Moritz (1992). "How U.S. Media Represent Sexual Minorities." in Peter Dahlgren and Colin Spraks, eds., *Journalism and Popular Culture.* London: Sage, p. 157.

2. Ibid., p. 158.

3. Peter Freiberg. "Gays and the Media," *Washington Blade* 24:18, 53.

4. "Media Guide to the Lesbian and Gay Community." Gay and Lesbian Alliance Against Defamation, Sec. 2, Part 1, p. 31.

5. The far right includes secular conservative political groups whose ties have been traced to the 1964 presidential campaign of Barry Goldwater and to the 1968 third party campaign of George Wallace, whose reactionary agenda attracted Southern whites, blue-collar and farm workers who had traditionally voted Democratic. The term "far right" is used throughout additionally to refer to what is also called the religious right, fundamentalist Christian organizations that work in the political arena for a conservative, anti-abortion, anti-gay agenda. The most prominent groups include the Free Congress Foundation, Concerned Women of America, the Moral Majority, the Eagle Forum, the Family Research Institute, the Heritage Foundation, the Christian Coalition, the Traditional Families Coalition, and the American Family Association.

6. Laura Flanders. "Hate on Tape: The Video Strategy of the Religious Right," *EXTRA!* 6:4 (June 1993), 5; and "Hidden Agenda: Behind and Anti-Gay Propaganda Video," *EXTRA!* 6:4 (June 1993), 6, citing *Freedom Writer.* Institute for First Amendment Studies, March-April 1993.

7. Ibid."Hate on Tape," p. 5.

8. Ibid., Hidden Agenda," p. 6.

9. See, for example, Herbert Gans (1979). *Deciding What's News.* New York:Vintage Press; Edward J. Epstein (1973). *News from Nowhere.* New York: Random House; and Gaye Tuchman (1978). *Making News.* New York: Free Press.

10. Fred Fejes and Kevin Petrich. "Invisibility, Homophobia and Heterosexim: Lesbians, Gays and the Media." Unpublished paper, June 1993, p. 30.

11. Ibid., p. 32.

12. "Media Guide," Sec. 2, Part 2, p. 42.

13. Freiberg, "Gays and the Media," p. 57.

14. Charlene L. Smith. "Undo Two: An Essay Regarding Colorado's Anti-Lesbian and Gay Amendment 2," *Washburn Law Journal* 32 (1993), 377.

15. GLAAD Newsletter, July /August 1993.

16. Smith, "Undo Two," p. 374.

CHAPTER 24. DON'T ASK, DON'T TELL:
LESBIANS AND GAY PEOPLE AND THE MEDIA

1. Larry Gross (1989). "Out of the Mainstream: Sexual Minorities and the Mass Media." In Ellen Seiter et al., eds. *Remote Control: Television, Audiences, & Cultural Power.* New York: Routledge, pp. 130-49.

2. Vito Russo (1987). *The Celluloid Closet: Homosexuality in the Movies.* New York: Harper and Row.

3. The Production Code required that "the sanctity of marriage and the home shall be upheld. Pictures shall not infer that low forms of sex relationship are the accepted or common thing." The code specifically precluded the picturing of "sex perversion or any inference" thereof.

4. John D'Emilio (1983). *Sexual Politics, Sexual Communities: The Making of a Homosexual Minority in the United States, 1940-1970.* Chicago: University of Chicago Press.

5. Robert C. Doty, "Growth of Overt Homosexuality in City Provokes Wide Concern," *New York Times* (December 17, 1963), A1.

6. Daniel Laskin, "The Herpes Syndrome," *New York Times Magazine* (February 21, 1982), 94.

7. Ron Milavsky. "AIDS and the Media." Paper presented at the annual meeting of the American Psychological Association, Atlanta, August 15 1988.

8. The shameful neglect of AIDS by the news media before Rock Hudson's death has been amply docnoumented (e.g., James Kinsella (1989). *Covering the Plague: AIDS and the American Media.* New Brunswick: Rutgers University Press; Randy Shilts (1987). *And the Band Played On: Politics, People and the AIDS Epidemic.* New York: St. Martin's Press) and readily traced to the pervasive homophobia and heterosexism of media institutions and decision-makers.

9. Larry Gross and Steven Aurand (1992). *Discrimination and Violence Against Lesbian Women and Gay Men in Philadelphia and The Commonwealth of Pennsylvania.* Philadelphia: Philadelphia Lesbian and Gay Task Force; and Gregory Herek and Kevin Berrill, eds., (1992). *Hate Crimes: Confronting Violence Against Lesbians and Gay Men.* Newbury Park, Calif.: Sage.

10. Andrea Weiss. "From the Margins: New Images of Gays in the Cinema." *CINEASTE* 15:1 (1986), 4-8.

11. Frank Rich. (1994) "What Now My·Love," *New York Times*, (March 6, 1994), E15.

12. Ibid.

13. George Gerbner, Larry Gross, Michael Morgan, and Nancy Signorielli (1994). "Growing Up With Television: The Cultivation Perspective." In Jennings Bryant and Dolf Zillmann, eds., *Media Effects: Advances in Theory and Research.* Hillsdale, N.J.: Lawrence Erlbaum Associates, pp.17-42.

CHAPTER 25. ON THE AVOCADO AND THE ASPARAGUS:
THE DANCE OF THE ARCHETYPES

1. E. Badinter (1989). *Man/Woman, the One Is the Other.* Trans. by Barbara Wright. London: Collins Harville.

CHAPTER 26. OF FAIRY GODMOTHERS AND WITCHES:
NETWORK TELEVISION AND THE TEACHER

1. Joseph Turow (1989). *Playing Doctor: Television, Storytelling, and Medical Power.* New York: Oxford University Press; Philip A. Kalish, Beatrice Kalish, and Margaret Scobey, (1983). *Images of Nurses on Television.* New York: Springer; and Richard Meyers (1981). *TV Detectives.* San Diego: A.S. Barnes.

2. See, for example, Eric Barnouw (1975). *Tube of Plenty: The Evolution of American Television.* London: Oxford University Press; Stuart Kaminsky, with Jeffrey H. Mahan, (1985).

American Television Dramas (Chicago: Nelson-Hall, 1985); David Marc, *Demographic Vistas: Television in American Culture*. Philadelphia: University of Pennsylvania Press; Brian Rose, ed. (1985). *TV Genres: A Handbook and Reference Guide*. Westport, Conn.: Greenwood; and Horace Newcomb 1974). *TV: The Most Popular Art*. New York: Anchor.

3. Melvin L. DeFleur. "Occupational Roles as Portrayed on Television," *Public Opinion Quarterly* 28 (1964), 57-74.

4. Roberta Wroblewski and Aletha C. Huston. "Televised Occupational Stereotypes and Their Effects on Early Adolescents: Are They Changing?" *Journal of Early Adolescence* 7:3 (1987), 283-97. See also Sidney W. Head. "Content Analysis of Television Drama Programs," *Quarterly of Film, Radio and Television* 9 (1954), 175-94; Melvin L. DeFleur and Lois B. DeFleur. "The Relative Contribution of Television as a Learning Source for Children's Occupational Knowledge," *American Sociological Review* 32 (1967), 777-89; J. F. Seggar and P. Wheeler. "World of Work on TV: Ethnic and Sex Representation in TV Drama," *Journal of Broadcasting* 17 (1973), 201-14; and Bradley Greenberg (1980). *Life on Television: Content Analysis of U.S. TV Drama*. Norwood, N.J.: Ablex.

5. Leah R. Vande Berg and Nick Trujillo (1989). *Organizational Life on Television*. Norwood, N.J.: Ablex, pp. 49-55.

6. Ibid., pp. 193-239.

7. Vicky Lytle. "From Our Miss Brooks to Bronx Zoo," *NEA Today*. 6:7 (February 1988),18.

8. George Kaplan. "TV's Version of Education (And What to Do About It)," *Phi Delta Kappan* 71:5 (1990), K1-K12.

9. Leslie Swetnam. "Media Distortion of the Teacher Image," *The Clearing House*. 66:1 (September/October 1992), 30-32.

10. George Gerbner (1973). "Teacher Image in Mass Culture; Symbolic Functions of the Hidden Curriculum.'" George Gerbner, Larry P. Gross, and William H. Melody, eds., *Communications Technology and Social Policy: Understanding the New "Cultural Revolution."* New York: Wiley, pp. 265-86.

11. Kaplan, "TV's Version," p. K1.

12. Ibid., p. K5.

13. Swetnam, "Media Distortion," p. 30.

14. Ibid., p. 31.

15. Ibid., p. 31-32.

CHAPTER 27. POST-RODNEY KING: THE RECIPROCAL GAZE

1. Jerome H. Skolnick and James J. Fyfe (1993). *Above The Law: Police and the Excessive Use of Force*. New York: The Free Press, p. xi.

2. Brian Duffy. "Days of Rage," *U.S. News & World Report* (May 11, 1992), 26.

3. Skolnick and Fyfe, *Above the Law*, p. 79.

4. Louis H. Carter and Wanda Foglia. "Law Enforcement That Wins Respect for Law," *Christian Science Monitor* (June 15, 1992), 18.

CHAPTER 28. DUELING STEREOTYPES OF POLITICIANS

1. Carol Schlagheck. "Enough is Enough, Say Columnists," *News Photographer* (September 1992), 57.

2. Maureen Dowd. "The Campaign You Didn't See," *American Photographer* (July 1988), 44.

3. Arthur Grace (1989). *Choose Me: Portraits of a Presidential Race*. Hanover, N.H.: University Press of New England, 1989, 12.

4. Richard M. Merelman, ed. (1992). *Language, Symbolism, and Politics*. Boulder, Colo.: Westview Press, 1992, pp. 2-3.

5. Gerald Critoph (1979). "The Contending Americas." In John A. Hague, ed., *American Character and Culture in a Changing World*. Westport, Conn.: Greenwood Press, p. 144.

6. Gerald N. Grob and Robert N. Beck (1970). *Ideas in America.* New York: The Free Press, p. 163.

7. Andrew Jackson (1960). "Veto of the Bank Bill." In Oscar Handlin, ed., *American Principles and Issues.* New York: Holt, Rinehart and Winston, p. 314.

8. "Can We Play Through," *Newsweek* (May 25, 1992), 6.

9. Carl Glassman (1994). "Why Is This Man Smiling? A Cultural Analysis of Presidential Campaign Photojournalism." Master's thesis, Hunter College of the City University of New York.

10. *Life* (January 1993), 10-11.

11. Martin J. Medhurst and Michael A. DeSousa. "Political Cartoons and American Culture: Significant Symbols of Campaign 1980," *Studies in Visual Communication* 8 (Winter 1980), 84-97.

12. Carol Squiers (1990). "Picturing Scandal: Iranscam, the Reagan White House, and the Photo Opportunity." In Carol Squiers, ed., *The Critical Image.* Seattle: Bay Press, pp. 131-32.

13. Matthew C. Morrison. "The Role of the Political Cartoonist in Image Making," *Central States Speech Journal* (Winter 1969), 252-60.

14. David Perkins. "A Definition of Caricature and Caricature Recognition," *Studies in the Anthropology of Visual Communication* (1975), 4-23.

15. Ibid., "Political Cartoons."

16. John Adler. "The Finer Art of Politics," *Newsweek* (October 13, 1980), 74-83.

17. Steve Platt. "The Right to be Offensive," *New Statesman and Society* (March 18, 1994), 40.

CHAPTER 29. LAWYER STEREOTYPES

1. Lawrence M. Friedman. "Law, Lawyers, and Popular Culture," *Yale Law Journal* 98:1574 (1989); and Robert C. Post, "On the Popular Image of the Lawyer: Reflections in a Dark Glass," *California Law Review* 75:379 (1987).

2. David Shaw (1984). *Press Watch.* New York: Macmillan, p. 113; also see Rennard Strickland. "Law and Lawyers in Popular Film," *Sooner Magazine* (Spring 1994), 25.

3. Jay Black, Bob Steele, and Ralph Barney (1993). *Doing Ethics in Journalism.* Greencastle, Ind.:Sigma Delta Chi Foundation, p. 11.

4. Sissela Bok (1979). *Lying: Moral Choice in Public and Private Life.* New York: Vintage Books; and Philip Patterson and Lee Wilkins (1991). *Media Ethics.* Dubuque: Brown and Benchmark, p. 11.

5. Clifford G. Christians, John Ferre, and P. Mark Fackler (1993). *Good News.* New York: Oxford University Press.

6. Post, *On the Popular Image*, p. 379.

7. Robert L. Haig. "Lawyer-Bashing: Have We Earned It?" *New York Law Journal* (November 19, 1993), 2.

8. Erik Hromadka. "Lawyers Battle Tarnished Professional Image," *Res Gestae* (October 1993), 152.

9. David Astor. "Lawyer Bashing is Debated at Meeting," *Editor & Publisher* (December 25, 1993), 32.

10. Ira Teinowitz. "Reviving Miller Lite: Can New Ads Do This?," *Advertising Age* (June 14, 1993), 3.

11. Hank Grezlak. "Lawyer Bashing Debated at Bar," *The Legal Intelligencer* (December 21, 1993), 1.

12. David W. Miller (1993). *Dead Lawyers and Other Pleasant Thoughts.* New York: Random House and (1993). *The New Yorker Book of Lawyer Cartoons.* New York: Knopf.

13. Miller, *Dead Lawyers.*

14. Astor, "Lawyer Bashing," p. 32.

15. Richard Zoglin. "All the News That's Fit," *Time* (June 20, 1994), 55.

16. Lawrence M. Friedman. "Law, Lawyers, and Popular Culture, *Yale Law Journal*

98:1579 (1989), 1605.

17. Shaw, *Press Watch*, pp. 111-31; David A. Harris. "The Appearance of Justice," *Arizona Law Review* 35:785 (1993).

18. Gary A. Hengstler. "Vox Populi," *ABA Journal* (September 1993), 64; and Harris, "The Appearance of Justice," p. 822.

19. Stephen Gillers. "Taking *L.A. Law* More Seriously," *Yale Law Review* 98:1607 (1989).

20. For an overview of film and television treatments of lawyers, see Stewart Macaulay. "Images of Law in Everyday Life: The Lessons of School, Entertainment, and Spectator Sports," *Law & Society* 21:185 (1987); Anthony Chase. "Lawyers and Popular Culture: A Review of Mass Media Portrayals of American Attorneys," *American Bar Foundation* 281 (1986); Steven D. Stark. "Lawyers and the Police as Television Heroes," *University of Miami Law Review* 42:229 (1987); Thom Weidlich. "A Cynical Age Sees Few Heroes in Its Lawyers," *National Law Journal* (November 29, 1993), S26; and Rennard Strickland. "Law and Lawyers in Popular Film," *Sooner Magazine* (Spring 1994), 25.

21. Weidlich, "A Cynical Age," p. S26.

22. See Note 18.

23. Kathleen Neumeyer. "Witness for the Persecution," *Los Angeles Magazine* (February 1994),66.

24. Hengstler, "Vox Populi."

25. Friedman, "Law, Lawyers," p. 1579.

CHAPTER 30. STEREOTYPING THE TRUE BELIEVERS: THE CLASH OF REDUCTIONISM AND SYMBOLISM

1. John Dart and Jimmy Allen (1993). *Bridging the Gap: Religion and the News Media.* Nashville: Freedom Forum First Amendment Center.

2. Thomas J. Billitteri. "Priest Urges Subscription Cancellations." *St. Petersburg Times* (January 18, 1994), 3B.

3. Larry Gross (1988). "The Ethics of (Mis)representation." In L. Gross, J.S. Katz, and J. Ruby, eds., *Image Ethics: The Moral Rights of Subjects in Photographs, Film, and Television.* New York: Oxford.

4. Paul H. Keckley Jr. "A Qualitative Analytic Study of the Image of Organized Religion in Prime-Time Television Drama," *Dissertation Abstracts International* 35:08 (1974), 5438A.

5. Will Herberg (1960). *Protestant-Catholic-Jew.* Garden City, N.Y.: Doubleday.

6. Joseph M. Murphy. "Black Religion and 'Black Magic': Prejudice and Projection in Images of African-Derived Religions," *Religion* 20 (1990), 323-37.

7. M.L. Stein. "Stereotyping in Editorial Cartoons," *Editor and Publisher* (June 21, 1986), 129-130.

8. Gary L. Bunker and Davis Bitton (1983). *The Mormon Graphic Image, 1834 - 1914.* Salt Lake City: University of Utah.

9. Dart and Allen, *Bridging the Gap.*

CHAPTER 31. STEREOTYPING OF MEDIA PERSONNEL

1. Associated Press, published in the *Southern Illinoisan*, Carbondale, Illinois (January 19, 1994), 5A.

2. P. J. Shoemaker and S. D. Reese (1991). *Mediating the Message.* White Plains, N.Y.: Longman. The authors use U.S. Bureau of Labor Statistics figures from 1986 to estimate that about 942,000 people were employed in communications jobs on a full-time, part-time, or free-lance basis. This includes 75,000 reporters and correspondents, 214,000 writers and editors, 61,000 broadcast announcers and newscasters, 87,000 public relations specialists, 323,000 marketing, advertising and public relations managers, 109,000 photographers and camera operators, and 73,000 actors, directors, and producers.

3. D.H. Weaver and G.C. Wilhoit (1986). *The American Journalist.* Bloomington, Ind.:

Indiana University Press found in their study of American journalists that from 1971 to the 1983, there was dramatic growth in the number of journalists in the twenty-five to thirty-four age category, while there were significant decreases in the number of journalists in the forty-five to fifty-four and fifty-five to sixty-four age groups, and the average age of journalists had declined by more than four years. However, the preliminary report of their 1992 restudy and D. Weaver and G.C. Wilhoit (1992). *The American Journalist in the 1990s*; preliminary report. Arlington, Va.: Freedom Forum, suggested a reversal of these trends and claimed that journalists are getting older again.

4. A. Borchgrave and R. Moss (1980).*The Spike*. New York: Crown Publishers.

5. S.R. Lichter, S. Rothman and L.S. Lichter (1986). *The Media Elite*. Bethesda, Md.: Adler and Adler.

6. M. Olasky (1988). *Prodigal Press*. Westchester, Ill.: Crossway Books, p. 41.

7. T. Goldstein (1985). *The News at Any Cost*. New York: Simon & Schuster, p. 18.

8. Ibid., p. 19.

9. J. Tebbel (1974). *The Media in America*. New York: Thomas Y. Crowell Company, p. 401.

10. Ibid., p. 402.

11. Ibid., p. 407.

CHAPTER 32. MEDIA VICTIMS

1. Wilson Hicks (1973). *Words and Pictures*. New York: Arno Press. Reprint of 1952 publication by Harper & Row.

2. Matt Bingham. "Spread 'em." *The Sagamore* 1 (October 11, 1993), 1.

3. Permission was not needed because the event took place on public property and in public view.

4. Patrick McKeand, publisher. *The Sagamore*, Indianapolis, October 12, 1993. Personal communication.

5. Trent McNeeley. "Diversity Goals and Being Politically Correct." Panel discussion, *The Working Press and How We Work*, Indianapolis Athletic Club, January 1989. Indianapolis: Indiana Professional Chapter of the Society of Professional Journalists, 1994.

6. Ajabu is an outspoken and controversial person. His message carries a tone of violence. He led a boycott against a Korean grocery store in a predominantly African American neighborhood. The Marion County (Indiana) prosecutor considered, but did not file, charges of extortion on the matter. Ajabu's son, Kofi, has been arrested and charged, with two others, in the brutal slaying of three Anglos in an upscale Indianapolis suburb. When the prosecutor was considering asking for the death penalty, Ajabu made public statements indicating that if his son lost his life, others would pay with their lives, including the mother of two of the victims. Prosecutors from both Marion and Hamilton counties are considering filing charges of obstruction of justice based on those threatening statements.

7. Tammy Dean. "Black Student Union Protests Campus Paper," *The Sagamore* 1:1 (October 18, 1993), 1.

8. Timothy L. Langston, dean of students, Indiana University-Purdue University at Indianapolis, Public Grounds, IUPUI, October 14, 1993. Noon rally remarks to protesting students and others.

9. Bepko is a lawyer and former dean of the law school at IUPUI.

10. Both Langston and Bepko made reference to the university administration making its views known to *The Sagamore*. In fact, no administrator called the editor or wrote a memo on the matter. Only the affirmative action officer, Charleston, called the faculty publisher about the picture.

11. Gerald L. Bepko, vice president, Indiana University, and chancellor, Indiana University-Purdue University at Indianapolis, Administrative Office Building, October 14, 1993. Conversation with protesting students and others.

12. Trevor Brown, letter to Gerald L. Bepko and William M. Plater, October 20, 1993.

13. Trent McNeeley. "Clarification of Oct. 11 Front Page Photograph," *The Sagamore* 1

(October 18, 1993), 1.

14. Dean, "Black Student Union."

15. Tammy Dean. "Ethics: Role of The Sagamore Explained to IUPUI Community," *The Sagamore* Voice 1 (October 18, 1993), 5.

16. Tony Garcia, *The Sagamore* Voice 3 (October 18, 1993), 5.

17. Kim L. Hooper. Letter to Trent McNeeley and James Brown, date unknown.

18. David Goetz. "'Nothing She Could Do'; Slain Student at IU Feared Ex-boyfriend, Friends Say," *Courier-Journal* (April 25, 1992), 1A.

19. Charles Whitney and Ellen Wartella used the DIALOG online information service to determine when the term "politically correct" was in wide use among mass media. Their search of thirty-three metropolitan dailies found the term "political" or "politically" just before "correct" or "correctness" in 101 entries in 1988, 306 in 1989, 638 in 1990 and 3,977 in 11.5 months of 1991. Thus, 1990 is the year beginning accelerated media use of the term. See Charles Whitney, and Ellen Wartella. "Media Coverage of the "Political Correctness" Debate," *Journal of Communication* 42:2 (March 1992).

20. The decision in *Doe v. University of Michigan*, 721 R. Supp. 852 (E.D. Mich. 1989), is available on the Internet at "ftp.eff.org/pub/CAF/law/doe-v-u-of-michigan" while another Internet hate speech link is "ftp.eff.org/pub/CAF/civil-liberty/campus-hate-speech.aclu".

21. Molefi Kete Asante. "The Escape into Hyperbole: Communication and Political Correctness," *Journal of Communication* 42:2 (March 1992), 141-47.

22. Patrick Boyle. "J-school Students Saved From Photos," *American Journalism Review* 16:1 (January 1994), 12.

23. Sheila Kennedy, director, Indiana Civil Liberties Union, Indianapolis. Personal communication, May 10, 1994.

24. Daniel Seligman. "PC Comes to the Newsroom," *National Review* 45:2 (June 21, 1993).

25. Elizabeth Kolbert. "We Interrupt This Program . . ." *New York Times* 4:1 (June 26, 1994), 18.

26. NBC actually broke in more than five minutes, according to a story in the *Rocky Mountain News* (network break from game coverage of forty-one minutes). Channel 13, WTHR, the NBC affiliate in Indianapolis showed thirty-six minutes of chase coverage on the station log for June 17, 1994.

27. Los Angeles Police Department. *Newsweek* 123:26 (June 27, 1994). Cover photograph of O.J. Simpson.

28. Matt Mahurin. *Time* 143:26 (June 27, 1994). Cover illustration of O.J. Simpson based on photograph by the Los Angeles Police Department.

CHAPTER 33. IMAGES THAT HEAL

1. In addition to a notice in *News Photographer* magazine, the trade publication for the National Press Photographers Association (NPPA), calls for images were sent via America Online, CompuServe and several discussion lists on the Internet.

2. Vicki Goldberg (1991). *The Power of Photography: How Photographs Changed Our Lives.* New York: Abbeville Press, p. 21.

3. Roland Barthes (1981). *Camera Lucida: Reflections on Photography.* New York: Hill and Wang.

CHAPTER 34. COMMON GROUND AND FUTURE HOPES

1. Thomas Kuhn (1970). *The Structure of Scientific Revolutions.* Chicago: University of Chicago Press, Chaps. 2-4, pp. 10-42.

2. Joseph T. Klapper (1965). "What We Know About the Effects of Mass Communication: The Brink of Hope." In *Information, Influence, and Communication.* Otto Lerbringer and Arthur J. Sullivan, eds., New York: Basic Books, p. 316.

3. Herbert Blumer. "What Is Wrong with Social Theory?" *American Sociological Review*

19 (February 1954), 3-10. See also Herbert Blumer (1969). *Symbolic Interactionism: Perspective and Method*. Englewood Cliffs, N.J.: Prentice-Hall.

4. Clifford Geertz (1973). "Thick Description." In his *The Interpretation of Culture*. New York: Basic Books, pp. 14, 30.

5. James W. Carey (1988). *Communication as Culture*. Boston: Unwin Hyman, pp. 14-23.

6. H. Richard Niebuhr (1941). *The Meaning of Revelation*. New York: Macmillan, p. 96. He describes his intention in *The Responsible Self* (New York: Harper and Row, 1963) as exploring "the nature and role of symbolic forms" (p. 151).

7. Thomas Nagel (1986). *The View From Nowhere*. New York: Oxford University Press, pp. 5, 7.

8. Martin Buber (1958). *I and Thou*, 2nd ed, trans. R. G. Smith. New York: Scribner's, p. 69.

9. Paulo Freire (1973). *Education for Critical Consciousness*. New York: Seabury Press, pp. 137-39.

10. Paulo Freire (1970). *Pedagogy of the Oppressed*. New York: Seabury, p. 69.

11. Albion W. Small (1903). "The Significance of Sociology for Ethics." In *The Dicennial Publication of the University of Chicago*, vol. 4. Chicago: University of Chicago Press, p. 119.

12. Quoted in Douglas Sloan (1980). "The Teaching of Ethics in the American Undergraduate Curriculum, 1876-1976." In Daniel Callahan and Sissela Bok, eds., *Ethics Teaching in Higher Education*. New York: Plenum Press, p. 18.

Bibliography

Altschul, Charles. (1992). "The Center for Creative Imaging and the Influence of Technology on Creativity." In *Ethics, Copyright, and the Bottom Line*. Camden, Me.: Center for Creative Imaging, pp. 59–61.

Arnheim, Rudolf. (1974). *Art and Visual Perception*. Berkeley: University of California Press.

Badinter, E. (1989). *The Unopposite Sex, the End of the Gender Battle*. Trans. by Barbara Wright. New York: Harper & Row.

Barnhurst, Kevin. (1994). *Seeing the Newspaper*. New York: St. Martin's Press.

——. (December 1991). "News as Art." *Journalism Monographs*.

Barthes, Roland. (1981). *Camera Lucida*. New York: Hill and Wang.

——. (1977). *Image Music Text*. New York: Hill and Wang.

Bateson, Mary. (1994). *Peripheral Visions: Learning Along the Way*. New York: Harper-Collins.

Berger, Arthur A. (1989). *Seeing is Believing An Introduction to Visual Communication*. Mountain View, Calif.: Mayfield Publishing.

Berger, John and Jean Mohr. (1982). *Another Way of Telling*. New York: Pantheon Books.

——. (1977). *Ways of Seeing*. London: Penguin Books.

Biederman, Irving. (1987). "Recognition–by–Components: A Theory of Human Image Understanding." *Psychological Review*, Vol. 94, No. 2, pp. 115–47.

Black, Jay, Steele, Bob, and Barney, Ralph. (1993). *Doing Ethics in Journalism: A Handbook with Case Studies*. Greencastle, Ind.: Sigma Delta Chi Foundation and the Society of Professional Journalists.

Bloomer, Carolyn M. (1990). *Principles of Visual Perception*. New York: Design Press.

Bolton, Richard, ed. (1992). *The Contest of Meaning Critical Histories of Photography*. Cambridge, Mass.: MIT Press.

——, ed. (1992). *Culture Wars, Documents from the Recent Controversies in the Arts*. New York: New Press.

Boorstin, D.J. (1961). *The Image: A Guide to Pseudo-Events in America*. New York: Harper Colophon Books.

Bornstein, K. (1994). *On Men, Women and the Rest of Us.* New York: Routledge.
Brod, H., ed. (1987). *The Making of Masculinities, the New Men's Studies.* Boston: Unwin Hyman.
Brownmiller, S. (1984). *Femininity.* New York: Fawcett Columbine.
Bruce, Vicki, and Green, Patrick. (1985). *Visual Perception Physiology, Psychology and Ecology.* London: Lawrence Erlbaum Associates.
Bryson, Norman, Holly, Michael Ann and Moxey, Keith, eds. (1991). *Visual Theory Painting & Interpretation.* New York: Harper Collins.
"Bye-bye 'Byrds.'" *Honolulu Advertiser* (May 10, 1994).
Cate, F. H. (1994). *Media, Disaster Relief and Images of the Developing World.* Annenberg Washington Program Communications Policy Studies, Northwestern University.
Christians, Clifford, Rotzoll, Kim, and Fackler, Mark. (1983). *Media Ethics: Cases and Moral Reasoning.* New York: Longman.
Conover, Theodore E. (1985). *Graphic Communications Today.* St. Paul: West Publishing.
Davies, Duncan, Bathurst, Diana and Bathurst, Robin. (1990). *The Telling Image The Changing Balance between Pictures and Words in a Technological Age.* Oxford: Clarendon Press.
Deely, John. (1990). *Basics of Semiotics.* Bloomington: Indiana University Press.
Dennis, Everette, and Merrill, John. (1991). *Media Debates Issues in Mass Communication.* New York: Longman.
Dondis, Donis A. (1973). *A Primer of Visual Literacy.* Cambridge, Mass.: MIT Press.
Dyer, R. (1993). *The Matter of Images, Essays on Representations.* London: Routledge.
Fineman, Mark. (1981). *The Inquisitive Eye.* New York: Oxford University Press.
Fiske, Susan T., and Taylor, Shelley E. (1984). *Social Cognition.* Reading, Mass.: Addison–Wesley.
Foss, Sonja K. (1992). "Visual Imagery as Communication." *Text and Performance Quarterly*, Vol. 12, pp. 85–96.
Friedhoff, Richard Mark, and Benzon, William. (1988). *The Second Computer Revolution Visualization.* New York: W. H. Freeman.
Fulton, Marianne. (1988). *Eyes of Time Photojournalism in America.* New York: New York Graphic Society.
Gardner, Howard. (1982). *Art, Mind, and Brain A Cognitive Approach to Creativity.* New York: Basic Books.
Ghiselin, Brewster. (1952). *The Creative Process.* New York: New American Library.
Gibson, James J. (1979). *The Ecological Approach to Visual Perception.* Boston: Houghton Mifflin.
Goldberg, Vicki. (1991). *The Power of Photography.* New York: Abbeville Press.
Gregory, R.L. (1970). *The Intelligent Eye.* New York: McGraw–Hill Book Company.
Gross, Larry, Katz, John Stuart, Ruby, Jay, eds. (1988). *Image Ethics.* New York: Oxford University Press.
Harada, Wayne. "Elvis and Hawaii: A Love Story," *Honolulu Advertiser* (August 17, 1977).
Haraway, D. J. (1991). *Simians, Cyborgs, and Women, the Reinvention of Nature.* New York: Routledge.
Hardt, Hanno. (April 1991). "Words and Images in the Age of Technology." *Media Development.*, Vol. 38, pp. 3–5.
Hatcher, Evelyn P. (1974). *Visual Metaphors A Methodological Study in Visual Communication.* Albuquerque: University of New Mexico Press.
Hicks, Wilson. (1973). *Words and Pictures.* New York: Arno Press.
Hochberg, Julian (1970). "Attention, Organization, and Consciousness." In Mostofsky, David, ed. *Attention: Contemporary Theory and Analysis.* New York: Appleton–Century–Crofts.
Hoffman, Howard S. (1989). *Vision & the Art of Drawing.* Englewood Cliffs, N.J.: Prentice Hall.
Hoistad, Gunnar. (April 1991). "How Vulnerable are Children to Electronic Images?" *Media Development*, Vol. 38, pp. 9–11.

Holmes, Nigel. (1985). *Designing Pictorial Symbols*. New York: Watson–Guptill Publications.

Hopcke, R. H., Carrington, K. L., and Wirth, S., eds. (1993). *Same-sex Love and the Path to Wholeness, Perspectives on Gay and Lesbian Psychological Development*. Boston: Shambhala.

——. (1989). *Jung, Jungians and Homosexuality*. Boston: Shambhala.

Hunter, Jefferson. (1987). *Image and Word The Interaction of Twentieth–Century Photographs and Texts*. Cambridge, Mass.: Harvard University Press.

Jean, Georges. (1992). *Writing the Story of Alphabets and Scripts*. New York: Harry N. A-brams.

Jung, C. J. (1964). *Man and his Symbols*. New York: Doubleday.

Kepes, Gyorgy, ed. (1966). *Sign Image Symbol*. New York: George Braziller.

Kling, J.W., and Riggs, Lorrin A., eds. (1971). *Experimental Psychology*. New York: Holt, Rinehart and Winston.

Koole, Wim. (April 1991). "Imagination Depends on Images." *Media Development*, Vol. 38, pp. 16–17.

Lambeth, Edmund. (1992). *Committed Journalism*. Bloomington: Indiana University Press.

Langer, Suzanne K. (1960). *Philosophy in a New Key*. Cambridge, Mass.: Harvard University Press.

——. (1953). *Feeling and Form A Theory of Art*. New York: Charles Scribner's Sons.

Leong, Russell, ed. (1991). *Moving the Image: Independent Asian Pacific American Media Arts*. Los Angeles: UCLA Asian-American Studies Center.

Lester, Paul Martin. (1995). *Visual Communication: Images with Messages*. Belmont, Calif.: Wadsworth Publishing Company.

——. (1991). *Photojournalism: An Ethical Approach*. Hillsdale, N.J.: Lawrence Erlbaum Associates.

——. ed. (1990). *The Ethics of Photojournalism*. Durham, N.C.: National Press Photographers Association.

Lodge, David. (1984). *Small World*. New York: Warner Books.

Louie, Walter. "Images of Asians in Media," panel discussion, University of Hawaii at Manoa, July 30, 1993.

Mahdi, L.C., Foster, S, and Little, M., eds. (1987). *Betwixt & Between: Patterns of Masculine and Feminine Initiation*. La Salle, Ill.: Open Court.

Margolin, Victor, ed. (1989). *Design Discourse History, Theory, Criticism*. Chicago: University of Chicago Press.

McCafferty, James D. (1990). *Human and Machine Vision Computing Perceptual Organization*. New York: Ellis Horwood Limited.

McLuhan, H. M. (1970). *From Cliché to Archetype*. With Wilfred Watson. New York: Viking Press.

—— and Powers, B.R. (1989). *The Global Village, Transformations in World Life and Media in the 21st Century*. New York: Oxford University Press.

Messaris, Paul. (1994). *Visual Literacy Image, Mind, & Reality*. Boulder, Colo.: Westview Press.

Morgan, John, and Welton, Peter. (1992). *See What I Mean?* London: Edward Arnold.

Paivio, Allan. (1971). *Imagery and Verbal Processes*. New York: Holt, Rinehart & Winston.

Parker, D.M., and Deregowski, J.B. (1990). *Perception and Artistic Style*. Amsterdam: North-Holland.

Parrillo, Vincent. (1990). *Strangers to These Shores*. New York: Macmillan.

Phelan, John M. (April 1991). "Image Industry Erodes Political Space." *Media Development*, Vol. 38, pp. 6–8.

Project Zinger. San Francisco State University: Center for Integration and Improvement of Journalism. 1991, 1992, 1993.

Rampell, Ed. "Thumbs Down: 10 Hawaii Films to Make You Lose your Luau," *Honolulu Weekly* (April 15, 1992).

Ritchin, Fred. (1992). "An Image-Based Society." In *Ethics, Copyright, and the Bottom*

Line. Camden, Me.: Center for Creative Imaging, pp. 19–35.
———. (1990). *In Our Own Image: The Coming Revolution in Photography*. New York: A-
    perture Foundation.
Rule, J. (1975). *Lesbian Images*. Garden City, N.Y.: Doubleday & Company, Inc.
Saint-Martin, Fernande. (1990). *Semiotics of Visual Language*. Bloomington: Indiana Uni-
    versity Press.
Scmitt, Robert C. (1988). "Hawaii in the Movies," *Hawaiian Historical Society*, 36-67.
Scott, J. W. (1988). *Gender and the Politics of History*. New York: Columbia University
    Press.
Sculley, John. (1992). "Computers, Communications and Content." In *Ethics, Copyright,
    and the Bottom Line*. Camden, Me.: Center for Creative Imaging, pp. 15–21.
Sebeok, Thomas A. (1991). *Semiotics in the United States*. Bloomington: Indiana University
    Press.
Shepard, Roger N. (1990). *Mind Sights Original Visual Illusions, Ambiguities, and Other
    Anomalies*. New York: W.H. Freeman.
Showalter, E.(1990). *Sexual Anarchy, Gender and Culture at the Fin de Siécle*. New York:
    Viking.
Signorielli, N. (1991). *A Sourcebook on Children*. New York: Greenwood Press.
Snitow, A., Stansell, C., and Thompson, S., eds. (1983). *Powers of Desire, the Politics of
    Sexuality*. New York: Monthly Review Press.
Sontag, Susan. (1978). *On Photography*. New York: Farrar, Straus and Giroux.
Spivak, G. C. (1988). *In Other Worlds, Essays in Cultural Politics*. New York: Routledge.
———. (1990). *The Post-Colonial Critic, Interviews, Strategies, Dialogues*. New York: Rout-
    ledge.
Stern, Jane and Michael. (1987). *Elvis' World*. New York: Alfred A. Knopf.
Stone, S. (1988). "A Transsexual Manifesto." In Scott, J. W. *Gender and the Politics of
    History*. New York: Columbia University Press.
Stoops, Jack and Samuelson, Jerry. (1983). *Design Dialogue*. Worcester, Mass.: Davis Pub-
    lications, Inc.
Stroebel, Leslie, Todd, Hollis, and Zakia, Richard. (1980). *Visual Concepts for Photo-
    graphers*. New York: Focal Press.
Thiel, Philip. (1981). *Visual Awareness and Design*. Seattle: University of Washington
    Press.
Tufte, Edward. (1983). *The Visual Display of Quantitative Information*. Cheshire, Ct.: Gra-
    phics Press.
Wade, Nicholas. (1990). *Visual Allusions Pictures of Perception*. London: Lawrence Erl-
    baum Associates.
Weitzman, L. J., Eifler, D., Hokada, E. and Ross, C. (1972). "Sex-Role Socialization in Pic-
    ture Books of Preschool Children." *American Journal of Sociology*, 77 (6).
Wel, William. "The Nature and Problem of Stereotypes," part V of a series, *On Diversity in
    Teaching and Learning*, University of Colorado at Boulder.
Wittig, M. (1992). *The Straight Mind and Other Essays*. Boston: Beacon Press.
Wolf, M. A., and Kielwasser, A.P., eds. (1991). *Gay People, Sex, and the Media*. New York:
    Harrington Park Press.
Worth, Sol. (1981). *Studying Visual Communication*. Philadelphia: University of Penn-
    sylvania Press.

Index

About the Contributors

JOHN BELL is an instructor at the New York City Technical College and contributes regularly to journals and conferences devoted to teaching and visual communications.

JOHN BISHOP is a writer and documentary filmmaker. Much of his work is in anthropology and folklore, including *The Land Where the Blues Began*, *New England Fiddles*, and *The Last Window*. He is in final editing on a film about a Himalayan village and another on an Islamic observance in Trinidad, and has recently shot a film in Cambodia on the court dance.

TOM BRISLIN is an associate professor of journalism at the University of Hawaii. He has spent more than half his life in the Pacific, working as a newspaper editor on Guam and in Hawaii. He teaches courses in journalism practice and ethics and administers the department's nationally recognized Carol Burnett Fund for Responsible Journalism Ethics Programs.

JAMES W. BROWN is the associate dean of the School of Journalism at Indiana University at Indianapolis. He has written extensively on the subjects of photojournalism, free speech, and database journalism and finds it amusing that his chapter is number 32.

RAMÓN CHÁVEZ is an associate professor in the School of Journalism and Mass Communication at the University of Colorado at Boulder. He is also now serving as the journalism school's first director of the Office of Student Diversity, created to promote the journalism program's minority recruitment, retention, and placement opportunities. He is one of the founders of the National Association of

Hispanic Journalists and of the El Paso Association of Hispanic Journalists.

CLIFFORD G. CHRISTIANS is a research professor of communications at the University of Illinois, Urbana-Champaign, where he directs the doctoral program in communications. He holds joint appointments as a professor of journalism and a professor of media studies. He has published numerous essays in various journals, edited or written several books on media ethics, served on editorial boards for dozens of academic journals, lectured in countries throughout the world, and has won four teaching awards.

J. B. COLSON teaches undergraduate and graduate courses in the practice, history, and criticism of photography in the Department of Journalism at the University of Texas. During the 1980s, his documentary photography of Mexico was exhibited widely there. His professional work, before coming to Austin, included photography in the U.S. Army Signal Corps, directing film production at Wayne State University, and film making for *Encyclopedia Britannica* and independent producers.

LINDA COULTER received her B.S. in journalism from the University of Idaho, Moscow, and an M.A. in communications from Wichita State University. She is currently working toward a Ph.D. in cultural studies at the University of Iowa.

CHARLES N. DAVIS is an assistant professor of the Department of Communication Arts at Georgia Southern University. He is a former journalist who covered a variety of topics for an international news service. He conducts research primarily on mass media law issues, but is also interested in societal issues and the mass media.

WAYNE DEEL is a thirty-one-year veteran in news photography covering Roanoke and southwest Virginia for the *Roanoke Times*. Among numerous state and national awards, he has won the Associated Press Photo of the Year for the state of Virginia twice. His pictures have been published in *Time*, *Newsweek*, and many large metropolitan newspapers across the country.

CRAIG DENTON is associate professor of communication in the University of Utah. He is the author of the graphic design textbook, *Graphics for Visual Communication*. His photographic documentary, *People of the West Desert*, looks at Jeffersonian democracy on the old frontier and new community building by religious groups on the eve of the twenty-first century.

BONNIE DREWNIANY is an assistant professor at the College of Journalism and Mass Communications at the University of South Carolina, where she teaches advertising. Her research interests include the portrayal of women and older people in advertising. She also prides herself in not knowing a thing about football.

DENI ELLIOTT is Mansfield Professor of Ethics and Public Affairs at the University of Montana and a professor in the department of philosophy there. She is also a Senior Fellow at the Institute for the Study of Applied Professional Ethics at Dartmouth College. She has published widely on questions of applied ethics in a variety of media.

WILLARD F. ENTEMAN is a former college president and professor of philosophy at Rhode Island College. He contributes regularly to journals and media workshops on the subject of media ethics.

SIMON FULFORD is a photographer whose work focuses on marginalized populations while reinforcing the common, human, and personal links between subject and viewer. His work has been exhibited across the country and his portraits are on permanent display at the Administration on Developmental Disabilities in Washington, D.C. as well as the Willowbrook Memorial on the campus of the City University of New York, College of Staten Island.

LAURA GACCIONE is a free-lance writer and photographer based in Bershire County, Massachusetts. Her photo essay on women's ice hockey "Reflections on New Ice," has been shown at Ohio State University, Northeastern University, and elsewhere.

LUCY A. GANJE is an assistant professor of graphic arts and director of the Native Media Center, School of Communication at the University of North Dakota. She grew up on the Cheyenne River Reservation in South Dakota, where her children and other family members are enrolled in the Cheyenne River Sioux Tribe. She is also an associate member of the Native American Journalists Association (NAJA).

CARL GLASSMAN is a professional photographer and teaches photojournalism as an adjunct professor in the Department of Journalism and Mass Communication at New York University.

TIM GLEASON is an associate professor in the University of Oregon School of Journalism and Communication. He teaches classes in mass media law, free press theory, media ethics, photojournalism, reporting, and information gathering. His research focuses on mass media law and mass media ethics.

LARRY GROSS is professor of communications in the Annenberg School of the University of Pennsylvania. He was editor of *Studies in Visual Communication* (1977–85) and associate editor of the *International Encyclopedia of Communications* (Oxford, 1989). He is also the editor of the *Between Men—Between Women* book series in lesbian and gay studies from the Columbia University Press and author of *Contested Closets: The Politics and Ethics of Outing* recently published by the University of Minnesota Press.

NANCY BETH JACKSON is an associate professor of journalism and mass communications at the American University in Cairo. She holds a doctorate in international studies from the University of Miami, Coral Gables, and has worked as a journalist in Africa, Asia, Europe, and Latin America as well as in the United States.

WALTER B. JAEHNIG is director of the School of Journalism at Southern Illinois University at Carbondale. He is a former reporter for the *Louisville Courier-Journal* and graduated from the Medill School of Journalism at Northwestern University. He has a doctorate in sociology from Essex University in England and formerly taught at Indiana University and the University of Wyoming.

formerly taught at Indiana University and the University of Wyoming.

LEE JOLLIFFE is an assistant professor at Drake University, with a long-term research interest in gender portrayal in the media. She began researching stereotyping of men when she and Turner Bond (her husband and a gender rights advocate) collaborated on a gender study in 1985. She also gained insight into men's issues by trading breadwinner roles with her homemaking husband.

BRUCE JORDAN holds a B.F.A. in photography and an M.A. in educational psychology. He is currently finishing an M.A. in photojournalism with a special emphasis in documentary photography at the University of Texas.

KEITH KENNEY is an associate professor in the College of Journalism and Mass Communications at the University of South Carolina. He teaches photojournalism, visual communications and communication theory courses and is the founding editor of the *Visual Communication Quarterly*.

PAUL MARTIN LESTER is an associate professor in the Department of Communications at the always sunny and shaky California State University, Fullerton, but is often too busy surfing the World Wide Web using Netscape to notice. Please feel free to visit his home page (http://www5.fullerton.edu/les/homeboy.html).

TRAVIS LINN is a professor and former dean in the Reynolds School of Journalism at the University of Nevada—Reno. He was a CBS News bureau chief from 1976 to 1984 and news director for WFAA-TV in Dallas from 1964 to 1973. His teaching areas include broadcast writing and production, media and society, and new media technology.

CAROLYN MARTINDALE is a professor and director of the journalism program at Youngstown (Ohio) State University (YSU) and the author of *The White Press and Black America* (Greenwood, 1986). She has written numerous articles on aspects of African American media portrayals and is co-editor of a forthcoming book analyzing news media portrayal of minority groups in America in the past sixty years. She is also a former daily newspaper reporter and has twice received YSU's Distinguished Professor Award.

KATHY BRITTAIN McKEE is an assistant professor of journalism at Berry College where she was granted tenure in 1994. She holds an M.A. in journalism and a Ph.D. in mass communication from the University of Georgia Grady College of Journalism. Her teaching and research areas include media ethics, law, and print journalism.

GLENN McGAHA MILLER is a self-taught photographer from Fort Collins, Colorado. His recent and ongoing projects include, "Whose Temple is this Anyway?", "My Trip to Dallas: A Tourist's Eye View of Deep Ellum," and "Our Trip to Disney: The Beaches of Orange County."

MARGUERITE MORITZ worked as a television news producer in Chicago before joining the faculty at the School of Journalism and Mass Communication at the University of Colorado at Boulder where she heads the electronic media sequence. She has a Ph.D. from Northwestern University and has written extensively on gays,

JACK A. NELSON is head of the journalism program in the Department of Communications at Brigham Young University in Provo, Utah. He has written often on disability issues and is responsible for the book, *The Disabled, the Media and the Information Age*.

JULIANNE HICKERSON NEWTON is head of the photojournalism sequence in the Department of Journalism at the University of Texas-Austin. She received a Ph.D. from the University of Texas and has considerable experience as a photojournalist and reporter for both print and broadcast media. She is also a former head of the Visual Communication Division of the Association for Educators in Journalism and Mass Communication (AEJMC) and director of a UT research project, "The Burden of Visual Truth: Seeing is Believing, Even When We Know Better."

PHILIP PATTERSON is Chairman of the Department of Communication at Oklahoma Christian University of Science and Arts. He is the co-author with Lee Wilkins of two books, *Risky Business: Communicating Issues of Science, Risk, and Public Policy* and *Media Ethics: Issues and Cases*. He is also the author of two trade books on media effects.

KATHERINE REED has a bachelor's degree in journalism from the University of Missouri-Columbia and a master's degree in English creative writing from Hollins College in Roanoke. After several years as a police reporter, she became a victim's advocate and consultant to the National Victim Center in Arlington where she helped train journalists to be sensitive to the rights of victims. She works as a copy editor and movie reviewer for the *Roanoke Times & World-News* and is looking for a publisher for her first novel.

SUSAN DENTE ROSS is a Ph.D. student in media law at the University of Florida, where she works as a research fellow in the Brechner Center for Freedom of Information. On leave from Lynchburg College in Virginia, she has also served on the faculty of the College of Journalism and Mass Communication at the University of North Carolina at Chapel Hill. She also owned and edited a weekly newspaper in Maine.

DONA SCHWARTZ is an associate professor at the School of Journalism and Mass Communication at the University of Minnesota. Her primary research area is visual communication and she works actively as a documentary photographer. Her book, *Waucoma Twilight*, exemplifies her approach to documentary as a "visual ethnography."

E. PAUL SECHRIST, jr., holds a B.S. in Agriculture and an M.S. in Guidance and Counseling. He is an academic counselor at Indiana University—Purdue University Indianapolis, and is a published poet, folksinger, and songwriter.

TED CURTIS SMYTHE is a distinguished scholar in residence at Sterling (Kan.) College. He is Professor of Communications Emeritus at California State University, Fullerton. He is author of several articles on contemporary and historical media and co-author with Michael C. Emery of *Readings in Mass Communication: Concept and Issues in the Mass Media*.

KIM WALSH-CHILDERS is an assistant professor in the College of Journalism and Communications at the University of Florida where she teaches reporting, feature writing, ethics, and computer-assisted reporting. She received her Ph.D. from the University of North Carolina-Chapel Hill.

PATSY G. WATKINS is an associate professor and chair of the Journalism Department at the University of Arkansas in Fayetteville. She holds bachelor's and master's degrees in journalism from the University of Texas and a Ph.D. in American Studies from the University of Iowa. Her professional experience includes magazine writing, editing and design, free-lance writing, graphic design, and small press book publishing.

LEE WILKINS is a professor in the Missouri School of Journalism Broadcast News Department. Her research and teaching interests are in media ethics and environmental communication. Most important for this volume, her father suffers from diabetic retinopathy—so writing the chapter provided her with an opportunity to learn a great deal about the blind and how society views them. She has co-authored a media ethics text and written articles on ethics, news values and political communication.

KRISTINE WOLFF is a master's candidate in the Department of Journalism at the University of Texas. Her current and future photographic work concerns the images of the family in the media that is often stereotypical, sexist, and materialistic.

MARSHA WOODBURY has a Ph.D. in computer-aided instruction at the University of Illinois at Urbana-Champaign. She earned her M.S. in Journalism there in 1991. She graduated from Stanford University in Communications, cum laude, in 1968, and immigrated to New Zealand, where she and her husband still own a sheep farm.

LEE ZUKOWSKI is a graduate student in the College of Journalism and Mass Communications at the University of South Carolina where she is finishing her master's degree in public relations.